Enhancing Employability in Higher Education through Work Based Learning

Dawn A. Morley
Editor

Enhancing Employability in Higher Education through Work Based Learning

palgrave
macmillan

Editor
Dawn A. Morley
Department of Higher Education
University of Surrey
Guildford, UK

ISBN 978-3-319-75165-8   ISBN 978-3-319-75166-5 (eBook)
https://doi.org/10.1007/978-3-319-75166-5

Library of Congress Control Number: 2018938661

© The Editor(s) (if applicable) and The Author(s) 2018
This work is subject to copyright. All rights are solely and exclusively licensed by the Publisher, whether the whole or part of the material is concerned, specifically the rights of translation, reprinting, reuse of illustrations, recitation, broadcasting, reproduction on microfilms or in any other physical way, and transmission or information storage and retrieval, electronic adaptation, computer software, or by similar or dissimilar methodology now known or hereafter developed.
The use of general descriptive names, registered names, trademarks, service marks, etc. in this publication does not imply, even in the absence of a specific statement, that such names are exempt from the relevant protective laws and regulations and therefore free for general use.
The publisher, the authors and the editors are safe to assume that the advice and information in this book are believed to be true and accurate at the date of publication. Neither the publisher nor the authors or the editors give a warranty, express or implied, with respect to the material contained herein or for any errors or omissions that may have been made. The publisher remains neutral with regard to jurisdictional claims in published maps and institutional affiliations.

Cover image © Tatiana Badaeva / Alamy

Printed on acid-free paper

This Palgrave Macmillan imprint is published by the registered company Springer International Publishing AG part of Springer Nature.
The registered company address is: Gewerbestrasse 11, 6330 Cham, Switzerland

Preface

'Enhancing employability in higher education through work based learning' is written at a time when there is increased focus on integrating real life work experience into degree courses. This repositioning of work based learning has been accelerated by debate on the learning gain of students' university experience through to employment. This book responds to this refocus by presenting innovative initiatives within higher education curriculum where work based learning is seen as a wide and transformative pedagogy for students.

The book is intended to inspire and guide all university staff who are instrumental in the integration of work and learning as part of students' university experience.

For ease of accessibility the book is divided into sections: setting up university infrastructures to support students in work based learning, teaching at university to prepare students for work based learning, university strategies to optimise students' learning while in the work based learning setting, supporting and supervising work based learning, using the university experience for work based learning for future employability and promoting students' work based learning for international collaboration and employment.

Each section contains chapters that are drawn from a variety of disciplines and universities from across the UK. The chapters showcase unique projects which detail the pedagogy and evaluation of their approach.

Guildford, UK   Dawn A. Morley

Contents

1 Introduction 1
   Dawn A. Morley

Part I Setting Up University Infrastructures to Support Students in Work Based Learning 11

2 Effective Management of the Tripartite Relationship of Educational Providers, Participants and Employers in Work Based Learning 13
   L. Rowe, D. Moss, and N. Moore

3 Personalising Work Based Learning for a Mass and Diverse Market 33
   J. Peach and M. Mansfield

4 Managing Degree Apprenticeships Through a Work Based Learning Framework: Opportunities and Challenges 51
   L. Rowe

Contents

Part II Teaching at University to Prepare Students for Work Based Learning — 71

5 Use of Simulation as a Tool for Assessment and for Preparing Students for the Realities and Complexities of the Workplace — 73
M. Hughes and A. Warren

6 Utilising Interprofessional Learning to Engender Employability — 91
M. Coward and A. Rhodes

Part III University Strategies to Optimise Students' Learning While in the Work Based Learning Setting — 111

7 Embedding Work Based Learning Opportunities into an Undergraduate Curriculum Through Participation in a Touring Dance Company — 113
C. Childs

8 Student Experience of Real-Time Management of Peer Working Groups During Field Trips — 133
Dawn A. Morley, A. Diaz, D. Blake, G. Burger, T. Dando, S. Gibbon, and K. Rickard

Part IV Supporting and Supervising Work Based Learning — 151

9 Building Students' Emotional Resilience Through Placement Coaching and Mentoring — 153
S. Eccles and V. Renaud

10	The 'Ebb and Flow' of Student Learning on Placement Dawn A. Morley	173
Part V	Using the University Experience for Work Based Learning for Future Employability	191
11	The Role of the Student Ambassador and Its Contribution to Developing Employability Skills: A Creation of Outward Facing Work Roles H. Baker and K. Sela	193
12	Enhancing Psychology Students' Employability Through 'Practice to Theory' Learning Following a Professional Training Year N. Winstone and R. Avery	213
Part VI	Promoting Students' Work Based Learning for International Collaboration and Employment	235
13	Exploring the Power of High-Level Postgraduate International Partnership Work Based Learning Programmes P. Weston, D. Perrin, and D. Meakin	237
14	Developing Global Citizenship: Co-creating Employability Attributes in an International Community of Practice N. Radclyffe-Thomas, A. Peirson-Smith, A. Roncha, A. Lacouture, and A. Huang	255
Index		277

Notes on Contributors

Rachel Avery is a chartered research psychologist and Head of Psychology at Caterham School—a leading independent, co-educational school. Rachel's PhD thesis explored the strategic use of attentional resources during learning which has fueled continued research and practice in applied problem solving in education.

Hollie Baker is an Outreach Manager in the Widening Participation and Outreach Department at the University of Surrey and a Fellow of the Higher Education Academy. As a Widening Participation practitioner, she is interested in the role of work based learning to support the progression of students from disadvantaged backgrounds.

Deborah Blake is a former student at Bournemouth University. She is employed by Footprint Ecology and works on projects including monitoring the Bird Aware Solent Initiative, obtaining data on recreational use at Ashdown Forest and researching potential disturbance to the Severn Estuary SPA. She is working towards obtaining Protected Species licences.

Grace Burger is a former student at Bournemouth University and master's student at the Royal Botanic Gardens Kew; studying plant and fungal conservation. Grace is currently researching the biodiversity benefits of silvopastoral farming in Peru and hopes to help bridge the gap between conservation and agriculture in the future.

Cathy Childs is a Principal Lecturer in Dance at the University of Chichester specialising in dance performance and pedagogy. Recent research includes *Figure and Rhythm* (2015) a collaborative project with Pallant House Gallery and the HEA funded (2016) pedagogic research, *Dance Map—The Employability Journey*.

Melaine Coward is Head of the School of Health Sciences at the University of Surrey. Her doctorate explored the methods by which reflection is taught to undergraduate nursing students across the UK. This work has informed the curricula within her own School whilst also influencing work at a national level with the NMC.

Thomas Dando is a former student at Bournemouth University currently researching the role of herbivores in rewilding at the University of Sussex. Thomas has previously conducted research on African wild dogs in South Africa and worked with the IUCN's small mammal specialist group, primarily focused on African small mammal species.

Anita Diaz is an Associate Professor in Conservation Ecology at Bournemouth University. She has a passion for engaging students in co-creating new research knowledge that informs wildlife conservation. She founded SERTs (http://www.cocreate4science.org/serts/) to inspire opportunities for authentic partnership between students and staff in a range of subject areas.

Sue Eccles is Acting Deputy Head of the Centre for Excellence in Learning at Bournemouth University. Her research is focused around the experiences of students as they transition into, through and out of HE and how providing and receiving coaching and mentoring impacts on students' personal and professional development.

Suzanne Gibbon is a former student at Bournemouth University currently returning to England after 18 months of work and travel in New Zealand, Australia and S.E. Asia. On return she hopes to find work in conservation with a key interest in human wildlife conflict and community engagement.

Adrian Huang is a lecturer on the BA Fashion Media & Industries and Diploma in Fashion programmes, Faculty of Design, LASALLE College of the Arts, Singapore. His professional experience spans the conceptualisation, making and marketing of fashion products, and the teaching of industry-specific skills and knowledge, particularly creative entrepreneurship.

Mel Hughes is Principal Academic in Social Work at Bournemouth University and academic lead for the BU PIER (Public Involvement in Education and Research) Partnership. Her expertise is on developing evidence based approaches for involving people with lived experience in user led research and health and social work education.

Anais Lacouture who passed away recently, was an Associate Lecturer in Fashion Merchandising in the School of Communication & Design at RMIT University, Vietnam. With a professional background as merchandiser and marketer for international luxury fashion brands, Anais was also an entrepreneur and founder of a contemporary ethical fashion brand, Maison Kenji.

Madeleine Mansfield is a researcher and proactive advocate of work based learning to support employability in higher education. As a lecturer, teaching fellow and current Associate Dean, Madeleine has embedded and supported multiple work based learning pedagogy projects within and across curricula, to increase early career professional development and life-long learning.

Denise Meakin is Deputy Head of Centre for Work Related Studies, University of Chester. She takes a lead role in accrediting businesses' education programmes to HE standards, and partnership and co-delivery arrangements. Her research interests and publications include quality assurance in partnerships and negotiated work based learning in HE.

Neil Moore is the MBA (WBIS) Programme Director, Centre for Work Related Studies at the University of Chester. He leads the Chartered Manager and Senior Leaders Master's Degree Apprenticeship (MBA) programme. His research interests include organisational ambidexterity, resilience and research methodology. He is an Associate Editor of the International Journal of Organisational Analysis.

Dawn A. Morley is a post doctorate researcher at Solent Learning and Teaching Institute, and formerly of the University of Surrey, specialising in work based learning and pedagogy. Her doctorate examined how student nurses learn in practice and this has informed the HEE funded STEP (Strengthening Team Based Education in Practice) project where Dawn acts as the external consultant.

Danny Moss is Professor of Corporate and Public Affairs at the University of Chester where he is Programme Leader for the Senior Leaders Master's Degree Apprenticeship programme, and Co-Director of the International Centre for Corporate and Public Affairs Research. He is co-editor of the Journal of Public Affairs.

Jeremy Peach is a Director of WBL at the University of Chester being involved with this form of pedagogy both as a Senior Lecturer, specialising in flexible, negotiated degrees and as a Head of Department for Social Work, Health and Counseling.

Anne Peirson-Smith is an Assistant Professor in the Department of English, City University, Hong Kong. With a background in PR, her research explores fashion communication and the creative industries. Anne co-authored, *Public Relations in Asia Pacific: Communicating Beyond Cultures* (John Wiley, 2009) and *Global Fashion Brands*: *Style, Luxury & History* (Intellect Books, 2014).

David Perrin is Director of the Centre for Work Related Studies at the University of Chester. He runs one of Europe's largest work based learning frameworks for undergraduate and postgraduate students. He has published widely in the field, with specialism in the accreditation of prior learning.

Natascha Radclyffe-Thomas is an HEA National Teaching Fellow, a UAL Senior Teaching Scholar and currently Course Leader BA (Hons) Fashion Marketing at the Fashion Business School, University of the Arts London. Natascha's doctorate explored culturally-situated creativity and she has published internationally on her pedagogic and fashion marketing research.

Vianna Renaud is a Placement Development Advisor for the Faculty of Media and Communication at Bournemouth University. Her doctoral research is exploring the impact of peer mentoring and coaching on managing the expectations and experiences of placement students. She is a Trustee for ASET and the UK Regional Coordinator for IASAS.

Alison Rhodes is Head of the Education Department within the School of Health Sciences at the University of Surrey. As a registered nurse, Alison's enthusiasm for practice development soon became apparent and motivated her to move into education. Her experiences have culminated in extensive professional knowledge and expertise in all aspects of learning and teaching.

Kate Rickard is a former student at Bournemouth University who is following an apprenticeship in Environment Conservation with Winchester City Council. She has led projects working with students and the local community to improve green spaces in their local area, and is helping to increase the biodiversity of the Winchester District.

Ana Roncha is a post-doctoral research fellow in Enterprise, Collaborations and Innovation at the Fashion Business School, University of the Arts London.

Ana's PhD focused on innovation, business development and value creation across fashion SMEs, and she has published internationally on the topics of strategic brand management and business model innovation.

Lisa Rowe is Deputy Head, Centre for Work Related Studies at University of Chester. Lisa has designed and launched the Chartered Manager and Senior Leaders Master's Degree Apprenticeships, working collaboratively with employers and professional bodies. Her current research interests include pedagogic theory, degree apprenticeships, skills development and resilience.

Katherine Sela works as Research and Evaluation Manager in the Widening Participation and Outreach Department at the University of Surrey. She has an MSc in Social Research Methods and has worked on a funded project for the National Union of Students and Leadership Foundation for Higher Education.

Angela Warren co-ordinates the PIER (Public involvement in Education and Research) Partnership at Bournemouth University. Her work with service users and carers aims to create activities which are meaningful for students' learning; providing opportunities to practice their skills in a safe environment, to prepare them for placements and future practice.

Pip Weston is a Senior Lecturer in the Centre for Work Related Studies at the University of Chester. She is link tutor and quality advisor for the University's strategic partnership with the Mountbatten Institute. She is enrolled on a professional doctorate exploring the relationship between Thriving at Work and HE WBL.

Naomi Winstone is a cognitive psychologist, Senior Lecturer in Higher Education at the University of Surrey and HEA National Teaching Fellow. As a Faculty Associate Dean for Learning and Teaching, she has worked with programme teams to develop authentic pedagogies and assessments that draw upon students' placement learning.

List of Figures

Fig. 3.1	The role of the work based learning tutor	38
Fig. 7.1	The development and three stages of the student learning experience © c.childs	120
Fig. 7.2	2015–16 3Fall Dance graduate employment and further study	127
Fig. 7.3	2014–15 3Fall Dance graduate employment	128
Fig. 7.4	2009–10 Dance graduate employment	129
Fig. 10.1	Student nurse learning in practice	186

List of Tables

Table 2.1	Modules compromising Chester Business Master's	21
Table 4.1	Profile of CMDA Cohorts 2016 and 2017 based upon projections	58
Table 7.1	3Fall Dance Company 2015–16 WBL schedule	121
Table 11.1	Activities participated in and future employability	202
Table 12.1	Descriptive statistics and correlation coefficients for all study variables: 'Work and Organisational Psychology'	225
Table 12.2	Descriptive statistics and correlation coefficients for all study variables: 'Psychology and Education'	225

1

Introduction

Dawn A. Morley

'Enhancing employability in higher education through work based learning' is written at a time of rapid change in higher education when universities are facing a deeper, and more commercial, accountability to their students. A culture has been created that requires student degrees to 'count' and that, as result of their studies, students will have a value-added experience or 'learning gain' (BIS 2015, 2016) that takes them forward into further study or employment. Globally, there is an increased emphasis on the 'student voice', and academic debate on the rise of student consumerism within higher education. Although this may vary across the student population, Tomlinson (2017, p. 464) concludes that from the students' perspective "there are many shared concerns; particularly around getting a beneficial and equitable 'return' and value from higher education".

Boden and Nedeva (2010, p. 41) identify that the 'third mission' of universities, to serve wider society, has been replaced by a "relational to functional" remit where "universities must now pursue direct, immediate

D. A. Morley (✉)
Department of Higher Education, University of Surrey, Guildford, UK

© The Author(s) 2018
D. A. Morley (ed.), *Enhancing Employability in Higher Education through Work Based Learning*, https://doi.org/10.1007/978-3-319-75166-5_1

and demonstrable economic utility". In the UK the changing relationship between student and their higher education institution has been formalised through significant policies such as the Teaching Excellence Framework (BIS 2015, 2016) and the new degree apprenticeships (UUK 2016). Both explicitly link the success of degrees with the ability to gain employment afterwards. This year, higher education has become increasingly dominated by the employability agenda and the challenges of enhancing students' chances for post degree employment in line with their educational investment.

Although the mechanisms to achieve 'learning gain' vary across the international higher education landscape, universities have met these increasing pressures by traditionally responding in two ways. The first embeds employability skills within university curricula as taught components of courses. The second increases students' exposure to real life practice by either sending students out to work placements or increasingly bringing the employers' influence into higher education courses.

Despite the many initiatives to embed employability skills within curricula, evidence suggests that generic skills development in higher education institutions is a less effective approach (Atkins 1999; Bridgstock 2009; Mason et al. 2009). Cranmer (2006) questions the development of employment skills outside of the work environment and recommends the policy of increasing work based learning and employer engagement in courses.

Irrespective of previous policies to introduce employability into higher education, universities are recognised for their tradition and expertise to facilitate the creation of well-rounded and reflexive employees of the future (UUK 2016). In the UK, it is not unusual for students to pursue a career away from the knowledge content of their university courses. Students, even in more vocational courses, are discovering that their future professional roles are in a constant state of flux and the ability to manage this can only be learnt from the integration of real life practice and practitioners within their education.

This book argues for a move away from stand-alone placement experiences for students in higher education to more sophisticated models where work based learning is integrated and used creatively in academic curricula. Boden and Nedeva (2010) advocate that the employability agenda is only partly satisfied by 'gaining a job'. Working towards employability involves the building of reflexive skills and attributes over longer periods of time. This book addresses the need to engage university staff and students in forward facing curricula that views future employability skills as part of the teaching and experience of higher education.

The core to the success of employability lies in the recognition of work based learning as a potentially transformative pedagogy where students can accelerate their development and maturity in ways that their academic learning may not reach. It is, however, important that this awareness acknowledges that work based learning is taught and supported in different ways to academic learning. Previous models of 'add on placements', that remained disconnected from the rest of the students' learning, dilute the potential of holistic student development and increases the risk of work and learning being viewed as two distinct entities accentuating a 'theory- practice' gap (Evans et al. 2010).

Under the right conditions, students' learning can challenge established practice in the workplace. Students can bring a fresh perspective to a placement where they may be the catalyst for re questioning and analysis of placement practice (Brown and Duguid 1991). Ellstrom (2001, 2011) provides an overview of the potential of students' learning to repeat practice (*adaptive learning*) or to augment practice (*developmental or innovative learning*). Argyris and Schön (1974) describe this difference as '*single loop*' and '*double loop*' learning; the latter being where wider, more creative solutions are sought on reoccurring issues. It is these types of employability skills that will mark out successful employees of the future and universities can be instrumental in creating these opportunities.

Schön (1983) argues that the complexity of professional decision making also needs to accommodate for the unplanned circumstances of practice. Often work situations arise where professional conformity to recognised theory does not allow solutions to "messes incapable of technical solution" (Schön 1983, p. 42). Schön (1983, p. 43) graphically describes the choice as the safe high ground of familiar practice against the swampy lowlands where practitioners "deliberately involve themselves in messy but crucially important problems and, when asked to describe their methods of inquiry, they speak of experience, trial and error, intuition, and muddling through". By learning in work environments, often less planned and controlled than the academic setting, students have real opportunities to challenge and extend their performance.

By doing so students can appreciate the complexity and nuances of managing themselves in an environment where their priorities are re-orientated to lifelong learning and the ability to move with greater confidence between different work roles.

The chapters within the book showcase examples from UK higher education work based learning practice that demonstrates an appreciation of this wider perspective. For the purposes of this book, 'work based learning', has been defined broadly as student development that may be based before, in and after students' experiences in the 'world of work'. By taking this wider approach the chapters demonstrate the initiative and creativity of academics in UK higher education who have recognised the significance of real life practice to their students' development and future employability. Some chapters provide examples of extracting core learning for employability, that may be passed by unnoticed by a student while on work placement, if it had not been made explicit in their work based learning. Other chapters focus on students' 'work readiness' and preparing them for work based learning in simulated settings as part of course or online learning.

The examples presented within the book are supported by theory, carefully detailed practice pedagogy and evaluated so readers may benefit from the book in their own institutions of higher education.

Section I: Setting Up University Infrastructures to Support Students in Work Based Learning

Section I, "Setting Up University Infrastructures to Support Students in Work Based Learning" provides an appreciation of the wider university infrastructures that support students' work based learning through the work of the Centre of Work Related Studies at the University of Chester (UK). The three chapters discuss the challenges of running large scale work based learning courses.

Chapter 2 examines the management of the tripartite relationship of educational providers, participants and employers in a work based postgraduate business programme. The chapter explores the challenges faced by providers and the prevalent themes and issues surrounding employer expectations of graduate employability and learner expectations of the workplace. The authors illustrate how a clearer understanding of stakeholder perspectives can enhance participant experiences, engage and develop academic skillsets and support employers as they aim to nurture and grow talent. Chapter 3 questions how large work based learning courses can be personalised for a mass and diverse market with a course that aims to develop workplace experiential learning and transferable skills. This chapter highlights the logistical and pedagogical challenges of such an approach, including the complexity of required support. Finally, Chap. 4 comments on managing Degree Apprenticeships through a Work Based Learning Framework. The opportunities and challenges of implementing and managing an innovative Chartered Manager Degree Apprenticeship within the new political reforms are explored. The author considers the academic implications of adapting a business and management degree to a workplace apprenticeship. It incorporates an evaluation of one of the earliest cohorts with viewpoints taken from each stakeholder, collectively identifying a complex range of themes and issues in designing, supporting and further developing apprenticeship programmes.

Section II: Teaching at University to Prepare Students for Work Based Learning

Section II, "Teaching at University to Prepare Students for Work Based Learning" showcases university teaching that enhances students' insight into the reality and nuanced nature of work based learning. The cognitive psychologist, Gary Klein, (Fadde and Klein 2010) believes that expertise in professional practice can be accelerated by focusing particularly on skills that require improvement. In the two chapters included, students from health disciplines immerse themselves in carefully managed teaching environments that allow them to grow particular aspects of their development.

The focus of Chap. 5 is on the use of simulation as a tool for assessing students' developing practice and for preparing students for the realities and complexities of the workplace. Testimonies are incorporated from academics, practitioners, service users and students regarding the efficacy of simulation models in assessing practice and in enabling students to use assessment and feedback (and feed forward) to improve their practice.

Chapter 6 presents the case study of an undergraduate module where an inter professional group of learners are taught to problem solve and reflect on their group work. The teaching approaches have taken favour reflection and experiential learning to solve 'problems' together that may arise within the clinical setting. In turn, this enhances the ability for students to learn from one another to develop their understanding of their own and other professions.

Section III: University Strategies to Optimise Students' Learning While in the Work Based Learning Setting

Section III, "University Strategies to Optimise Students' Learning While in the Work Based Learning Setting" presents two chapters where universities, in the diverse disciplines of dance and ecology, have created opportunities for real time professional practice for their students. In both examples the opportunity for students to work in practice, through situations created by their own academics, gives them exposure to real life work situations and experiences that they will only meet again in employment.

In Chap. 7 work based learning opportunities are embedded into an undergraduate curriculum through participation in a touring dance company. Using a module case study, the pedagogic approaches to work based learning through real time practice with professional choreographers, performing in theatres and gaining teaching experiences in schools and colleges is explored. Challenges within the arts sector to gain employment upon graduation have placed increasing emphasis on providing relevant embedded experiences whilst studying. The shared objectives of the dance performers, administrators and technicians give students the opportunity to work creatively together at '3Fall Dance Company.' In Chap. 8 undergraduate ecology students experience the real-time management of fieldwork during a ten day, cross university fieldtrip where student groups are peer managed by a student team leader. The support of student group leaders to autonomously manage their groups in an authentic work setting accelerates leaders' work readiness and employability skills. The resultant disseminated leadership role, and exposure to professional experts during the trip, further stimulates student leaders' awareness of their longitudinal professional development.

Section IV: Supporting and Supervising Work Based Learning

Section IV, "Supporting and Supervising Work Based Learning" presents two unique ways that students' needs are supported on placement. Schön (1983) introduces coaching, rather than formal teaching mechanisms, to explicitly assist students' build on previous knowledge and develop a critical appreciation of practice (Gobbi 2012).

Chapter 9 explores how the combined approach of coaching and mentoring supports media students on work placements in building emotional resilience. Literature indicates that peer coaching amongst students can have a positive impact on their academic performance and the chapter explores the effectiveness of the Placement Development Advisor (PDA) in supporting students' development of emotional resilience in order for students to become successful media professionals. Chapter 10 argues for a more integrated mentorship model where students are supported by both a named supervisor but also 'helpful others'. When properly managed these individuals combine to support learning from different aspects in a community of social learning and the author recommends how an integrated model of student support can be applied to all HE students learning on placement.

Section V: Using the University Experience for Work Based Learning for Future Employability

Section V, "Using the University Experience for Work Based Learning for Future Employability" discusses two examples of how students use their work based learning experience in the context of the university setting. The first contribution explores the role of the student in both internal and external university work based learning opportunities and the effect on the development of future employability skills for the students involved. The second contribution demonstrates how students effectively use their placement learning in their final academic year of their degree.

Chapter 11 examines the role of the student ambassador created in a university Widening Participation and Outreach Department and the contribution of this role to student employability skills. The student ambassador role is a unique opportunity that enables students to experience work based learning in the context of the university where they are an integral part of the department whilst both learning and working. This chapter focuses on surveys and case studies of ambassadors who have taken a professional training year, or have graduated and progressed into employment, to understand the impact of their role on personal development and employability. Chapter 12 explores how experiences during a Professional Training (Sandwich) Year can be harnessed to support academic learning once students return to university study with an increase in students' self-reported preparedness for work. The authors detail how a Reality-Based Learning model (Smith and Van Doren 2004) informs instructional design in two Level 6 Psychology modules, employing authentic activities and assessments, reflection and problem-based learning.

Section VI: Promoting Students' Work Based Learning for International Collaboration and Employment

Section VI, "Promoting Students' Work Based Learning for International Collaboration and Employment" provides two chapters taken from the differing disciplines of business and the creative industries where the importance of providing an international dimension to work based learning is supported in two very different ways. The increased interest in bringing internationalisation into student curricula is marked by the work of policies such as The UK Strategy for Outward Mobility (Go International 2017) which aims to increase the proportion of UK domiciled students who access an international experience as part of their UK higher education. Like the chapters included in this section, Go International (2017) recognises that "studying, working or volunteering abroad for even a short period as part of their university experience enables students to develop many skills sought after by employers".

Chapter 13 explores post graduate students' reflections of their experiential learning on a work based learning international internship programme jointly developed by the University of Chester and the Mountbatten Institute. Using data gained from student evaluations, together with quotes obtained from students' reflective learning logs, the chapter explores students' perceptions of what they perceive they have gained from this experience which they can take forward into their future careers. As such it provides a unique insight into the nature and value of an international learning experience. In Chapter 14, the authors review a transformative global classroom project that links undergraduate students in the UK and Asia to facilitate cross-disciplinary peer collaboration. The authors explore how international collaborations can simulate some of the complexities of working in the modern creative industries and highlight how social media platforms can facilitate blended learning that seeks to develop both digital literacies and global citizenship.

References

Argyris, C., & Schön, D. (1974). *Theory in practice: Increasing professional effectiveness*. San Francisco: Jossey Bass.

Atkins, M. J. (1999). Oven-ready and self-basting: Taking stock of employability skills. *Teaching in Higher Education, 4*(2), 267–280.

Boden, R., & Nedeva, M. (2010). Employing discourse: Universities and graduate 'employability'. *Journal of Education Policy, 25*(1), 37–54.

Bridgstock, R. (2009). The graduate attributes we've overlooked: Enhancing graduate employability through career management skills. *Higher Education Research & Development, 28*(1), 31–44.

Brown, J. S., & Duguid, P. (1991). Organisational learning and communities of practice: Toward a unified view of working, learning and innovation. *Organisation Science, 2*(1), 40–57.

Cranmer, S. (2006). Enhancing graduate employability: Best intentions and mixed outcomes. *Studies in Higher Education, 31*(2), 169–184.

Department of Business, Innovation and Skills. (2015). *Fulfilling our potential: Teaching excellence, social mobility and student choice*. London: BIS.

Department of Business, Innovation and Skills. (2016). *Success as a knowledge economy: Teaching excellence, social mobility and student choice*. London: BIS.

Ellstrom, P.-E. (2001). Integrating learning and work: Problems and prospects. *Human Resource Development Quarterly, 12*(4), 421–435.

Ellstrom, P.-E. (2011). Informal learning at work: Conditions, processes and logics. In M. Malloch, L. Cairns, K. Evans, & B. O'Connor (Eds.), *The Sage handbook of workplace learning* (pp. 105–119). London, California, New Delhi, and Singapore: Sage.

Evans, K., Guile, D., Harris, J., & Allan, H. (2010). Putting knowledge to work: A new approach. *Nurse Education Today, 30*, 245–251.

Fadde, P. J., & Klein, G. A. (2010). Deliberate performance: Accelerating expertise in natural settings. *Performance Improvement, 49*(9), 5–14.

Go International. (2017). Homepage. Retrieved September 5, 2017, from http://go.international.ac.uk/about-us

Gobbi, M. (2012). "The hidden curriculum". Learning the tacit and embodied nature of nursing practice. In V. Cook, C. Daly, & M. Newman (Eds.), *Work-based learning in clinical settings* (pp. 103–124). London and New York: Radcliffe Publishing.

Mason, G., Williams, G., & Cranmer, S. (2009). Employability skills initiatives in higher education: What effects do they have on graduate labour market outcomes? *Education Economics, 17*(1), 1–30.

Schön, D. (1983). *The reflective practitioner: How professionals think in action*. Aldershot: Ashgate Publishing Limited.

Smith, L. W., & Van Doren, D. C. (2004). The reality-based learning method: A simple method for keeping teaching activities relevant and effective. *Journal of Marketing Education, 26*, 66–74.

Tomlinson, M. (2017). Student perceptions of themselves as 'consumers' of higher education. *British Journal of Sociology of Education, 38*(4), 450–467.

Universities UK. (2016). *The future growth of degree apprenticeships*. Universities UK.

Part I

Setting Up University Infrastructures to Support Students in Work Based Learning

2

Effective Management of the Tripartite Relationship of Educational Providers, Participants and Employers in Work Based Learning

L. Rowe, D. Moss, and N. Moore

Introduction

An increasing concern amongst many graduate employers has been the perceived poor quality of graduates entering employment. Some of the most common employer criticisms include a lack of commercial awareness, unrealistic work expectations and poor work readiness (Confederation of British Industry (CBI) 2011; Chartered Association of Business Schools (CABS) 2014). Moreover, many of the skills shortages observed amongst undergraduate students, appear to be equally common amongst postgraduate students, particularly given the forecast that one in seven jobs will require a postgraduate qualification by 2022 (Wilson and Homenidou 2012). The inference here is that the UK is likely to face a significant graduate and postgraduate skills gap by 2022 unless corrective action is taken. Growing concerns about business graduate skills are likely to force many universities to re-examine and reconfigure the content of, and their approach to, business education.

L. Rowe (✉) • D. Moss • N. Moore
University of Chester, Chester, UK
e-mail: lisa.rowe@chester.ac.uk

© The Author(s) 2018
D. A. Morley (ed.), *Enhancing Employability in Higher Education through Work Based Learning*, https://doi.org/10.1007/978-3-319-75166-5_2

This chapter focuses on the increasingly problematic and challenging postgraduate marketplace where universities not only face criticism regarding the skills levels of their graduates but also where they also have to work hard to attract the most talented students and graduates. Here universities are not only competing against each other, but increasingly face a growing challenge from a range of private sector providers and employer-led graduate schemes. To gain a better understanding of if and how postgraduate provision is evolving to meet the needs of employers in the twenty-first century, we have adopted a '360 degree', tripartite perspective on the postgraduate marketplace, exploring the interaction between the key players—students, employers and universities/educational institutions. Arguably, it is only when all three perspectives are brought together and understood fully, that it is possible to construct a sustainable postgraduate strategy and effectively locate learning in the workplace (Boud and Solomon 2001; Raelin 1997).

In addition, this chapter examines the experiences and challenges of developing and managing an innovative 12 month intensive work based Masters programme (the Chester Business Master's—CBM), which is located in the University's Centre for Work-Related Studies (CWRS) and draws heavily on the core principles of reflective learning based around a negotiated learning contract. Here the strengths and weaknesses of the programme are examined through the 'tripartite lens' of the students, employer and university perspectives. The structure and key features of the Chester Business Master's (CBM) are explored in more detail in a longitudinal case study presented later in this chapter.

Background Context

In exploring the experiences and lessons learned in developing and delivering the CBM programme this chapter will provide insights into the benefits and challenges that accrue from delivering a work based, rather than traditional, postgraduate business curriculum. This approach arguably can offer a recipe for reframing contemporary and future postgraduate business strategies. More specifically this chapter seeks:

- To explore the changing drivers and patterns of demand for business school postgraduate students in this context;
- To examine the relevance and potential of postgraduate work based learning programmes and the introduction of workplace focused business school curricula
- To demonstrate the benefits and challenges of adopting a work based/ workplace focused postgraduate curricula.

As a precursor to exploring the lessons that can be drawn from the experience of the CBM programme we use the 'tripartite lens' to explore the key debates relating to each of the key perspectives (i.e. employer, student and university).

Employer Perspective

While it would be wrong to suggest that employers speak with a single collective voice, it seems that employer representative bodies do broadly condemn the work-readiness and capabilities of many graduates. Larger employers in particular, have been outspoken about the apparent 'skills deficit' amongst graduates and how this may impact on the competitiveness of British industry. According to CABS (2014), 89% of employers feel that graduates are not 'work-ready' and that courses should have work experience embedded within them, whilst four in five employers rank employability skills above degree subject (CBI 2011). Employers have highlighted the need to develop graduates' soft skills including communication and team working (Archer and Davison 2008; Hughes et al. 2013). Moreover, over 80% of employers concur that graduate skills are often exacerbated by unrealistic work expectations and a worrying lack of commercial awareness (CBI 2011).

While one might expect that the education system might be blamed for not addressing skills deficits, there appears to be recognition within the business literature that it is difficult to develop employability skills within the mainstream academic curriculum. The consensus view is that such skills, and the tacit knowledge associated with them, would be developed more effectively within a live business environment (Ng and

Feldman 2009). Of course, universities have not been oblivious to such criticisms and have attempted to adapt their offering to develop skills that are more aligned to the needs of contemporary businesses. Measures, such as including broader hard skills development, bringing in industry projects and speakers to augment teaching (Forsyth et al. 2009; Wilson 2012) and engaging with businesses to review the curricula (Plewa et al. 2015), represent initiatives to enhance the ways in which graduates function in the workplace. However, it is not merely a case of handing over the task of curriculum design to employers. There is a broad consensus that some form of work experience is critical to developing individuals' career related competencies (Murakami et al. 2009). Placements undoubtedly provide students with a valuable work experience opportunity that can develop vocational skills and competencies, but in recent years undergraduate placement opportunities declined to 7.2% (HESA 2014). Likewise, CABS (2014) reported that less than 25% of organisations were willing to offer business school students the opportunity to complete an internship or placement because of the additional supervisory workload with associated cost implications of placement (Weinstein 2007) exacerbated by the perceived lack of commitment from many of today's graduates (Jackson 2010; Byrom and Aiken 2014).

Examining the challenge of supplying talent to regional industry the Wilson Review (2012, p. 9) advocated the establishment of a multi-dimensional 'skills supply chain between universities and local business' to meet the needs of local enterprise partnerships and retain talent within regions. Such initiatives suggest that employers are often unaware of the benefits of graduates and how to access them from their local university (CABS 2014).

Moreover, Barber et al. (2004) found that employers often failed to fully appreciate the scope of work that a placement student might bring to their organisation. Similarly, Archer and Davison (2008) noted that without senior management 'buy-in' placements were often seen as being of minor importance and as incurring costs rather than adding benefits (CABS 2014). This lack of support for a work placement agenda across industry may accelerate the impending skills crisis, which is likely to be further exacerbated by the projected workforce replacement demand for 13 million jobs by 2020, resulting from a need to fill retiring and career changer professional and managerial posts (Wilson and Homenidou 2012; HESA 2014).

In summary, from the employer's perspective, the landscape particularly as far as the availability of younger talented people is concerned, does not look healthy. The message for employers is that they need to play a more active role in shaping the agenda for both educators and graduates entering the world of work.

Student Perspective

Relatively little research has been conducted into student expectations of postgraduate study particularly in relation to programmes built around work based experience. Yet perhaps not surprisingly in the light of higher tuition fees, students now place a stronger emphasis on progression to employment (Mark 2013). Indeed, the CBI (2011) found that 79% of students believe that their course will improve their job opportunities and the vast majority cite enhanced employment prospects as their main motivation for completing a postgraduate programme. This emphasis on enhancing employment prospects is reflected by research into postgraduate student expectations and priorities. Here there is an understandable concern about future employment prospects and a growing demand for transferable, vocational skills, which are fully embedded within programmes (Purcell et al. 2009; Hall et al. 2009). The rise in the overall financial burden of study has inevitably had a strong influence on student expectations and concerns related to perceptions of poor value encompassing issues such as comparative time spent in industry over time spent in the classroom (Byrom and Aiken 2014).

There is considerable evidence to suggest that where employers have been involved in both course design and providing relevant work experience, there is significant improvement in the number of employment offers received by students within six months of graduation (Williams and Cranmer 2006). However, effective programme design, incorporating work experience, is still no guarantee of finding employment. Indeed, evidence suggests that 1 in 10 either choose, or are forced, to seek employment overseas, and 1 in 3 leave regional homes to seek work in London

(HESA 2014). It is also significant that over 80% of graduates do not welcome the idea of gaining employment within SMEs, despite the fact that numerically SMEs constitute the largest potential employment sector (Highfliers 2016).

Although postgraduate students earn approximately £5500 p.a. more than their peers (London School of Economics 2010), it appears that those from disadvantaged backgrounds are often deterred from postgraduate study because of cost issues (HEFCE 2013). However, it is misleading to assume that a rational economic model underpins decisions about postgraduate study. There remains insufficient research into the views of students with regard to the extent to which they believe postgraduate courses help to develop employment skills, and hence represent 'good value for money' (Tymon 2013).

Even where programmes do incorporate workplace experience many participants struggle to cope with combining study and employment. One inference here is that students on work based learning placements often need high levels of pastoral and tutor support.

A further issue that has gained traction is the need for greater emphasis on 'peer support' and 'peer learning'. Weinstein (2007) and Helyer (2015) identified that some work based programmes failed to plan for how students can support each other. Since work based learning students spend the majority of their time working in isolation, it is sometimes more difficult to establish networking bonds with their peers and engage in "social capital development" (Pedler 2012, p. 318). Here Brown et al. (2014) have suggested that such isolation can be partially addressed by setting up Action Learning Groups in order to provide on-going peer support.

From a student perspective engagement in work based learning programmes, rather than more traditional postgraduate education, would appear to address many of the concerns that students hold about the cost-benefit of engaging in a further programme of study. The lack of substantive research into student perceptions of postgraduate, and particularly work based learning, study makes it difficult to draw conclusions about the perceived merits of each type of programme. What is clear is that whatever the advantages of work based learning in terms potential employability, such programmes are not entirely without significant challenges. Here issues of perceived 'isolation' and limited opportunities for peer networking and peer support, need to be addressed if the other benefits of such programmes are to be realised.

University Perspective

Much of the literature relating to postgraduate study is critical of HEIs' failure to prepare students for the workplace. What emerges from the limited literature is the strong sense of instrumentality which emphasises the cost and utility of university-based programmes, the skills deficit of many graduates and the perceived value of workplace experience embedded in programme design and delivery. What becomes clear is that in attempting to juggle and balance these considerations, universities face complex challenges in managing programme design and delivery while simultaneously engaging with industry and recruiting and retaining students.

Boud and Solomon (2001) focused on the introduction of work based learning programmes and argued that they change the character of the university-student learning-employer workplace 'equation'. Such change is manifest in many ways, perhaps most notably in terms of multiple conceptual and practical challenges to institutional identity, structures and work practices. Indeed, Boud and Solomon (2001) emphasise, that with the introduction of work based learning, decisions about what is to be learned and how and where learning will take place are no longer the sole prerogative of the academic. Rather, a set of 'learning partnerships' involving universities, employers and the learner emerge and when taken together these have the potential to facilitate the co-production of knowledge. This raises some fundamental epistemological questions about the ownership and location of work based learning and knowledge creation processes.

A central theme within the literature is the pedagogical dimension of work based learning development which highlights the link between "explicit and tacit knowledge and theory and practice" (Raelin 1997, p. 572). Emphasis has centred on individual learner-negotiated processes drawing on learning models (Kolb 1984; Honey and Mumford 1986) stressing the central importance of critical thinking and reflection (Gibbs

1988; Schön 1987). Other authors, such as Garnett et al. (2008), have drawn on the notion of 'intellectual capital', using Stewart's (1997) division into 'human capital', 'structural capital' and 'client capital' as a basis to explore the benefits of university-employer work based partnerships.

The extant literature also highlights changes in the conventional HE-industry relationship and how these have led to challenges that have the potential to impact on the future success, and perhaps even survival, of some universities. A fundamental issue here is that despite universities and employers having a stake in work force development, and in the ways in which work based learning may evolve, they often struggle to collaborate because there is "no common language between them" (Roodhouse and Mumford 2010, p. 27).

Thus, the university perspective of work based learning exhibits a strongly instrumental emphasis, focused on examining the most cost effective ways in which universities can meet the needs of both employers and students. There is also strong interest in pedagogical issues and in particular, how universities can best offer the distinctive learner-negotiated processes associated with such programmes.

In the remainder of this chapter we use the tripartite lens to explore how the issues outlined above play out in the context of the CBM programme and identify the consequences for our understanding of work based learning and the development of postgraduate programmes.

Case Study: Chester Business Master's

The key aim of the programme was to address the core challenge faced by most graduates seeking employment. Namely to provide them with the opportunity to undertake an extended mainstream work placement experience; something which many employers cited as missing from the profiles of most graduate applications. The programme comprises of a number of intensively taught business related modules that help prepare students for the real world. Assessed project work is undertaken in two extended 20 week work based placements, addressing the needs of employers, participating students and the University in terms of meeting employability, skills development and recruitment goals. As such, the

Table 2.1 Modules compromising Chester Business Master's

Modules	Credit
Reflective learning module	20 credits
Business Environment module	20 credits
Placement based Business Consultancy project I	60 credits
Business Research Methods module	20 credits
Placement based Business Consultancy project II	60 credits

CBM provides an effective lens with which to examine the tripartite relationship. Its structure is summarised as follows (Table 2.1).

A longitudinal study was carried out to assess the effectiveness of the CBM programme. Data was collected from two cohorts of students and 12 employers. The first student group comprised of 12 learners who graduated in 2015 and the second comprised of 15 students who were participating on the programme in 2016. Hence those participating were either inexperienced existing students or recently graduated new entrants to fulltime work and therefore very different to the more experienced professionals typically seeking to enhance their existing knowledge and skills through work based learning programmes. Participants were surveyed using a combination of telephone interviews and questionnaires.

Employers were predominantly based in the North-West region of the UK. They varied in terms of their size, sector and experience of placement provision. The most experienced had provided placements since the inception of the programme whereas for others placement provision had not been undertaken previously. In many cases larger organisations with greater budgets were bound by complex recruitment procedures and often operated their own internal graduate programmes; while smaller organisations commonly struggled with resource scarcity and a lack of funding knowledge that could help to create appropriate placement opportunities. These factors impacted upon recruitment for placements, with a 20% take-up rate aligning with previous research (CABS 2014).

In terms of the overall success of the programme not only was the feedback from both students and employers extremely positive, also the contributions and benefits to the regional economy were significant with over 100 projects conducted for client organisations to date 25% of these in SMEs. A total of £420,000 was paid in salaries and talent was retained in the region. Less easily quantifiable contributions, but nevertheless potentially significant, include increases in client revenue and efficiency and potential jobs created and/or saved resulting from the consultancy projects undertaken by placement students.

The following sections draw upon the data to explore each of the tri-partite perspectives relating to CBM.

Employer Perspective

Responses from placement providers identified a number of key issues. First employers expressed concern about the time and effort involved in vetting and recruiting suitable placement students. Moreover, despite their commitment to engage in and support the placement scheme, some employers expressed frustration at the time and resources spent on rejecting poor candidates whose CVs and interview skills were of an unacceptable standard. This finding perhaps speaks of more fundamental issues surrounding the UK HEIs and how they prepare students for work. In contrast, other employers were surprised by the high calibre of candidates presented for interview, as one managing director of a small distribution company endorsed: *"We decided to take two students, such was the calibre of the candidates."*

Beyond the recruitment phase, some employers also identified the additional challenge of managing the placement process. In particular, the demands of monitoring and supporting placement students was recognised as a strain on resources and in more extreme cases was cited as an issue that could lead to unexpected problems such as placements failing mid-term.

The interview data collected after each placement indicated that despite these challenges, employers recognised the benefits of 'growing their own talent'. Indeed managing director of a small refrigeration company commending the programme as the company had *"gained a high calibre and talented new recruit"*. Some comments suggest that CBM had helped to overcome many of the negative perceptions surrounding the calibre and work-readiness of graduates. As one director of a small engineering company said: *"Our placement student has fully met, and in many* ways, exceeded the expectations we had for the Masters programme. This has been a very good experience and one we expect to make full use of in future years." Likewise, the response from large organisations was equally positive with a senior director from a global translation company commenting: *"Our intern has really hit the ground running. So far the quality and level of her results far exceed our original expectations."*

Student Perspective

The experiences and feedback from students indicated that they found the intensive 12-month structure of CBM extremely demanding. The transition from undergraduate to Master's level, coupled with entry into the world of work, and the demands of greater reliance on autonomous work based learning proved to be a very challenging experience for most students.

A further issue that emerged was the high level of student expectation about what the programme, and particularly what the placement, might deliver. Despite comprehensive and clear pre-course information most expected graduate level roles in their placement and a number expressed some surprise when not selected to join their preferred company. Student failure at placement interview was most often because, despite their strong academic standing, students were sometimes unable to convince employers of their suitability for the placement. Poor quality CVs and underdeveloped interview skills also meant that some candidates failed multiple interviews.

In addition, in common with other work based learning programmes, the reduced taught contact hours found on CBM caused some initial student concern and dissatisfaction as they struggled to come to terms with adapting to a new mode of study alongside satisfying workplace expectations. These concerns were most readily expressed by students who had graduated from highly structured undergraduate programmes, and who also had limited real world work experience.

Student concerns were partially addressed through additional tutor liaison via email, telephone and Skype. Online facilitation was improved and action-learning groups were introduced to increase peer support and reduce student isolation. However, some students continued to find it difficult to adapt and reaction to action learning groups was mixed: *"I had some really good one-to-one conversations with members of my group when we had sessions together, but obviously the number of these meetings was limited,"* which was echoed another student who commented *"more contact time with my group would have been beneficial in terms of developing my ideas"*.

As the students progressed they began to recognise the value of the programme. This was confirmed by unsolicited comments including: *"The programme has given me an insight into the real-life business world, as well as getting the academic and theoretical understanding that you would receive from a conventional Masters."* Notwithstanding the fact that a small number of students found it difficult to adapt to, and benefit fully from, the experience and opportunities that CBM offered, the majority did benefit directly from their participation, both in terms of completing the master's degree and securing full time employment. Indeed over two thirds of CBM alumni remained with the same employer and many secured graduate level roles. Given that most students chose the programme primarily to accelerate their career prospects, it is not surprising that overall feedback was extremely positive, for example: *"This programme really has jump started my career and enabled me to obtain a role I had never thought possible prior to undertaking CBM"* and *"As a result of the programme I went on to gain graduate employment in my sponsoring company."*

University Perspective

For universities, the success or failure of a new programme is invariably gauged primarily in terms of the achievement of target recruitment and fee income. One notable feature of programmes such as CBM is the labour-intensive nature of the work involved in sourcing and managing work placements, which inevitably limits the scope to markedly grow student numbers. Such considerations often result in a somewhat ambivalent view of this type of work based programme within increasingly resource-constrained universities. This focus on achievement of academic results and the recruitment of target numbers can clearly be found in university documentation and discussions about CBM and other work based programmes.

Against the current background of financial austerity, it is perhaps not surprising to find less emphasis on the development of soft skills sought by employers in the workplace. As a consequence, it is not surprising that there remains a significant and widening gap between university and employer perceptions of work-readiness and the role that universities should play in ensuring graduates possess necessary workplace skills.

Arguably, the university has benefited enormously from the kudos and profile raising news coverage, case studies and word of mouth publicity that the CBM programme has generated. However, while happy to bask in the afterglow of the publicity some have questioned the longer-term economic viability of such programmes if numbers cannot be grown significantly. Here there seems to be limited recognition of the potential 'halo effect' of such programmes on wider student recruitment.

From the university and faculty perspective, a further potential benefit lies in the under-exploited research potential from the 112 consultancy projects that have been completed since the inception of the programme. While many of the students expressed an interest in investigating the knowledge transfer and publishing opportunities that could accrue from their project work in reality this proved to be problematic for a number of reasons. Most notably there were issues of commercial or other sensitivities that prevented publication of data. In some cases, even though the data may have had little or no immediate commercial value, host companies nevertheless, did not wish for information to be released into the public domain. Thus, while the pool of work based projects might prove a potentially valuable source of publishable research, like other aspects or considerations with this type of work based programme, the issues are not always straightforward and need to be considered 'in the round' taking account of the implications for all parties.

Conclusion

In this chapter, we have adopted a tripartite lens comprising student, university and employer perspectives, to explore the benefits of adopting a work based learning approach to the design of a contemporary business

Masters programme. Utilising this tripartite lens has helped to bring into stark relief the sometimes differing expectations and interests of the three key stakeholder groups involved in any business programme development—the students as customers, the University as provider and employer organisations as employers of programme graduates. Arguably, only when all three perspectives are understood and taken into account will it be possible to design or adapt programmes that best satisfy the needs and interests of all three stakeholder groups.

As we have highlighted earlier, universities and HEIs are having to operate in an increasingly resource constrained world in which financial concerns have come to the fore and often dominate thinking to the exclusion of any other considerations. Moreover, it seems clear that recent growth in undergraduate student numbers has peaked and further significant growth in numbers is unsustainable going forward because of demographic trends and changing demands on the part of students and employers. In short, against the backdrop of rising costs the market has and is continuing to change and evolve as the 'customer' (students and employers) for university services becomes more discerning and demanding. Moreover, university and HE institutions are no longer only competing with each other to attract students, they are increasingly facing competition from a growing number of commercial providers especially in the more vocational subject fields such as business and management and law.

Indeed, against the backdrop of the proliferation of work based or work related programmes being offered by a combination of university and private sector providers, which arguably has led to considerable confusion in the marketplace as what exactly constitutes 'work based learning'. It is all the more important for universities/HE institutions offering 'genuine' work based learning programmes to up their game in terms of engaging closely with employers and potential participants to reinforce and differentiate the distinctive nature of their programme offering.

An important lesson to emerge from our experience of developing the Chester Business Masters programme, which was built on a foundation of careful tripartite engagement with employer organisations, students and university management, was recognition of the particular skill sets needed by the staff charged with engaging with employer organisations in particular. As was emphasised earlier in this is chapter, the success of any reasonably sized work based learning programme relies on establishing and managing a relatively large-scale work placement scheme required to underpin a successful high yield programme. Here it was apparent that developing and maintaining such an employer network requires the type of 'relationship management' skills normally associated with a sales and marketing professional, and is not a task that can be readily allocated to a traditional academic member of staff, many of whom may lack any such training or professional experience. Indeed, putting the wrong type of person in such a role might prove extremely damaging to the success and credibility of any work based learning programme such as the Chester Business Masters, by reinforcing stereotypes that some employers may hold of academic institutions as detached from the reality of day-to-day of business operations and management.

A tripartite perspective also implies the need to take account of university imperatives particularly with respect to the financial viability of any programme provision. As was highlighted earlier, work based learning programmes such as the Chester Business Masters can be extremely resource intensive particularly in terms of identifying maintaining employer placement networks and hence are unlikely to be capable of attracting or sustaining the large taught cohort numbers associated with more traditional postgraduate business provision. Hence it is difficult to see how such work based learning programmes can be grown to form the centrepiece of an all-new postgraduate strategy for the twenty-first century.

Moreover, our study undoubtedly echoes many of the issues identified earlier in the literature review, focusing notably on a mismatch of expectations and demands of employers relating to the capabilities of graduates emerging from HE institutions looking to enter the workforce; and equally the expectations of many graduates who appear to be less than adequately prepared to enter the world of work. To what extent universities and HE institutions as a whole can play a valuable role closing these 'expectations gaps', and whether work based learning programmes may be one of the most effective ways to address such gaps is something on which arguably the 'jury is still out'. As we have sought to suggest in this chapter, a key starting point in bridging these 'expectation gaps' lies in facilitating much better communications between all key stakeholders; employers, students and university management, to understand each other's perspective and identify any issues of conflict or ambiguity. This is not just a question of having the 'right' mechanisms or channels for communications, but also requires that the right people lead such communications and have the power to effect any necessary changes to the way in which the relationships are managed and how any resulting work based learning programmes operates. Where such individuals lack 'power' to effect change can often prove a stumbling block particularly within universities because of the bureaucratic procedures often associated with programme design and approval.

In principle at least, work base learning programmes such as the Chester Business Master's programme, if resourced effectively and appropriately can address many of the concerns raised by both employers and students, particularly in terms of providing students with high quality work experiences and thereby enhancing their workplace skills, and capabilities. For employers, the programme has effectively served as something of a recruitment funnel ensuring they can effectively vet and trial graduates in an extended workplace setting before committing to hiring them. Equally, graduates can use their work placement to try out workplace settings to ensure it is suited to their needs and lives up to their expectations before accepting an employment offer. In this sense, this type of work based learning programme is something of a 'win-win' for both employers and potential graduate employees. However, as emphasised earlier, this type of programme, which offers a high degree of individual counselling and support (CV writing, interview technique, pastoral care and employment advice) cannot easily be replicated on a large scale and as such will always tend to function as something of a 'flagship' programme, championing the cause of stronger tripartite relationships between employers, students and the Universities. While perhaps not easily scalable, such work based learning programmes can open the way for the development of a range of other possible collaborations between the universities/HE institutions and industry that can help tackle the 'expectation gaps' that have impacted negatively on graduate employment and employer satisfaction statistics.

In terms of future developments, the introduction of Degree Apprenticeship programmes promises an additional opportunity for employees to engage in both undergraduate and postgraduate education and also facilitates the development of professional competence through work based learning. However, whether the long held and deeply embedded difficulties and challenges of managing the tripartite relationships between students, employers and universities can be resolved satisfactorily remains to be seen.

References

Archer, W., & Davison, D. (2008). *Graduate employability: What do employers think and want*. UK: The Council for Industry and Higher Education.

Barber, L., Pollard, E., Millmore, B., & Gerova, V. (2004). *Higher degrees of freedom: The value of postgraduate study*. Institute for Employment Studies.

Brown, A., Rich, M., & Holtham, C. (2014). Student engagement and learning: Case study of a new module for business undergraduates at Cass Business School. *Journal of Management Development, 33*(6), 603–619.

Boud, D., & Solomon, N. (2001). *Work-based learning: A new higher education?* London, UK: McGraw-Hill Education.

Byrom, T., & Aiken, V. (2014). Doing it differently: Re-designing the curriculum to face the challenges of student work-based learning opportunities. *Higher Education, Skills and Work-Based Learning, 4*(3), 271–283.

Chartered Association of Business Schools. (2014). *21st century leaders building practice into the curriculum to boost employability*. Retrieved May 22, 2017, from http://www.associationofbusinessschools.org/sites/default/files/21st_century_leaders_june2014_-_final_report.pdf

Confederation of British Industries. (2011). *Education and skills survey: Building for growth-business priorities for education and skills*. Retrieved May 22, 2017, from http://www.cbi.org.uk

Forsyth, H., Laxton, R., Moran, C., Banks, R., & Taylor, R. (2009). Postgraduate coursework in Australia: Issues emerging from university and industry collaboration. *Higher Education, 57*(5), 641–655.

Garnett, J., Workman, B., Beadsmoore, A., & Bezencenet, S. (2008). Developing the structural capital of higher education institutions to support work-based learning programmes. In *The Higher Education Academy Workforce Development: Connections, frameworks and processes* (pp. 18–30). Retrieved

May 22, 2017, from https://www.heacademy.ac.uk/system/files/wfd_developing_the_structural_capital_of_higher_education_institutions.pdf

Gibbs, G. (1988). *Learning by doing: A guide to teaching and learning methods.* Oxford: Further Education Unit, Oxford Brookes University.

Hall, M., Higson, H., & Bullivant, N. (2009). The role of the undergraduate work placement in developing employment competences: Results from a 5-year study of employers. In *DECOWE International Conference* (pp. 24–26).

Helyer, R. (2015). *The work-based learning student handbook.* Palgrave Macmillan.

High Fliers Research Ltd. (2016). *The graduate market in 2016.* London: High Fliers Research Ltd. Retrieved May 22, 2017, from http://www.highfliers.co.uk/download/2016/graduate_market/GMReport16.pdf

Higher Education Funding Council for England. (2013). *Postgraduate education in England and Northern Ireland: Overview report.* Retrieved May 22, 2017, from http://www.hefce.ac.uk/pubs/year/2013/201314/

Higher Education Statistics Agency. (2014). *Free online statistics—Students and qualifiers.* Retrieved May 22, 2017, from https://www.hesa.ac.uk/stats

Honey, P., & Mumford, A. (1986). *Using your learning styles* (2nd ed.). Maidenhead: Peter Honey.

Hughes, T., Sheen, J., & Birkin, G. (2013). Industry graduate skills needs. Summary report for the National Centre for Universities and Business. *CFE Research, 2013.* Retrieved May 22, 2017, from http://www.ncub.co.uk/reports/cfe.html

Jackson, D. (2010). An international profile of industry-relevant competencies and skill gaps in modern graduates. *The International Journal of Management Education, 8*(3), 29–58.

Kolb, D. (1984). *Experiential learning: Experience as the source of learning and development.* London: Prentice Hall.

London School of Economics Centre for Economic Performance. (2010). *The social composition and future earnings of postgraduates.* Retrieved April 13, 2018, from https://www.suttontrust.com/research/the-social-composition-and-future-earnings-of-postgraduates/

Mark, E. (2013). Student satisfaction and the customer focus in higher education. *Journal of Higher Education Policy and Management, 35*(1), 2–10.

Murakami, K., Murray, L., Sims, D., & Chedzey, K. (2009). Learning on work placement: The narrative development of competence. *Journal of Adult Development, 16*(1), 13–24.

Ng, T. W. H., & Feldman, D. (2009). How broadly does education contribute to job performance? *Personnel Psychology, 62,* 89–134.

Pedler, M. (2012). *Action learning in practice* (4th ed.). London: Routledge.

Plewa, C., Galan-Muros, V., & Todd, D. (2015). Engaging business in curriculum design and delivery: A higher education institution perspective. *Journal of Higher Education, 70*(1), 35–53.

Purcell, K., Elias, P., Atfield, G., & Behle, H. (2009). *Plans, aspirations and realities: Taking stock of higher education and career choices one year on*. Findings from the second Futuretrack survey of 2006 applicants for UK Higher Education. Retrieved May 22, 2017, from https://www.hecsu.ac.uk/assets/assets/documents/futuretrack/FT2_Nov09_links.pdf

Raelin, J. (1997). A model of work-based learning. *Organisational Science, 8*(6), 563–578.

Roodhouse, S., & Mumford, J. (Eds.). (2010). *Understanding work-based learning*. London: Gower.

Schön, D. (1987). *Educating the reflective practitioner*. San Francisco, CA: Jossey Bass.

Stewart, T. (1997). *Intellectual capital: The new wealth of nations*. London: Nicholas Brealey.

Tymon, A. (2013). The student perspective on employability. *Studies in Higher Education, 38*(6), 841–856.

Weinstein, K. (2007). *Action learning: A practical guide*. London: Gower.

Williams, G., & Cranmer, S. (2006). Employability skills initiatives in higher education: What effects do they have on graduate labour outcomes? *Education Economics, 17*(1), 1–30.

Wilson, R. A., & Homenidou, K. (2012). Working futures 2010–2020. *UKCES Sectoral Report*. Retrieved May 22, 2017, from http://dera.ioe.ac.uk/15957/1/working-futures-sectoral-report.pdf

Wilson, T. (2012). *A review of business-university collaboration*. Department for Business, Innovation and Skills. Retrieved May 22, 2017, from https://www.gov.uk/government/uploads/system/uploads/attachment_data/file/32383/12-610-wilson-review-business-university-collaboration.pdf

3

Personalising Work Based Learning for a Mass and Diverse Market

J. Peach and M. Mansfield

Introduction

This chapter has been designed to contribute to practice in the field of Work Based Learning (WBL). The focus is University of Chester's unique approach to WBL and the opportunities and challenges of a university-wide, centralised, credit bearing module for second year (Level 5) students. The University of Chester, based in the North West of England, has had the 'Enhancing your Employability through Work Based Learning' module as part of its curricula for over 25 years. The module provides an authentic learning experience to undergraduate students, offering scaffolded and guided reflection via module assessment. The overarching aims are to aid the development of transferable employability skills, to support students in critically reflecting on them, to gain new personal insights and to articulate the skills developed. Additionally, through a process of engagement with both employers and tutors it is

---

J. Peach (✉) • M. Mansfield
University of Chester, Chester, UK
e-mail: j.peach@chester.ac.uk

designed to increase student autonomy and responsibility. The module is facilitated by over 60 academic colleagues supporting circa 1600 students, representing around 70% of the Level 5 (second year) cohort.

This chapter critically explores academic issues involved in personalising learning by adopting an experiential reflective pedagogy. We explore the logistical issues of managing such a large, professionally diverse, cross-faculty cohort of undergraduate students including the challenges of getting buy in from faculties to support the venture and ensuring academic rigour. In doing so it draws from student, employer and staff perspectives to offer insights into promoting student work-readiness across diverse disciplines, industries and pedagogic approaches in a common module framework.

Work Based Learning at the University of Chester

UK universities are coming under increasing pressure from government to strengthen university and employer engagement (The Dearing Report 1997; Wilson 2013; BIS 2016a) which emphasises a drive for institutions to ensure they are developing employable graduates. The tracking of student employability success may also come under greater scrutiny via the potential implementation of long-term employment measures, via external sources such as the HM Revenue and Customs (HMRC) in addition to the proposed changes to the Destinations of Leavers from Higher Education survey (DLHE). Far from employability reaching a level of maturity within HEIs, the speed and prominence of the Teaching Excellence Framework (TEF) (BIS 2015), implementation means the agenda is very much in the spotlight (Tudor and Mendez 2014). Indeed, the advent of subject specific TEF may raise the criticality of developing student employability to even the most sceptical.

Over half of job vacancies between now and 2022 are predicted to require high-level graduate skills and knowledge with graduates being likely to be facing multiple careers in a Gig Economy (McKinsey Global Institute 2016). This requires graduates who are agile, have an understanding of workplace requirements, can demonstrate transferable skills, and a growth mindset (Raelin 2008). The ability to help enhance student employability and meet these demands through WBL, aided through authentic work experiences, are well documented (Johnson and Burden 2003; Helyer 2011; Helyer and Lee 2014). It provides the opportunity to apply and develop knowledge, integrate theory with practice, explore possible future career areas helping students to be better prepared and to have better control of their own lives and employment (Wilson 2013). The Shadbolt review of graduate employability in computer science highlights the particular importance of work experience in improving not only employability, but also in shaping graduates' expectations about the world of work (Department for Business, Innovation & Skills 2016b).

A key approach to WBL at the University of Chester is through the module 'Enhancing your Employability through Work Based Learning'. This is credit rated at twenty Level 5 (second year) credits with students required to complete a work placement of at least 150 hours, normally over a five-week period, timetabled to take place during May and June. Assessment is in the form of a 4000-word report, in which students reflect on their learning and development in placement and also produce a personal and professional development plan.

This module is designed for a mass market; in 2015/16 a total of 70% of the university second year students undertook this module, representing all faculties, and accessed a placement at the same time. However, the assessment of experiences and reflection of individual skill development creates a personalised student learning experience. The module does not focus on degree or profession-specific skill development, but instead focuses on transferable skills and the notion of learning in the workplace. It is our assertion that this better equips students for work and career development in the short and longer term. However, the omission of degree specific skill development is not without critics and can cause debate with some students and academic colleagues.

Students are responsible for securing their own placement, which are normally based in the UK, with support from a dedicated specialist placement coordinator. Students may seek their own placement or apply for opportunities actively sourced by placement coordinators, who also act as a gatekeeper for placement providers. In 2015/16 the WBL team secured 1069 placement opportunities from the business community.

Coordinators approve each placement to ensure it provides the opportunity to develop workplace transferable skills and that the placement organisation complies with health and safety polices and insurances. Students may undertake a placement congruent with their studies or wider career aspirations. For example, in 2015/16 over 200 students, who were not undertaking a teaching qualification, embarked on a placement in an educational setting. Students are able to secure a placement anywhere in the UK. In 2015/16 circa 46% of students secured a placement opportunity using their own contacts (usually based close to their home) and this helps to provide a greater number, diversity and quality of placement opportunities than could be met in the Chester locale alone. In addition, as some students work to support themselves financially, they are able to utilise their own part-time work. In these instances, however, students are encouraged to negotiate additional tasks that extend their organisational knowledge and work-place skills.

Student Journey

Most students are introduced to the module in their first year (level four), when a member of the WBL team, attends a programme lecture and encourages them to start to prepare for their placement by updating their CV, thinking about the type of placement they wish to undertake and their preferred location.

In level five (second year) students from October to March students are timetabled to attend a series of lectures, delivered by the WBL team, in which the module is formally introduced and guidelines for placement acquisition and academic requirements are explored. Each student is allocated and given unrestricted access to a designated placement coordinator, who has specialisms and networks in the students' chosen area. Their role is to help explore options for both placement and wider career opportunities and prepare students for placement acquisition through support with letter writing, telephone skills, CV development, and interview skills. In addition, students are signposted to the Careers and Employability Department.

All students are required to attend placement preparation workshops in the first week of May. Students are then in their placement from May to June. At the start of the placement (or prior, where possible) each student must work with the placement provider to complete a Placement Objectives Document. This is a formal agreement of the role, key objectives and expected skill development outcomes. Assessment takes place at the end of their placement and is a 4000 word report comprising of three-part reflective critical analyses based on a set of graduate skills, which employers report as gaps and are congruent with the Careers and Employability model of a Chester Graduate, the TEF, QAA research, and professional bodies' approach to demonstrating competence. This report is also designed to increase students' ability to articulate transferable skills.

Academic Tutors

WBL Academic Tutors are drawn from academic staff across the university, and are responsible for the module supervision of up to 25 students over a two month period. In brief, a tutor is expected to:

- Lead induction sessions in the first week of May. All resources are provided by the WBL team, which the tutor has the option to use.
- Communicate with, and be the main contact for, students and placement providers during the placement period to:
  - Provide guidance
  - Resolve difficulties
  - Escalate the problem to the Director of WBL if required
- In the fourth week of June, complete a summative assessment (in Grademark) using a prepared 'rubric' and undertake moderation of another tutor's assessment.

To help tutors fulfill their role they are able to attend staff development sessions facilitated by the WBL team, where they are introduced to the module, its requirements, their role, assessment process and assessment criteria. A group of eight experienced WBL tutors undertake moderation of all submissions and three external examiners provide additional scrutiny.

The support from designated academic tutors is a key component of the module and a critical success factor for student engagement. However, the role is challenging and multifaceted, as may be seen in Fig. 3.1. Tutors represent the university, acting as a key conduit between students, the WBL team and placement providers.

This line of communication enables them to step in and resolve problems at an early stage, should they occur. Tutors also provide an essential quality assurance and enhancement role, which is focused on academic standards, such as that of assessment. They are also key to helping maintain standards within the placement itself, ensuring students are given opportunities to develop transferable employability skills. This includes

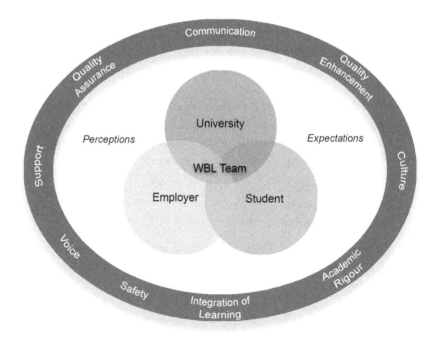

Fig. 3.1 The role of the work based learning tutor

guiding placement providers and students with regards to particular needs, managing their exceptions and perceptions. For example, students can become concerned that their work role is not at the level they anticipated. This can be due to a myriad of reasons but often the concern is in the initial days, where the placement provider is allowing time for training and familiarisation. Conversely, expectations of providers can be unrealistic with regard to students' understanding and level of skill. Therefore, mediation and problem resolution through support and effective communication are key tutor skills.

Pedagogic Rationale

WBL, at University of Chester, provides an experience that serves as a basis for meaningful critical reflection that is the pedagogic basis of the module. The assessment process supports greater meaning and learning to be derived by providing a bridge between the experience and theoretical conceptualisation. Students are required to undertake a process of deliberate systematic critical reflection on a specific experience, the learning is then fed forward into an assessed, personal and professional development plan, which as Schön (1984) highlights, helps facilitate improvement of practice and leading to positive outcomes (Sherwood and Horton-Deutsch 2012). The process resonates with Smith and Martin's (2014) research which shows the congruence between the skills of reflection and being a professional. The assessment process asks students to move beyond questions such as 'What did I do?' and 'Can I do it differently next time?' to ask 'Who am I?' and 'Is this who I want to be?' (Johns 2002). It is to try, as Brookfield (1998) has argued, to uncover and question deeply held assumptions that have been both socially and personally developed within a specific cultural context.

The challenges of developing reflective practice in higher education are well documented (Brockbank and McGill 1998; Johns 2002; Smith and Martin 2014). Meaningful engagement from students unused to expressing their thoughts, feelings and perceived weaknesses to an unknown audience can cause some students to feel sensitive, vulnerable and adopt potential defensive behaviours (Helyer 2015). For some, simply the process of writing in the first person, so they have ownership, is challenging as they have been conditioned by academic conventions to only write in the third person. However, changes in the job and graduate employment market requires a change from being a passive recipient of knowledge through didactic methods of instruction, to a growth mindset, the acceptance of self-responsibility in the learning process and gaining mastery of knowing how to learn (Rogers 1969), of which reflexivity is a key part (Brockbank and McGill 1998; Maudsley and Strivens 2000). In short, being a reflective practitioner enhances what may be brought to a job role and career development (Schön 1984; Billett 2011).

There is much research to support the notion that critical reflection is enhanced when students are given the time, space and tools by which they can reflect (Kolb and Kolb 2005) and it is a collaborative venture. Dewey and Schön transferred reflection as a concept of habitual wondering to a systematic examination of an event or problem (Farrell 2012). As such, to aid the development of critical reflection students are introduced to concepts such as reflection-in-action, and reflection-on-action, central to Schön's (1984) thinking, and models based on the work of Kolb (1984), Gibbs (1998) and Boud et al. (1985). These provide a framework with which to structure both their thinking and their assessment. Whilst critical reflection in reality is often messy and non-linear, unlike the neat learning models may suggest, they provide a useful access point for all students and enable the personalised activity of reflection to be structured in pedagogically robust way. With guidance from tutors students are able to select and use whichever framework best suits the context of their placement and experiences.

Within the WBL module students develop a Personal and Professional Development Plan (PPDP) for their future development. Within a 'Specific Measurable Agreed Realistic and Timed' framework, these 'SMART' goals have a long association within critical reflective practices (Brown et al. 2016) and importantly they provide a focus, and structure for implementation. The developmental nature of the process has become an essential part of WBL at University of Chester. This reflection-for-action (Kneale 2002) seeks to empower students to participate more fully in the development of their learning. It gives some control over what and how they learn it that is intended to foster notions of lifelong learning

(Quality Assurance Agency 2009). Ongoing engagement with PPDP via personal tutors in the final year of study is encouraged, to support meaningful engagement in academic skill development and employability (Head and Johnston 2012; Croot and Gedye 2006).

As students are encouraged to be autonomous and active learners, the key part of being a WBL tutor is the ability to listen and guide rather than instruct (Helyer 2015). Situated learning is supported via engagement and interaction with 'expert partners' in the form of employers and module tutors (Rogoff et al. 1996). This creates opportunities for students to master both job specific and transferable skills. In line with Vygotsky's (1978) notion of social learning, Brown et al. (1989, p. 34) refer to this type of learning as cognitive apprenticeship where students are able to "acquire, develop and use cognitive tools in [an] authentic domain activity through social interaction and the social construction of knowledge."

Evaluation

Each year the WBL team at the University of Chester undertakes detailed evaluation of the module from stakeholder feedback including module tutors, students and placement providers. This evaluation draws from evaluation questionnaires distributed to stakeholders and is supported by semi-structured interviews using nonprobability sampling with representatives from each stakeholder group.

Whilst it is often, anecdotally, reported that 'all students work' this isn't the case for the University of Chester with only around 50% undertaking some form of part time work alongside their studies. For those that engage in work experience it is often limited to low skilled experience. Crucially the module requires students to reflect on their experiences and articulate their skills. This, according to a Little (2007) and Graduate Recruiters is critical to students competing for graduate levels job on leaving university, whilst the number of graduate vacancies is expected to rise the employment market for graduates is challenging and competitive (Helyer and Lee 2014). A significant number of students report greater self-confidence, personal and professional growth through meaningful engagement with the module. In 2015/16, module evaluation showed 72% of students reporting that they had learnt new skills and knowledge as a result of the module and 78% recommending the module to other students.

Many students reported that they felt daunted about securing a placement and having to 'push' themselves, but 70% of students found the learning support helpful. Some students require significant support as they are not yet work ready. In 2015/16, the WBL team dealt with circa 50 students with issues that required urgent and ongoing attention. In addition, there is an increasing number of students with health challenges, in particular mental health, some of which do not manifest themselves until the student is in placement and away from the safe supportive university environment. Whilst all students are adult learners, the WBL team and academic tutors are always mindful of the duty of care we owe all students and act quickly to resolve problems. Thankfully, students reported that they valued the placement team support they were given and felt they had developed resilience, which in turn helped them develop personally and professionally.

Whilst international students' English language skills are more than sufficient to gain a place at University, for some these are not considered as sufficient or satisfactory for the workplace by employers. For these students a workplace simulation in the form of a consultancy project, supervised by a member of staff, has been created. This ensures all students have access to the same opportunities for experiential reflection.

The centralised structure, in which the WBL framework and staff sit enables the team to maximise student opportunities, act quickly to resolve problems through teamworking and shared networks, consistency of decision making and cost effectiveness. However, it can lead to lack of involvement and understanding of the module across the university. As such the team have to spend time communicating and internally marketing the programme to colleagues. There is a perennial issue of recruiting sufficient numbers of academic tutors who have interest in WBL *and* have space within their own workloads to devote sufficient time to support students and assess work. Tutor workshops are designed to explore operational elements but also the underlying philosophical issues of

WBL. Engaging tutors in how they perceive their role in the work based learning process is significant as the pedagogy may be very different from that they have experienced or value.

In 2015/16 feedback was obtained from 466 Placement Providers and the analysis provides further evidence of the multiple benefits gained by students and employers (Johnson and Burden 2003; Helyer and Lee 2014). The vast majority of placement providers, (92% of respondents) thought that having a student on placement helped bring a fresh perspective to an organisation and challenged their thinking by being able to look in detail at a particular process informed by theory or a particular demographic, which aligns to Wenger's (1998) ideas concerning communities of practice. The direct result of the experience led a number to offer further paid or other unpaid work experience opportunities to students. This was further supported by 98% of placement providers who suggested that their experience of hosting a student was a positive one due to the attitude shown by students and the relationship they had developed with the university.

> *Very rewarding and eye opening experience.*
> *We have hosted six placements now, and they have all been fantastic; they have really engaged and participated, and everybody has gained from their involvement in our organisation.*
> *[The student] was a breath of fresh air and has been a fantastic addition to our team, we will be sorry to see her leave.*

The perception of WBL as a mechanism for skill development was supported with 99% of placement providers agreeing that WBL helps prepare students for employment by developing key skills that they either did not have or lacked confidence in. The skills were also re-enforced through formal mechanisms such as the pre-placement meetings, the structured format of agreeing roles and responsibilities and through the appraisal, which 96% of placement providers found to be highly beneficial to the learning process.

Employers also highlighted that they were able to influence the curriculum, albeit in a small way, and enjoyed the involvement in student's development and supporting learning. In addition, they asserted that students helped bring a different perspective on their company and influenced practice, in some case the placement was a partnership of mutual learning.

> *I think it is brilliant scheme that allows students an opportunity to think about their future options.*
> *This year has been a fantastic experience. One student in particular has really excelled herself and will be offered future work with us.*

It is critical for universities to engage with employers and build strong relationships to maximise mutual partnership value (Brook and Corbridge 2016). Clearly to meet these demands it cannot be confined to career departments and job seeking skills, it needs to be a much more integral part of the curriculum if it is to succeed, which is an advantage of University of Chester's approach. WBL supports the concept of corporate social responsibility and helps the university play a significant role in the local and wider economy. Organisations, often SMEs and charities, speak about the crucial developmental work our students undertake through WBL. This is through the work of the WBL team, who work throughout the year to develop and maintain strong relationships with placement providers. Our 2015/16 evaluation showed that 96% of providers found that the communication from the University prior to the placement was clear and sufficient and 97% found that issues occurring during the placement were resolved to their satisfaction. This is critical as it both ensures ongoing engagement with WBL (96% wishing to host a student in 2016/17 and/or recommending doing so to their colleagues or other organisation) and also opens up other opportunities for the organisations and the university, such as knowledge transfer or research projects. It is also worth noting that placement providers welcome being involved in formally planning work and the written agreement that sets out all party's roles and responsibilities and proving a formal opportunity for providers to feedback on performance is welcomed and aligns to good practice.

> *We are delighted with the positive contribution made by the Chester University placement this year to a major public awareness project. Their work quality and commitment was a significant factor in the success of the project.*

Helyer and Lee (2014) highlight that a key factor in the usefulness of work experience is the duration; cited by Lowden et al. (2011) as preferably 6 months or longer. Also, sandwich placements tend to aid students' employability after their degrees, evidenced by the STEM accreditation reviews published in May 2016 (HEFCE 2016). Whilst the programme and activities of WBL at University of Chester is a year-long, the placement activity is only five weeks. This is not a specifically referred to in written feedback but anecdotal evidence suggests that this allows sufficient learning to take place, is long enough to appreciate the organisation yet does not overly disrupt employers' activities, create an overreliance on the student or indeed disrupt teaching. Organisations that are able and willing often take advantage of the opportunity to extend the WBL placement, albeit outside the module boundaries, however many do not. The notion of greater integration into the curriculum in the first year (Level 3 or 4) and in their final year (often but not exclusively Level 6) is the next stage of WBL development at University of Chester, as this may help better prepare students for the module, their employability needs and subsequently provide more opportunity for them to reflect on and build on their placement and learning with tutor support.

Being an assessed, mandatory, and credit bearing approach not only validates work based learning but also helps promote and facilitate student learning. Additionally, for the University of Chester it can enhance pedagogy by providing a different student experience where learning is situated and socially mediated (Eames and Bell 2005) which can provide an authentic learning experience that challenges comfort zones of tutors, students and employers. Given this, it is a tripartite symbiotic relationship that has been engendered. There are mutual and multiple benefits for the university, for employers and for students.

Conclusion and Recommendations

Our ongoing evaluation of the module has led to incremental changes and refinements in the approach. Through our own reflections and evaluations, we consider the pre placement preparation of students as a crucial, but often underappreciated part of the success of WBL at Chester. Feedback, which is gained annually from all stakeholders, demonstrates that the value of preparation in each stage of the process. This is because our approach supports the development of the following:

Learning How to Learn

The curriculum is predominantly derived from context of application of the learning (i.e. the workplace) as well as learners' current knowledge and experience. The pedagogy is also experiential in nature, centred on the application of learning in the workplace and evidence-based assessment of progress and achievement. However, this type of pedagogy may be unfamiliar to students and support in 'learning how to learn' is vital and therefore supported via tutor input.

Orientated into the Workplace

Gaining an understanding of organisational behaviour such as cultures, structures, and how to manage their entry into their work role and work team in addition to staying safe and healthy at work.

Developing Resilience

Whilst some thought is given to the benefits of WBL it is often primarily concerned with the placement activity. It is our view that the pre-placement activities of securing a placement is of equal recognition. Whilst this may concern practical issues of, for example getting the requisite Disclosure and Barring Service check, in reality the subtle difference to Chester's approach is to support the students to secure a placement. As such searching for opportunities, developing their CV, letter of application and interview technique is highly developmental and replicates the process many students will undertake pre or post-graduation. However, the capacity to recover quickly from difficulties and developing emotional resilience can require support and many students would benefit from greater help and advice. This is an ongoing challenge for the WBL team, and is likely to increase in difficulty as the diversity of our student body increases.

An often unseen benefit of the module is that it aids the concept of corporate social responsibility, a key part of the University of Chester's vision and mission statements. Organisations, often SMEs and those in the third sector, speak about the crucial developmental work students undertake through WBL, and as such a symbiotic relationship is engendered with benefits to all stakeholders.

We consider ongoing development of the module critical, and are already reviewing how WBL may be enhanced in a number of ways. Firstly, we are seeking to offer more bespoke placements for students in highly specialised studies and reviewing how support for securing such placements may be further enhanced. Secondly, we are looking to enrich the application process, particularly in supporting students in writing competency based applications and preparing for interviews and assessment centres. Thirdly, we are exploring the introduction of effective communities of practice through action learning sets, and the more effective utilisation of personal and professional development plans. We hope that further engagement by personal academic tutors and support departments at the university will help ensure plans are supported and realised.

In summary, students consistently report that they gain great confidence in the workplace and key transferable academic skills and excellent academic results, with 96% of students successfully completing the module in 2015/16. The use of standardised frameworks and models successfully allows the WBL team to ensure pedagogic consistency across diverse academic disciplines, employment opportunities and student experiences.

References

Billett, S. (2011). *Curriculum and pedagogic cases for effectively integrating practice-based experiences*. Sydney: Australian Learning and Teaching Council.

Boud, D., Keogh, R., & Walker, D. (1985). *Reflection: Turning experience into learning*. Oxford: Routledge.

Brockbank, A., & McGill, I. (1998). *Facilitating reflective learning in higher education*. Buckingham: SRHE/Open University Press.

Brook, C., & Corbridge, M. (2016). Work-based learning in a business school context: Artefacts, contracts, learning and challenges. *Higher Education, Skills and Work-Based Learning, 6*(3), 249–260.

Brookfield, S. (1998). Critically reflective practice. *Journal of Continuing Education in the Health Professions, 18*(4), 162–184.

Brown, G., Leonard, C., & Arthur-Kelly, M. (2016). *Writing SMARTER goals for professional learning and improving classroom practices*. Taylor and Francis Online. Retrieved April 4, 2017, from http://dx.doi.org.voyager.chester.ac.uk/10.1080/14623943.2016.118712

Brown, J., Collins, A., & Duguid, P. (1989). Situated cognition and the culture of learning. *Educational Researcher, 18*, 32–42.

Croot, D., & Gedye, S. (2006). Getting the most out of progress files and personal development planning. *Journal of Geography in Higher Education, 30*(1), 173–179. Retrieved January 9, 2017, from http://www.tandfonline.com.libezproxy.open.ac.uk/doi/abs/10.1080/03098260500499857

Dearing, R. (1997). *Higher education in the learning society: Report of the national committee of enquiry into higher education*. London: HMSO.

Department of Business, Innovation and Skills. (2015). *Fulfilling our potential: Teaching excellence, social mobility and student choice*. London: BIS.

Department of Business, Innovation and Skills. (2016a). *Success as a knowledge economy: Teaching excellence, social mobility and student choice*. London: BIS.

Department of Business, Innovation and Skills. (2016b). *Computer science degree accreditation and graduate employability: Shadbolt review*. London: BIS.

Eames, C., & Bell, B. (2005). Using sociocultural views of learning to investigate the enculturation of students into the scientific community through work placements. *Canadian Journal of Science, Mathematics and Technology Education, 5*, 153–169.

Farrell, T. S. C. (2012). Reflecting on reflective practice: (Re)visiting Dewey and Schon. *Tesol Journal, 3*(1), 7–16. Retrieved December 27, 2016, from http://onlinelibrary.wiley.com.libezproxy.open.ac.uk/doi/10.1002/tesj.10/abstract

Gibbs, G. (1998). *Learning by doing: A guide to teaching and learning methods*. London: Further Education Unit.

Head, K. S., & Johnston, J. H. (2012). Evaluation of the personal development portfolio in higher education: An explorative study. *Nurse Education Today, 32*(8), 857–861.

HEFCE. (2016). *Graduate employment and accreditation in STEM*. Retrieved February, 2017, from http://www.hefce.ac.uk/skills/gradstemreview/stemreview/

Helyer, R. (2011). Aligning higher education with the world of work. *Higher Education, Skills and Work-Based Learning, 1*(2), 95–105.

Helyer, R. (2015). Learning through reflection: The critical role of reflection in work-based learning (WBL). *Journal of Work-Applied Management, 7*(1), 15–27.

Helyer, R., & Lee, D. (2014). The role of work experience in the future employability of higher education graduates. *Higher Education Quarterly, 68*(3), 348–372.

Johns, C. (2002). *Guided reflection: Advancing practice.* Oxford: Blackwell Publishing.

Johnson, S., & Burden, T. (2003). *Young people, employability and the induction process.* York: Joseph Rowntree Foundation.

Kneale, P. (2002). Developing and embedding reflective portfolios in geography. *Journal of Geography in Higher Education, 26*(1), 81–94.

Kolb, A. Y., & Kolb, D. A. (2005). Learning styles and learning spaces: Enhancing experiential learning in higher education. *Academy of Management Learning & Education, 4*(2), 193–212.

Kolb, D. (1984). *Experiential learning: Experience as the source of learning and development.* London: Prentice-Hall.

Little, B. (2007). *Learning and employability, series one: Employability and work-based learning.* York: Higher Education Academy.

Lowden, K., Hall, S., Elliot, D., & Lewin, J. (2011). Employers' perceptions of the employability skills of new graduates. Glasgow: University of Glasgow SCRE Centre and Edge Foundation Mountbatten Institute.

Maudsley, G., & Strivens, J. (2000). Promoting professional knowledge, experiential learning and critical thinking for medical students. *Medical Education, 34*(7), 535–544.

McKinsey Global Institute. (2016). *Independent work: Choice, necessity, and the gig economy.* Retrieved February 21, 2017, from www.mckinsey.com/mgi

Quality Assurance Agency. (2009). *Personal development planning: Guidance for institutional policy and practice in higher education.* Retrieved January 8, 2017, from http://www.qaa.ac.uk/en/Publications/Documents/Personal-development-planning-guidance-for-institutional-policy-and-practice-in-higher-education.pdf

Raelin, J. A. (2008). *Work-based learning: Bridging knowledge and action in the workplace.* San Francisco: Jossey-Bass.

Rogers, C. (1969). *Freedom to learn: A view of what education might become.* Columbus, OH: Charles Merill.

Rogoff, B., Matusov, B., & White, S. (1996). Models of teaching and learning: Participation in a community of learners. In D. Olson & N. Torrance (Eds.), *The handbook of cognition and human development* (pp. 388–414). Oxford, UK: Blackwell.

Schön, D. A. (1984). *The reflective practitioner: How professionals think in action.* New York: Basic Books.

Sherwood, G. D., & Horton-Deutsch, S. (2012). *Reflective practice transforming education and improving outcomes.* Indianapolis: Sigma Theta Tau International. Retrieved December 27, 2016, from https://ebookcentral.proquest.com/lib/openuk/reader.action?docID=3383922

Smith, S., & Martin, J. (2014). Practitioner capability: Supporting critical reflection during workbased placement—A pilot study. *Higher Education Skills and Work-Based Learning, 4*(30), 284–300.

Tudor, S., & Mendez, R. (2014). Lessons from covey: Win-win principles for university-employer engagement. *Higher Education, Skills and Work-Based Learning, 4*(3), 213–227.

Vygotsky, L. S. (1978). *Mind in society: The development of higher psychological processes.* Cambridge, MA: Harvard University.

Wenger, E. (1998). *Communities of practice: Learning, meaning, and identity.* Cambridge: Cambridge University Press.

Wilson, T. (2013). *The social revolution.* Keynote Speech at ASET Annual Conference, Greenwich University, London, 3–5 September 2013.

4

Managing Degree Apprenticeships Through a Work Based Learning Framework: Opportunities and Challenges

L. Rowe

Introduction

The Higher Education Institute (HEI) employer interface has attracted much attention in recent years, particularly in light of current dissatisfaction with graduate work-readiness. Concurrently, pressure upon new entrants to the workplace is accelerating through an unprecedented pace of change in technology, requiring currency of employability skills and resilience for individuals to adapt, thrive and perform effectively in an increasingly unpredictable global environment. In 2014 a new form of apprenticeship was proposed in England to simultaneously address these skills shortages whilst offering a genuine alternative to undergraduate degree programmes. Hailed as "the greatest opportunity ever seen for anyone concerned with skills and employment" (Jeffrey 2016, p. 1) early HEI adopters have already successfully collaborated with employers to launch business management degree apprenticeships with initial cohorts nearing completion of their first year.

L. Rowe (✉)
University of Chester, Chester, UK
e-mail: lisa.rowe@chester.ac.uk

The chapter proposed here is therefore highly significant for two reasons. The first is to inform HEI practice and pedagogic development, particularly in terms of work based learning degree apprenticeship design and delivery within the new political apprenticeship reforms, which are attracting renewed interest across the globe. This is one of the first evaluations to be published upon this type of programme, affording a unique opportunity to explore how pedagogic approaches to building graduate employability can be improved.

Secondly it considers the effectiveness of the emerging generation of work based business degree apprentices in terms of performance, retention and engagement as a result of well-developed employability skills. This degree apprenticeship challenges academically led, full time provision with a 20% off the job learning model. An explicit employer led focus cumulates in a separate synoptic end point assessment, altering the fundamentally traditional approach to embedding employability skills into something far more tacit in nature, through negotiated projects, reflective learning and employer mentoring.

In order to examine the effectiveness of this new pedagogic approach, the chapter focuses upon the design and development of a business management degree apprenticeship. It explores current literature concerning work based learning pedagogy and reflective practice, the role of the employer as a mentor and the development of employability skills. It incorporates an exploratory case study based upon one of the earliest cohorts in England, collectively identifying a complex range of themes and issues for each stakeholder in designing and developing degree apprenticeships.

The chapter concludes with recommendations for HEIs who wish to take advantage of this new and fast changing political agenda through their own development of similar, highly innovative and lucrative initiatives.

Background

The introduction of degree apprenticeships is one of the biggest changes in HE for decades providing a sustainable prospect to simultaneously develop relevant talent and a viable alternative to traditional programmes, and an opportunity to improve social mobility (City and Guilds 2015; Jeffrey 2016; Institute of Apprenticeships (IfA) 2017). One of the earliest launched is the Chartered Manager Degree Apprenticeship (CMDA), creating a lucrative opportunity for many business schools. The first cohorts commenced in September 2016 with a rapid acceleration of 3000 by 2018 predicted and a Senior Leaders Master's Degree Apprenticeship imminent (Universities United Kingdom (UUK) 2017).

An aspiration to develop educational systems to meet the needs of employers and the wider economy is driving this change (Lee 2012; Wall and Perrin 2015). Despite record levels of graduates in the UK it has long been argued that educators do not provide relevant and efficient learning for transfer to the workplace leading to poor graduate work-readiness and under-developed transferable skills (Archer and Davison 2008; Hughes et al. 2013; Chartered Association of Business Schools 2014). The fundamental concept of degree apprenticeships is that higher qualifications are designed, and subsequently delivered in partnership with employers and professional bodies, solving employability and professional competence issues. Funding is embedded into a levy from April 2017 for large employers with a payroll exceeding £3 million, whilst smaller organisations receive notable support, representing a huge opportunity for universities (BIS 2016). In spite of challenges facing the sector, HEIs who are prepared to evolve and adapt to create high quality programmes and infrastructures will be able to benefit from, and indeed largely influence the success of the levy (Morley 2017; Hill 2017).

Curriculum Design—Embedding Employability Skills

The challenges in embedding employability skills directly into mainstream academic curriculum are widely evidenced, along with the recognition that arguably more relevant and practical opportunities to develop tacit and professional knowledge readily exist within live business environments (Archer and Davison 2008; Hughes et al. 2013; Billett 2014). The fundamental concept of degree apprenticeships requires closer engagement with employers and professional bodies to directly tackle employability and professional competence issues. Although this presents an entirely unique opportunity to embed employability strategies through collaborative design and delivery, there are resource implications for employers who will need to provide additional support and guidance to apprentices. The implicit expectation is that managers will need to develop and adopt new approaches to support and manage colleagues as they progress through programmes, combining work-related study with full time employment.

In an era of unprecedented change and mobility classed as the fourth industrial revolution, employees are entering a relentless and rapidly changing workplace, where seemingly stable jobs can quickly evolve or dissipate in lieu of emergent competencies within a "knowledge intensive economy" (Bridgstock 2009, p. 31; CIPD 2012; Kossek and Perrigino 2016).

Consequentially employers are less concerned with trained graduates, forcing adaptive pedagogic development with greater emphasis upon assessment of non-technical, transferable skills (Harvey 2003; Jackson 2016).

Research into skills development and deployment in early careers could better support HEI pedagogy but it largely focuses upon mid-career development, leaving early professional journeys relatively under-explored (Trede et al. 2012; Jackson 2016). Consequently, a more holistic concept of employability emerges, cultivated through an extensive range of practical and theoretical competencies which informs skilled practice and identity, in turn contributing towards performance (Hinchliffe and Jolly 2011; Pegg et al. 2012). Similarly the CMDA standard focuses keenly upon performance through knowledge, skills and behaviours whilst overtly referencing underpinning psychological conditions (CMI 2015; UK Commission for Employment and Skills (UKCES) 2016). Crucially 80% of apprentices' time must be spent 'on the job' creating opportunities for skills driven curricula. Responsibility for sustainable and adaptive workforces can no longer remain the preserve of HE, but compression of study may place an unprecedented burden upon apprentices, particularly in "high prestige occupations" which includes managerial and leadership positions (Kossek and Perrigino 2016, p. 780). The synoptic end point assessment may lead to a disjointed sequential process which could create an excessively sharp distinction between the degree and professional competence assessment, also risking HEI income (Schön 1987; Lee 2012).

Work Based Learning Pedagogy

It is widely accepted that our modern learning society demands a culture promoting opportunities for lifelong learning, developing conceptual, helicopter and analytical thinking skills. Reduced demand for technically trained graduates has led to a preference for reflective employees who can analyse, critique and synthesise experiences, developing themselves accordingly (Harvey 2003). The emphasis is upon empowering and enhancing learners to demonstrate a range of qualities, particularly the ability to think and work 'outside the box' (Wisher 1994). This requirement for learners to self-develop skills is forcing HEIs to adapt from the deep-rooted continuum of 'process based' teaching towards experiential and reflective learning, classic hallmarks of work based learning designed in collaboration with employers (Kolb 1984; Raelin 1997; Boud and Solomon 2001; Smith and Paton 2014). Indeed, the term 'work based learning' draws upon notions of 'lifelong learning', 'employability' and 'flexibility' and can "embrace all forms of learning that are generated or stimulated by the needs of the workplace…" (Unwin and Fuller 2003, p. 7). The differences found in ways in which work based learning is referred to and understood may arguably be a product of the more densely populated work based learning 'landscape' in recent years, with an increasingly diverse range of academic and training institutions and employer organisations engaged in a variety of different partnership arrangements. Here, for example, the idea of 'flexibility', which is seen as a central characteristic of work based learning programmes has implications for the type of learning arrangements, settings and associated modes of delivery, levels and assessment methods. By inference, work based learning may take a variety of different forms in response to the learner and learning organisation's needs.

Authors such as Boud and Solomon (2001) have set out some defining characteristics of work based learning programmes, which emphasise the importance of the HE–organisational partnership as a setting for mutual learning benefits to both the organisation and HE institution, as well as the individual learner. Other defining characteristics include: the negotiated nature of the learning contract, the flexibility and often customisation of the learning pathway for each participant that reflects the individual's existing capabilities and learning needs in the workplace, the work-driven nature of the curriculum, and the fact that most learning takes place in the workplace setting rather than in the 'classroom'.

UK work based learning has largely remained the preserve of nursing, medicine and social work despite Western economic performance's implicit link to human capital and knowledge stock which requires development of interactive pedagogy and experiential learning (QAA 2017). Since business school occupational disciplines require some of the most advanced cognitive skills, initiatives to integrate lifelong self-learning through reflective, transformative practice are critical to ensure skills currency and employability (Cranmer 2006). However this requires a radically different pedagogy incorporating learner space and time for project supervision, critical thinking and problem solving, subsequently creating resourcing and timetabling problems within confined HEI systems (World Economic Forum 2009; Kossek and Perrigino 2016).

On the job learning is already one of the most effective training practices, second only to in-house training with line manager coaching (CIPD 2012). Self-development requires encouragement of far broader positive attitudes with a 'can do' approach in order to develop a professional identity, career security and growth, but the context in which skills will be established and verified is largely beyond HEI control (Bridgstock 2009; Pegg et al. 2012; Jackson 2016; UKCES 2016). Individual roles and projects may not have academic credibility or parity and there are risks concerning manipulation of content and lack of objectivity (Lester and Costley 2010). Conversely employer expectations of intercultural interactions between students resulting in cross-pollinated ideas have not materialised, largely because work based learners have less regular opportunities to access HEI skills development interventions (Bishop and Hordern 2017).

Apprentices are more reliant upon workplace supervision, the quality of which may vary with opportunities to learn affected by organisational type, size and sector, intangible cultures and norms (Billett 2014; Jack and Donnellan 2010). Some may benefit from committed role model mentors, who can effectively enable and influence, allowing seamless integration of curricula and workplace. In addition the UK continues to suffer from weak management practice with 2.4 million untrained 'accidental managers' and just 28% of new graduates receiving any training but it is unclear how this, coupled with an increasingly consumerist approach towards employment and education, might affect degree apprenticeships (Accenture 2015; CMI 2017). Ironically, the new generation of degree apprentices may accrue more relevant management qualifications than their superiors upon whom their development relies.

Given the vast array of complexities facing HEIs, it is unsurprising that many will seek to eliminate the pedagogic challenges discussed by designing "academy-based" rather than "academy-aligned" degree apprenticeship programmes (Dalrymple et al. 2014, p. 78).

Case Study

Overview

This case study is a reflective narrative of a HEI's experience of delivering the CMDA within an existing work based learning framework, building upon an earlier review of apprenticeship development (Rowe et al. 2016). Data gathered during June and July 2017 was based upon the first cohort of eight first year CMDA apprentices and four employers. This comprised documented evidence and semi-structured interviews with academics, apprentices and employers. Anecdotal data from other HEIs and employers strengthens the validity of findings.

Recent reports suggest that the CMDA will attract nearly 3000 apprentices by 2018, forming 36% of all apprenticeship standards (UUK 2017). 60 enterprising HEIs are currently engaged in degree apprenticeship activity, but development is incremental, due in part to internal challenges of embedding new processes and procedures. Pedagogies vary but there is growing evidence of learner-centered curricula developing through experiential learning and reflective practice.

Case Study Findings

A profile overview and projections for cohorts 1 and 2 already reveal some interesting variances shown in Table 4.1. Growth is predominantly regional, aligning with current research (UUK 2017) although some national interest is developing. This is due to the programme's work based design incorporating block workshop delivery supported by electronically based learning materials. It also supports employability skills development, aligning with additional professional body qualifications beyond other more traditional frameworks.

Recruitment

Despite encouraging projections the institution remains cautious given the challenges highlighted and this mood continues to be reflected across the sector (UVAC 2017). HEIs are well versed in the vagaries of funding, and delivery expense ratios creating a circumspect response to time consuming, resource intensive programme development. Design and delivery of employer led degrees is problematic with painfully slow adaptation of outwardly facing processes inhibiting enterprise. Many are understandably reticent with one Russell Group respondent saying: *"We will wait and see how you and others fare."* Even the most experienced work based learning providers have been surprised at the inability to forecast apprenticeship numbers and the protracted timeframes required to develop relationships and programmes with employers. Application processes have been further complicated by employer led HRM recruitment and training policies as well as the traditional view of apprenticeship hiring cycles, forcing HEIs to adapt from their protracted marketing

Table 4.1 Profile of CMDA Cohorts 2016 and 2017 based upon projections

Cohort	Levy	Number	Gender	Age range	Status	Geographical spread
2016–2019	75% levy	8	88% female	18–47	75% new employees	0–10 miles
2017–2020	87% levy	58	48% female	18–36	17% new employees	6–46 miles

campaigns and compress processes to meet demand. Entry requirements may be compromised without clear alignment of HEI and employer selection criteria.

The initial cohort has led to a cohesive employer HEI interface, transitioning smoothly in most instances. However, there is potential for resurgent issues to develop as cohorts grow. Whilst some employers recognise the opportunity to recruit new talent, the earliest providers confirm a trend to reconfigure internal training policies to recoup levies, highlighting concerns that existing training and development programmes may merely transfer into degree and master's apprenticeships, failing to address a stalled social mobility agenda (CBI 2016). The majority of participants are employed within levy paying organisations, which have been quick to recognise the opportunity. As one oil terminal operations director said: *"The new degree apprenticeship has given members of my senior management team the chance to gain a formal academic qualification and professional registration credibility without impacting on their ability to carry out their work commitments."*

A growing complication is the portability of qualifications from more experienced applicants. Whilst a work based framework can accommodate transfer of prior accredited and relevant learning (APCL), it is more difficult to award credit for prior experiential learning (APEL) whilst also meeting professional body and apprenticeship standards. Applicants without prior work based learning experience must take core reflective and project planning modules to successfully complete the programme, classed as new learning within funding rules. A highly complex cohort is emerging with varying entry points, APCL claims and payment schedules. The requisite Level 2 Maths and English qualifications for apprenticeship completion has elicited a belligerent response from several senior employees.

Local school support for degree apprenticeships has been sporadic, with many maintaining focus upon University league tables. Even so there is no shortage of applicants with over 200 registrations by July 2017 for just 17 new opportunities. Indeed, there is a general lack of entry-level opportunities with very limited CMDA vacancies available nationally, perhaps because of an emerging disconnect between the standard and the likely employee status of school leavers. Whilst degrees are viewed as a mechanism to equip aspiring graduates, apprenticeships require embedded skills development, here aligning only to employees who are enabled to practice management and leadership.

Early adopters of degree apprenticeships are not necessarily unhappy with this outcome. For now, the CMDA is more aligned to an executive education model, diversifying programme portfolios and allaying fears over the dilution of other courses. Additionally, the applicant pool has created an unintentional database. Rather than viewing apprentices and undergraduates as separate entities, a more cohesive marketing strategy can broaden opportunities and strengthen access for non-traditional students amidst a decreasing youth population (UUK 2017). The soaring popularity of management frameworks has led to criticism of the IfA's commitment to boosting social mobility, and as increasing numbers find out about this unprecedented opportunity, competition for depleted vacancies means that the oft cited 'ladder of opportunity' remains challenging to access (HM Government 2013; Department for Education 2017).

Resources

Reliance upon funding and short recruitment cycles herald a departure from guaranteed, front-loaded income, creating a significantly different cash flow, with more risk-averse institutions unwilling to resource vulnerable activity. Pressurised academics have little opportunity to disrupt their existing activities, making it difficult to garner cross faculty and departmental support for shared delivery models. End point contractual agreements are expensive and risky given the difficulty in forecasting starts and retention rates, plus there are additional costs for professional body administration, business development and workplace visits. Such constraints have led to demands for economies of scale, raising the prospect of larger class sizes which may ultimately threaten key components of work based learning practice including individually negotiated learning modules, breadth of assessment methods, reflective practice and the provision of full formative feedback. Despite extensive experience in delivering work based learning pedagogy, many cross-functional departments require strategic adaptation to student facing mechanisms, resulting in difficult conversations over the status of stakeholders. Indeed as one NHS Trust succinctly put it: *"Let us be clear. These are our employees first, not students."*

Curriculum Design

Whilst Degree Apprenticeships clearly have huge potential to provide a significant income stream, their inception is difficult and time-consuming work. Many employers and apprenticeship standards require alignment to professional bodies but the synoptic end point assessment means that skills and competencies remain a risky separate entity. A robust work based learning framework naturally focuses upon skills development and can be tailored to adapt to employer needs, thus reducing this risk. A less attractive option is to re-draft traditional module content, resulting in a plethora of learning outcomes to ensure that both practical and theoretical competencies are tested.

In addition to the practicalities of assessment, it is important that curriculum design supports employers who are contributing towards the cost of apprenticeships, paying salaries and committing to 20% off the job learning. Here employers are beginning to recognise the advantages of HEIs committed to work based learning pedagogies, resulting in programmes which *"are not too invasive"* (large manufacturing SME). Negotiated, experiential project content, designed in collaboration with employers provides tangible outcomes, attracting superb feedback from employers. One multinational manufacturing company said: *"The work that the apprentices have completed here is of such a high standard that I am now in a position to move this forward and put the plans into practice. I really did not expect work of this standard so early into their programme."* A micro SME was similarly positive about their apprentice's projects: *"This gives us an opportunity to do things that we wouldn't ordinarily have the time, or the skills to do. It has taken us several steps forward and the benefits are significant."*

The first cohort has attracted a diversity of age and backgrounds, which has led to some incredibly successful and cohesive workshops to date: *"I think the different perceptions, expectations, probably helped it be quite a dynamic session, with strong engagement. Young and old were able to compare time management strategies quite well—different calls on their time and different strategies, but spinning ideas off each other."* Two modules are specifically designed to develop apprentices' skills and capabilities associated with reflective processes and to encourage the vision necessary for action planning. These attributes have already been evident through each apprentices' personal and professional development within each module, and critically through their proactive generation of experiential learning opportunities, demonstrating their understanding of the potential for the workplace to become a catalyst for learning. The highly experienced programme leader has congratulated the cohort, confirming already that: *"They have really grasped the principle that they need to learn as well as produce."* Even during the first module there was a general move *"from activists to leaders"* (Honey and Mumford 1986), with relevant skills development evidenced through a personal SWOT analysis and 360 degree feedback in subsequent Level 4 modules. Critical appraisal and reflective essays are key assessment methods, based upon common models and components of reflection (e.g. Gibbs 1988; Johns 2006; Driscoll 2007). This framework effectively challenges the apprentices to critically analyse situations, reducing criticism leveled at graduates regarding their tendency toward descriptive writing. The experience of leading projects and development of reflective practice to drive employability skills is evident: *"I worked alongside five other apprentices on an integrated marketing communications campaign, developing helpful theoretical and practical knowledge. We worked effectively as a team and I have enhanced my project planning skills."*

Workplace Supervision

Degree study alongside full time employment creates a tough learning environment requiring resilience, determination and drive. Punishing workloads and external influences including health, redundancy and family have weakened retention rates to just 75% in year one. Previous work based learning modes have sustained the ability to negotiate completion rates, but compressed models reduce contractual commitments, meet funding rules and expedite fee payments. A sustained effort to retain and engage learners and employers is of paramount importance, both in university and in the workplace. The CMDA standard addresses this to some extent in the implicit requirement to identify and assign employer mentors, however the reality of monitoring this will be challenging as cohorts grow. Within this cohort the role of the mentor is well defined, forming a distinct role from HR Managers to Managing Directors, depending on organisational size. All had maintained direct line management responsibility, supporting development through appraisals, project development and HEI liaison. As in the classroom, generational disconnect has not been an issue with one MD saying: *"The degree of enthusiasm that I think you get is of course part of being eighteen. It's very, very motivating for the company."*

Clearly the quality of employer recruitment processes will to some extent predicate the success of the programme but reliance upon their support of academic progress and project development remains largely untested to date. Personal academic tutors and managers may interchangeably assume apprentice-mentoring roles whilst in smaller or less hierarchical structures, a variety of workplace staff may formally or informally mentor. Some HEIs have already built an academic mentor support system into their apprenticeships, and others are developing employer training sessions and guidance packs. Although on-site visits are resource intensive, they have formed a valuable opportunity to surface priorities and issues at the earliest stage, particularly with all stakeholders present to discuss progress, mentoring, project content and programme administration. These visits serve to support and encourage apprentices to take ownership of their career development. The negotiation of bespoke projects requires skilled navigation of individual agendas through open dialogue to facilitate appropriate content and meet academic rigour. As one employer put it: *"It's really good to be involved and great to forge relationships with you. The degree is for both of us and we should support her".*

Conclusion

This is the first publication to consider the efficacy of the design and development of a work based business management degree apprenticeship. In evaluating the pedagogic design of the CMDA, it offers a useful framework for others to consider, whilst raising awareness of potential challenges and benefits. Indeed, both are considerable, particularly in the light of lucrative funding opportunities, but there must be careful consideration given to resourcing, particularly client and programme management as cohorts grow and profiles inevitably change to potentially challenge undergraduate provision. Such diversification of HE delivery fits perfectly into work based learning frameworks, providing efficient and relevant learning across a variety of contexts and faculties. The opportunity to work with employers, radically update and develop curricula and practice, and subsequent involvement with cutting edge research activity cannot be underestimated. These transformative teaching strategies support employability, social mobility and widening participation of HE, evidenced by some of the earliest adopters already scoring highly in teaching excellence framework measures (CMI 2017). Indeed, the earliest emergent data suggests that there is better distribution of higher apprenticeship learners across HEFCE's five participation of local areas (POLAR) quintiles than traditional HE programmes (UVAC 2017). Rich and overwhelmingly positive employer and academic feedback is testament to the effectiveness of the curricula and the issues surrounding employability have largely dissipated, as a result of the employer leading future graduate skills development. Local talent will be easier to retain as the opportunity to study and work locally becomes more attractive. The employer's role as mentor has also been successful to date, with clear cost benefits derived from tripartite relationships and innovative project completion.

There is a cautionary note however, for whilst many of the challenges raised in the literature appear to have been successfully overcome in this pilot study, findings were based upon a small cohort and may not be representative of a larger sample size, longitudinal study or more diverse cohort profile. Much of its success has resulted largely from an enhanced HEI employer interface and sustained academic collaboration with employers and apprentices. Resourcing is a critical issue here and further constraint through rising numbers will bring pressure to bear upon programme teams. It is acknowledged therefore that some of the issues raised within the literature may not yet surfaced and the findings cannot be generalised across other disciplines. More longitudinal research is needed, with larger sample sizes across a range of disciplines and pedagogic frameworks.

Despite such limitations, the prediction for degree apprenticeship growth is predicted to increase across the UK by 650% in 2017/18. It would be unwise to ignore this agenda and universities who grasp the challenge now by investing in the development of work based learning frameworks are likely to see significant and sustained benefits (UUK 2017).

Recommendations

Several recurrent themes have emerged from early adopters of the CMDA resulting in key recommendations for future degree apprenticeship development. Of primary importance is resourcing, in the first instance requiring a centralised apprenticeship function with a project board or strategy group comprising senior staff to oversee progress, agree direction and fully map end to end processes for degree apprenticeship design and delivery. This ensures engagement from a number of cross institutional departments to ensure efficient and responsive progress for activities including improvement of employer engagement and employer facing mechanisms, cross-faculty development of frameworks and programmes to enable sharing of core work based learning modules, the sharing of resources for all administrative processes and a cohesive and comprehensive marketing offer incorporating a range of access routes into HE.

At faculty level there is a need to engage enterprising, employer facing practitioners to design and deliver programmes in collaboration with employers and professional bodies through the implementation of work based learning frameworks. This new pedagogic approach requires academic support with apprenticeship portfolios, engagement with end point assessors and the provision of guidance for new trailblazer groups in subject specific areas. Creation and publication of supportive strategies for employers is also recommended, comprising mentoring guidance and/or training for employers. There is also a necessity for academics to begin researching and publishing data based upon findings as programmes develop and grow, and to collaborate with other HEIs already delivering work based learning apprenticeships to ensure that best practice is shared across the sector.

References

Accenture UK Graduate Employment Survey. (2015). Retrieved July 26, 2017, from https://www.accenture.com/t20150706T235021__w__/usen/_acnmedia/Accenture/Conversion-Assets/DotCom/Documents/Global/PDF/Dualpub_17/Accenture-UK-University-Grad-Research-2015.pdf

Archer, W., & Davison, J. (2008). *Graduate employability*. The Council for Industry and Higher Education.

Billett, S. (2014). Integrating learning experiences across tertiary education and practice settings: A socio-personal account. *Educational Research Review, 12*, 1–13.

BIS. (2016). *Apprenticeship levy: How it will work*. London: Department for Business, Innovation and Skills. Retrieved July 26, 2017, from www.gov.uk/government/publications/apprenticeship-levy-how-it-will-work/apprenticeship-levy-how-it-will-work#accessing-money-paid-under-the-apprenticeship-levy

Bishop, D., & Hordern, J. (2017). *Degree apprenticeships: Higher technical or technical higher (education)?* Gatsby Charitable Foundation.

Boud, D., & Solomon, N. (Eds.). (2001). *Work-based learning: A new higher education?* Buckingham: SRHE and Open University.

Bridgstock, R. (2009). The graduate attributes we've overlooked: Enhancing graduate employability through career management skills. *Higher Education Research and Development, 28*(1), 31–44.

Chartered Institute of Personnel and Development. (2012). *Learning and talent development survey*. London: CIPD.

Chartered Manager Institute. (2015). *All you need to know about the new Chartered Manager Degree Apprenticeship*. Retrieved July 26, 2017, from http://www.managers.org.uk/insights/news/2015/november/all-you-need-to-know-about-the-new-chartered-manager-degree-apprenticeship?sc_trk=follow%20hit,{86CB756B-AB02-44E6-995A-305C69252B29},accidental+manager

Chartered Manager Institute. (2017). *Higher education providers awarded gold medals for teaching excellence*. Retrieved July 26, 2017, from http://www.managers.org.uk/insights/news/2017/june/further-education-institutions-awarded-gold-medals-for-teaching-excellence?sc_trk=follow%20hit,{86CB756B-AB02-44E6-995A-305C69252B29},tef

City and Guilds Group Industry Skills Board. (2015). *Making apprenticeships work—The employers' perspective*. Retrieved July 26, 2017, from www.cityandguilds.com/~/media/Documents/Courses-and-Quals/Apprenticeships/Making%20Apprenticeships%20Work_Full%20report_web%20 version%20pdf.ashx

Confederation of British Industries. (2016). *Radical rethink required for apprenticeship levy: Business concerned about levy but committed to skills*. Retrieved April 13, 2018, from http://educationandskills.cbi.org.uk/reports

Cranmer, S. (2006). Enhancing graduate employability: Best intentions and mixed outcomes. *Studies in Higher Education, 31*, 169–184.

Dalrymple, R., Kemp, C., & Smith, P. (2014). Characterising work-based learning as a triadic learning endeavour. *Journal of Further and Higher Education, 38*(1), 75–89.

Department for Education. (2017). *Apprenticeship framework starts and apprenticeship standard starts by level*. Retrieved December 16, 2017, from https://data.gov.uk/dataset/fe-data-library-apprenticeships

Driscoll, J. (2007). *Practising clinical supervision: A reflective approach for healthcare professionals*. Elsevier Health Sciences.

Gibbs, G. (1988). *Learning by doing: A guide to teaching and learning methods*. Oxford: Further Education Unit, Oxford Brookes University.

Harvey, L. (2003). *Transitions from higher education to work*. A briefing paper prepared by Lee Harvey (Centre for Research and Evaluation, Sheffield Hallam University), with advice from ESECT and LTSN Generic Centre colleagues. Retrieved July 26, 2017, from http://bit.ly/oeCgqW

Hill, S. (2017). *Universities can help make a success of the apprenticeship levy*. Retrieved April 13, 2018 from https://wonkhe.com/blogs/universities-can-help-make-the-apprenticeship-levy-a-success/

Hinchliffe, G. W., & Jolly, A. (2011). Graduate identity and employability. *British Educational Research Journal, 37*(4), 563–584.

HM Government. (2013). *The future of apprenticeships in England: Implementation plan*. Retrieved July 26, 2017, from https://www.gov.uk/government/uploads/system/uploads/attachment_data/file/253073/bis-13-1175-future-of-apprenticeships-in-england-implementation-plan.pdf

Honey, P., & Mumford, A. (1986). *Using your learning styles*. Maidenhead: Peter Honey.

Hughes, T., Sheen, J., & Birkin, G. (2013). *Industry graduate skills needs*. Summary report for the National Centre for Universities and Business, CFE Research. Retrieved July 26, 2017, from http://www.ncub.co.uk/reports/cfe.html

Institute for Apprenticeships. (2017). *The institute 6 months on: Purpose, vision and corporate objectives*. Retrieved December 16, 2017, from https://www.instituteforapprenticeships.org/about/the-institute-6-months-on

Jack, G., & Donnellan, H. (2010). Recognising the person within the developing professional: Tracking early careers of newly qualified child care social workers in three local authorities in England. *Social Work Education, 29*(3), 305–318.

Jackson, D. (2016). Re-conceptualising graduate employability: The importance of pre-professional identity. *Higher Education Research and Development, 35*(5), 925–939.

Jeffrey, C. (2016). *Is your vision the same or similar to mine—Can you see what I see?* Association of Employers and Learning Providers. Retrieved July 26, 2017, from www.aelp.org.uk/ news/aelp-blog/details/is-your-vision-the-same-or-similar-to-mine-can-you/

Johns, C. (2006). *Engaging reflection in practice: A narrative approach*. London: Wiley-Blackwell.

Kolb, D. (1984). *Experiential learning: Experience as the source of learning and development*. London: Prentice Hall.

Kossek, E. E., & Perrigino, M. B. (2016). Resilience: A review using a grounded integrated occupational approach. *The Academy of Management Annals, 10*(1), 729–797.

Lee, D. (2012). Apprenticeships in England: An overview of current issues. *Higher Education, Skills and Work-Based Learning, 2*(3), 225–239.

Lester, S., & Costley, C. (2010). Work based learning at Higher Education level: Value, practice and critique. *Studies in Higher Education, 35*(5), 561–575.

Morley, D. (2017). Degree apprenticeships are a ray of light in a gloomy sector. *Times Higher Education*. Retrieved August 5, 2017, from https://www.timeshighereducation.com/blog/degree-apprenticeships-are-ray-light-gloomy-sector

Pegg, A., Waldock, J., Hendy-Isaac, S., & Lawton, R. (2012). *Pedagogy for employability*. York, UK: Higher Education Academy.

Raelin, J. (1997). A model of work-based learning. *Organisational Science, 8*(6), 563–578.

Rowe, L., Perrin, D., & Wall, T. (2016). The Chartered Manager Degree Apprenticeship: Trials and tribulations. *Higher Education, Skills and Work-Based Learning, 6*(4), 357–369.

Schön, D. (1987). *Educating the reflective practitioner*. San Francisco, CA: Jossey Bass.

Smith, A. M., & Paton, R. A. (2014). Embedding enterprise education: A service based transferable skills framework. *The International Journal of Management Education, 12*(3), 550–560.

The Chartered Association of Business Schools. (2014). *21st century leaders building practice into the curriculum to boost employability*. Retrieved July 26, 2017, from http://www.associationofbusinessschools.org/sites/default/files/21st_century_leaders_june2014_-_final_report.pdf

The Quality Assurance Agency for Higher Education. (2017). *Quality assuring higher education in apprenticeships: Current approaches*. Retrieved July 26, 2017, from http://www.qaa.ac.uk/en/Publications/Documents/Quality-assuring-higher-education-in-apprenticeships-2017.pdf

Trede, F., Macklin, R., & Bridges, D. (2012). Professional identity development: A review of the higher education literature. *Studies in Higher Education, 37*(3), 365–384.

United Kingdom Commission for Employment and Skills. (2016). *Employer skills survey 2015: UK results*. Retrieved July 26, 2017, from https://www.gov.uk/government/publications/ukces-employer-skills-survey-2015-uk-report

Universities United Kingdom. (2017). *Degree apprenticeships: Realising opportunities*. Retrieved July 26, 2017, from http://www.universitiesuk.ac.uk/policy-and-analysis/reports/Documents/2017/degree-apprenticeships-realising-opportunities.pdf

University Vocational Awards Council. (2017). *Policy, partnership and practice: Degree apprenticeships, higher education, skills and work-based learning*. UVAC National Conference, 21 November, Birmingham.

Unwin, L., & Fuller, A. (2003). *Expanding learning in the workplace: Making more of individual and organisational potential*. National Institute of Adult Continuing Education (England and Wales), Leicester.

Wall, T., & Perrin, D. (2015). *Žižek: A Žižekian gaze at education*. London: Springer.

Wisher, V. (1994). Competencies: The precious seeds of growth. *Personnel Management, 26*(7), 36–39.

World Economic Forum. (2009). *Educating the next wave of entrepreneurs: Unlocking entrepreneurial capabilities to meet the global challenges of the 21st century*. 2009 Report, World Economic Forum, Switzerland. Retrieved July 26, 2017, from www.ncge.org.uk/publication/educating_the_next_wave_of_entrepreneurs.pdf

Part II

Teaching at University to Prepare Students for Work Based Learning

5

Use of Simulation as a Tool for Assessment and for Preparing Students for the Realities and Complexities of the Workplace

M. Hughes and A. Warren

Introduction

The focus of this chapter is the use of simulation as a tool for assessing students' developing practice and for preparing students for the realities and complexities of the workplace. The chapter draws on a range of adult learning theories and literature exploring experiential learning and reflexivity and models of effective assessment and feedback which enable students to develop their knowledge, skills and practice in the workplace, for example, the use of 'feed-forward' (Duncan et al. 2013) in both formative and summative assessment. The benefits of incorporating simulation activities and stakeholder involvement into professional degree programmes as a way of preparing students for the realities and complexities of the workplace and as a tool for fostering deeper learning, insight, reflexivity and criticality for future employability are considered.

M. Hughes (✉) • A. Warren
Bournemouth University, Poole, UK
e-mail: mhughes@bournemouth.ac.uk

© The Author(s) 2018
D. A. Morley (ed.), *Enhancing Employability in Higher Education through Work Based Learning*, https://doi.org/10.1007/978-3-319-75166-5_5

The chapter sets out examples of simulation activity in social work, adult nursing and paramedic science programmes at Bournemouth University and incorporates testimonies from academics, practitioners, service users and students regarding the efficacy of simulation models in assessing practice and in enabling students to use assessment feedback and feed forward to improve their practice. Three models of simulation are explored, each one involving stakeholders (service users and carers) who have first-hand experience of the scenario the simulation activity is based on and who form part of the assessment and feedback process. The chapter draws on the experiences and reflections of the authors who coordinate the work of the BU PIER (Public Involvement in Education and Research) partnership in the Faculty of Health and Social Sciences at Bournemouth University.

Professional Context

The Nursing and Midwifery Council (NMC) Standards for pre-registration nursing education and the updated standards for education which were put out for consultation in 2017, specify the requirement for service users and carers to be involved in the structure, design and delivery of programmes, alongside inclusion in the selection process and assessment of students. The updated 2017 standards are clear in the need for programmes to involve service users and carers in a range of activities and for students to have the opportunity to 'receive constructive feedback throughout the programme from a range of relevant stakeholders, including service users and carers to aid reflective learning' (R3.12 NMC 2017). The opportunity to engage in simulation based learning is also identified (R3.5 NMC 2017).

Similarly, in 2014, the Health and Care Professions Council (HCPC 2014) introduced a standard of education and training which requires service users and carers to be meaningfully involved in programmes they approve (currently 16 professions including social work in England, paramedic science, physiotherapy and occupational therapy in England, Scotland and Wales); a requirement which had been in place for social work education, under previous regulators, since 2003 and is anticipated to underpin standards developed by the new regulator for social work from 2018.

Within our own faculty, this has led to an extensive range of activity with service users and carers contributing to curriculum design and re-validation, admissions processes, simulation and role plays, assessments of students' work, group facilitation and contributing to and delivering lectures. In a study the BU PIER partnership conducted to explore the impact of involvement on social work students' subsequent practice (Hughes 2017) social workers identified four types of impact: enhanced awareness of the lived experience, taking on board suggestions of good practice from service users and carers, developing a more critical 'real life' understanding, and a culture of recognising service users and carers as experts.

In this study, and in a separate thematic analysis of over 2000 student evaluations of BU PIER partnership activities between 2014 and 2016, it was evident that students particularly valued opportunities to consult and engage in conversations with service users and carers outside of the practice setting and to receive feedback from service users and carers on their knowledge, skills and competencies. Students identified three types of learning from having this contact: increased knowledge; improved practice (how best to intervene) and enhanced emotional resilience (ability to cope with and explore emotionally challenging subjects). Involving service users in health and social work education was shown to directly contribute to a student's ability to meet the professional requirements of their disciplines and in preparing them for employment.

Simulation

One such activity commonly used across health and social work programmes is that of simulation where a practice scenario or experience is re-created or imitated to enable a student to put their learning into action, to practise skills, and to be assessed.

A number of benefits of simulation have been identified within the wider literature such as authenticity and realism, an ability to foster deeper learning, reflexivity and criticality and to enhance students' skills, confidence and self-efficacy (Pearson and McLafferty 2011; Duffy et al. 2013; Osborne et al. 2016; Cant and Cooper 2017). Liaw et al. (2012), however, identified from their study that whilst simulation activity increased student confidence, this didn't correlate with enhanced clinical performance. They express caution that simulation could lead to an overestimation of self-confidence.

The activity of simulating practice experiences is underpinned by adult learning theories which suggest that for adults to learn effectively, learning needs to draw on previous experiences and be purposeful and relevant to their life (Knowles 1990). Simulations are commonly used in health and social work education prior to students undertaking practice learning as part of preparation and assessment of readiness (Duffy et al. 2013; Katz et al. 2014) or to introduce more complex scenarios that students have yet to encounter, providing them with experiences from which they can learn and reflect.

Kolb's (1984) experiential learning model identifies four distinct stages of learning from experience or learning from doing. To achieve an effective simulation activity which enhances knowledge, skills and confidence, students need to be supported to engage in all four stages of Kolb's learning cycle: concrete experience, reflective observation, abstract conceptualisation and active experimentation. As with Argyris and Schön's (1974) reflective cycle, the learning comes from being able to reflect in and on action rather than just the action itself. Argyris and Schön (1996, p. 21) described this process as "thinking on your feet" and "keeping your wits about you" which is necessary for employment in professions dealing with risk and complexity.

There are simulation models which do not use service users which have been shown to prepare students for aspects of employment. Kostoff et al. (2016), for example, organised opportunities for pharmacy students to practise using the SBAR communication tool (situation-background-assessment-recommendation/request) over the telephone with nursing students to develop skills in communicating between team members in urgent situations.

Conducting role plays with the part of the service user played by actors is another example, and has long been a tradition in social work and nursing education (Mooradian 2007; Bogo et al. 2011; Logie et al. 2013; Katz et al. 2014; Olson et al. 2015; Manning et al. 2016). Using actors or staff has the benefit of creating a more standardised patient or service user experience for assessment purposes. Such models lend themselves particularly well to OSCEs (Objective Structured Clinical Examinations) commonly used in health programmes and by the NMC to test the competence of nurses and midwives and more recently adapted for use in social work (Katz et al. 2014). Studies have identified the benefits of using actors or staff to create more complex scenes for health and social work education such as trauma and emergency response scenarios (Manning et al. 2016; Olson et al. 2015) and a chaotic home environment (Mole et al. 2006) whilst still providing opportunities for students to create and respond to real life scenarios and to interact with people playing the roles of service users or families. Manning et al. (2016) however conclude that learner engagement is dependent on the simulation actors and scenarios being realistic and believable.

Increasing, particularly in health programmes, are the use of virtual patients or computer generated mannequin simulations (Washburn et al. 2016; Loomis 2016; Nimmagadda and Murphy 2014) which have proven to be effective in enabling students to develop and practice medical interventions, improve diagnostic accuracy, clinical skills and interprofessional and team working (Washburn et al. 2016). Technology enhanced simulations ensure a standardised measure of assessment, provide multiple opportunities for students to practice and develop their skills and remove the ethical and logistical challenges of involving service users in scenarios which may impact on their own wellbeing (Washburn et al. 2016).

The benefits of involving service users however, is in the authenticity of the lived experience and in the role the service user then plays in assessing the students' performance and providing feedback and feed forward. The same can be said for any professional programme seeking to engage stakeholders such as customers or employers in simulation activities. Duffy et al. (2013) found that when moving from a model of using drama students to service users in assessed social work role plays, students and academics expressed concern regarding the lack of standardisation and unpredictable nature of the role plays but following the activity, identified this as one of the main strengths of the model. Students could respond to the real reactions and emotions of service users and assessors could observe these responses. This enhanced the authenticity of the practice being assessed and, as such, was effective in preparing students for the realities of the workplace where interventions are not always predictable.

Assessment Models—Feedback and Feed Forward

Assessment of students' knowledge, skills and competence is a fundamental part of the learning process (Boud 1999) and for preparing students for employability in their chosen profession. For professional programmes, in particular, assessment provides a framework by which students can demonstrate evidence toward eligibility for professional registration. More recently, literature has focused on dissatisfaction of students with the quality and nature of assessment and feedback provided in higher education (Boud and Molloy 2013; Race 2014), leading to attempts to engage students more actively in the assessment process with a focus on feed forward which students can use to improve and enhance their knowledge and practice (Baker and Zuvela 2013). Emphasis is on collaborating with students to foster growth and development; an approach more congruent with adult learning theories which promote autonomous learning and enabling learners to think for themselves (Hughes 2013) rather than more traditional didactic models of learning where the academic or teacher is seen as the person who imparts knowledge to a passive learner.

As Crisp et al. (2006) acknowledge, however, university regulations often assume that assessment is undertaken by academic staff, which overlooks the increasing practice and benefits of involving stakeholders such as practitioners, student peers and service users. Crisp et al. (2006), Duffy et al. (2013) and Anka and Taylor (2016) all report on studies where educators have raised concerns about incorporating service user feedback in their assessment citing that service users may be too tolerant of poor performance or base their feedback on popularity rather than competence. MacLean et al. (2017), following a review of 19 studies using simulated patients in nursing education, concluded that whilst there is a strong evidence base for involving service users in evaluating students' practice in simulation activities, they found little evidence of this happening.

The surfacing of power relations in the assessment process and the way by which service users inform final decisions are necessary if we are to avoid tokenistic involvement which fails to impact on the quality and relevance of the feedback or the final outcome. Methods we have sought to achieve this are outlined within the following case studies.

Case Study One: Social Work

The first case study is taken from a social work preparation for professional practice unit where students engage in an assessed role play with a service user or carer in a simulated home visit setting. Sessions are based in the Faculty's skills suite where bays are set up as lounge, kitchen and bedsit environments. Students are required to demonstrate basic interpersonal skills (use of appropriate questions, empathy, building a rapport and active listening) whilst breaking difficult news. Scenarios include informing a service user or carer that the care provider is going to change, that the support group they attend is closing, or that they are leaving and there isn't yet a replacement. Each of the scenarios was developed by the service users and carers themselves, based on examples which were real or realistic to their own lived experience.

When developing the assessment activity with service users, we discussed the concerns about the emotional impact of re-living real experiences. Service users were encouraged to choose scenarios which were realistic rather than real, in order to protect themselves. The service users taking part however all chose scenarios which had happened to them as they identified this as a way of improving the experience for others. In hindsight our own desire to 'protect' whilst demonstrating a duty of care, could be explained by issues of power and control and perhaps an assumption on our part regarding a person's perceived vulnerability. People with lived experience have a range of expertise and experience they can draw on and become involved for many different reasons. One service user said: *'I feel that my opinions and my experience is valued. I am unable to work as a nurse due to my health and this is my way of still being involved and contributing to the caring professions'.*

Having conducted the assessed role plays over four years our evaluations show a number of advantages of the scenarios being based on real experiences. Service users and carers incorporate the lived experience into their feedback to the student *'when that happened to me I....'* 'what

I found helpful in the way you did it was….' 'In real life, it wasn't possible for the service to…'. Students consistently evaluate the linking of the feedback and assessment to actual experience as valuable in their own understanding and development. For example, as two BA first year students reported:

> *I found the role play participation really useful. It helped me with my confidence and it was useful having tips on how to improve*
> *I realised the importance of communication, how body language, eye contact and choice of words can make a big difference*

As discussed in relation to adult learning theories, it makes the learning purposeful and relevant.

In terms of emotional impact, we have yet to experience a situation where a service user has identified a detrimental effect of taking part in assessed simulations but a number of steps are taken to ensure that service users have control over the process and are supported. Service users choose the scenario themselves, they attend a preparation session, and have the opportunity to shadow a session before taking part so they are aware of their role and the support available. A de-briefing session is conducted at the end of the morning and the number of role plays conducted by each person is limited to five. The unit facilitator is present in the room throughout but is not part of the role play process so is able to respond to concerns or queries if needed.

Adequate preparation, support and de-briefing are consistently highlighted in the literature regarding service user involvement (Skoura-Kirk et al. 2013; Naylor et al. 2015). Service users involved in this activity report being valued and a respected part of the process which avoids concerns raised in the literature of the service user being an invisible part of the process or considered an outsider (Rhodes 2012; Skoura-Kirk et al. 2013; Anka and Taylor 2016),

The role play forms part of an assessment of the students' safety and readiness to undertake direct practice in the first year of their qualifying programme. As part of the simulation activity and overall assessment, students receive immediate verbal feedback from the service user and observer (a social work practitioner) at the end of the ten minute role play and students are given the opportunity to discuss their performance. This provides the opportunity for the student to reflect on both the activity itself and the feedback and feed forward received by considering the impact of their practice on the service user and on identifying how they can use this to inform their own developing practice.

The discussions enable the student to engage in the stages of Kolb's experiential learning model by facilitating their reflective observation, abstract conceptualisation and active experimentation. The aim is to create a conversation with the first question being to the student—so how do you feel that went? Both the observer and the service user are able to support the student to self-evaluate, as recommended by Boud (1995) as a way of fostering autonomy and self-directed learning, in addition to providing feedback and sharing their own perspectives such as how it felt to be the service user during the intervention.

The activity provides the student with the opportunity to practice an intervention, be assessed and gain feedback from a qualified social worker and someone who has used social work services, gain experience in having their practise observed and develop their own skills in receiving and being open to constructive feedback. Once the student has left, the practitioner and the service user decide on whether to award a pass based on set criteria in terms of inter-personal skills demonstrated during the interview and openness to receiving the feedback and ability to reflect after. If, for example, a student demonstrates some skills required but made mistakes, their awareness of this and ability to identify what they would do differently, can lead to a pass mark, whereas a student who is defensive to the feedback or struggles to acknowledge the impact or what they would do differently, will receive a fail and given opportunity to re-submit following further guidance.

Service user involvement in simulation and assessment is not without its challenges. The social work role play scenario outlined here is conducted separately with three cohorts of social work students (MA, BA and PG Dip Social work) totalling around 80 students per year. The input described and the infrastructure required to support it, is significant. Social work programmes in the UK receive funding to involve service users in the delivery of social work education as well as funding for skills days, enabling us to put these resources in place. For larger cohorts of students on other programmes, this has proved much more difficult to achieve as the next scenario demonstrates.

Case Study Two: Adult Nursing

In an adult nursing programme, students conduct a simulated handover in a hospital bedside setting. In this activity, students undertake a nurse, student nurse or assessor role and are provided with written feedback from the service user after the activity. Particular emphasis is placed on the students' effective and accurate sharing of information in a manner which demonstrates industry requirements for increased patient centred focus in health care, alongside better communication, as identified in the Francis Report (2013) and the independent inquiry into the care provided at Mid Staffordshire NHS Foundation Trust between 2005 and 2009.

Whilst having the same access to the Faculty skills suite, in this case a simulated hospital ward, and to service user coordinator support, the nursing programme has cohorts of around 350 students per year through two intakes and over two campus sites, all of who undertake the assessed activity as part of the Therapeutic Communication in Adult Nursing unit. The challenge has been to create an activity which is meaningful for students' learning and provides accurate and rigorous assessment of their skills at this stage of their programme. As with the example from social work, the success of this unit can be attributed to the collaboration between the lead academic, the service user coordinator and the service users involved.

Due to large numbers, students undertake the activity in groups of three taking on a nurse, student nurse or assessor role. This has raised concerns regarding parity of experience with the nurse role being most active. Opportunities for discussing the feedback with the patient-service user are limited due to time constraints placing more emphasis on the need for clear and constructive written feedback and assessment. In the initial cycles of the activity we realised that there were disparities in the length, style and tone of the feedback being provided by the service users with some being particularly negative and critical; an experience which contradicts some of the concerns previously expressed about service users being too tolerant of poor practice.

As part of our own processes of reflecting in and on action, we have made a number of changes to significantly improve the learning experience for students and the quality of the assessment process, in most cases based on the feedback provided to us by the service users themselves who made suggestions on how the activity could be improved. These included clarifying expectations and professional requirements regarding student competence at each stage of the course, amending the feedback forms so they are more concise and easier to complete and delivering workshops to enable service users to develop skills and feel more confident in giving constructive feedback. This led to some noticeable improvements including the service users demonstrating increased confidence in giving feedback; both in completing the form and in offering 'real time' verbal feedback immediately after the assessment. Despite these challenges, the simulation activity remains particularly well evaluated by students. Many comment on how the activity has afforded them the opportunity to practise their skills in a safe environment, with time to reflect before they begin their next placement. Along with the acquisition of assessment and handover skills, students gain a greater awareness of the specific needs of the individual and how the manner in which they conduct the assessment may need to be modified e.g. always facing a patient who has a hearing impairment, in order for them to lip read.

The activity is evaluated by students as a meaningful learning experience which has an impact on their future practice. This is demonstrated by the following comments:

I found the activity useful as it felt real. Definitely it gave an understanding of real hospital assessment; what to pay attention to and how to approach individualised care of the patient's needs. Our patient showed us understanding to take over to practice, ideas to reflect upon.

I will remember this for the rest of the course. It helped me understand some areas of improvement that could help me in practice.

Case Study Three: Paramedic Science

The final example is from our BSc Paramedic Science programme where applicants to the course undertake a simulated activity as part of their interview day. Simulations are based on an OSCE model, as previously discussed, as applicants undertake a series of assessed simulations where they are required to respond to different scenarios. One of the OSCE stations or simulations is conducted by service users with others conducted by practising paramedics and academics from the course. The use of simulations as part of the admissions process is new to paramedic science and our faculty. It originated from a review of the admissions process within paramedic science and the need to ensure that processes were leading to recruitment of the best applicants. The team observed that many applicants were able to 'say the right thing' at interview by listing their skills, professional values and qualities, but weren't always able to put these into practice once on the course. The purpose of using simulations in the assessment of candidates was to give applicants this opportunity to demonstrate what they could do.

The simulation with service users is conducted by two members of the BU PIER partnership who alternate between the service user or assessor role. Whilst the scenario was initially suggested by the programme lead ('you are required to inform the person that their pet has died'), this was changed by the service users as part of the planning process to informing the service user that a relative had been involved in a road traffic accident. The programme lead reflected that his intention had been to incorporate a light hearted scenario; however the service users involved wanted it to be more realistic and felt that the applicants should be assessed in relation to how they managed the potential impact on the person they were sharing the news with.

In preparation for the new admissions format, those involved conducted a run through with academics, practitioners and six service users; with current students taking on the applicant roles. Piloting the simulations enabled those involved to make changes to the format and structure of the day such as the simulation timings being changed from 10 minutes with two minutes to record their assessment to seven minutes with three minutes to record, the paper work was amended to make completion easier and the scenario was changed as mentioned above. Students fed back on the format by comparing it to their own admissions experience. They preferred the focus on applicants' people skills as opposed to their knowledge as they believed this was a more effective measure of potential. The academic team reflected on how the use of simulation as part of the admissions process (in addition to a group activity), also enabled them to observe an applicant's openness to feedback and ability to cope with a challenging situation. It was evident from all involved that the opportunity to pilot the activity had been fundamental to the design process.

Using Simulation as Part of the Assessment Process

From all three case studies, key themes emerged regarding the benefits of using simulation as a tool for assessment. Students reported that engaging in simulations and receiving feedback opened their eyes to the reality of practice situations, provided opportunities to practice and make mistakes without the immediate pressure of being in the workplace, and to develop a less simplistic view of the practice field they wish to go into once qualified. A survey of paramedic science applicants found that whilst some reported that the simulations were unexpected, many commented on having valued the challenge, particularly if they felt they had performed well. Specific comments included "*it felt exciting*" and "*it gave me a glimpse into the job*".

In all three case study examples, there has been feedback from some students preferring to have more detailed information on the nature and content of the scenario in advance so they could prepare. In our experience however, this has led to students 'over-preparing' by writing questions and in some cases trying to script the session. The benefits cited by academics and service users are that students have to be responsive to a scenario and how it unfolds and that this is a more realistic reflection of what would happen in practice.

Where an assessment of a simulated activity involves observing student reactions and responses to unplanned scenarios, we have found that managing expectations and providing a clear assessment framework enables students to adequately prepare and to engage positively in the simulation activity even when they may not be able to predict what happens.

Transferability

Examples used throughout this chapter have been drawn from health and social work programmes and the work of the BU PIER partnership in involving service users in simulation activities. Learning from these experiences is transferable as stakeholder involvement in simulation as a method of assessment and of enhancing preparation of students for the workplace is of relevance across disciplines and industries. A number of themes can be identified regarding what purpose the simulation has, how it informs student learning and subsequent professional practice and in how it can be used to assess students' competence and ability to put into practice what they have learnt.

Simulating professional and practice experience provides students with the opportunity to learn from experience and to gain feedback and be supported to engage in reflective learning. The experience is enhanced if it is realistic. Involving stakeholders such as service users, customers, practitioners and employers gives credibility and authenticity to the scenario and results in students engaging and committing more fully to the activity than when they feel it is fake or unrealistic. Using simulation as an assessment tool enables assessors to observe the students' practice in action and base their assessment on what they do, not what they say or think they do. It enables students to engage and learn from practice scenarios which they may not yet have had the opportunity to experience and to be supported to self-evaluate and gain feedback from that experience.

References

Anka, A., & Taylor, I. (2016). Assessment as the site of power: A Bourdieusian interrogation of service user and carer involvement in the assessment of social work students. *Social Work Education, 35*(2), 172–185.

Argyris, C., & Schön, D. (1974). *Theory in practice: Increasing professional effectiveness*. San Francisco: Jossey-Bass Classics.

Argyris, C., & Schön, D. (1996). *Organisational learning II: Theory, method and practice*. Reading, MA: Addison Wesley.

Baker, D. M., & Zuvela, D. (2013). Feed forward strategies in the first-year experience of online and distributed learning environments. *Assessment and Evaluation in Higher Education, 38*(6), 687–697.

Bogo, M., Regehr, C., Logie, C., Katz, E., Mylopoulos, M., & Regehr, G. (2011). Adapting objective structured clinical examinations to assess social work students' performance and reflections. *Journal of Social Work Education, 47*(1), 5–18.

Boud, D. (1995). Meeting the challenges. In A. Brew (Ed.), *Directions in staff development* (pp. 203–213). Buckingham: SRHE & Open University Press.

Boud, D. (1999). Situating academic development in professional work: Using peer learning. *International Journal for Academic Development, 4*(1), 3–10.

Boud, D., & Molloy, E. (2013). Rethinking models of feedback for learning: The challenge of design. *Assessment and Evaluation in Higher Education, 38*(6), 698–712.

Cant, R. P., & Cooper, S. J. (2017). Use of simulation-based learning in undergraduate nurse education: An umbrella systematic review. *Nursing Education Today, 49*, 63–71.

Crisp, B., Green Lister, P., & Dutton, K. (2006). Not just social work academics: The involvement of others in the assessment of social work students. *Social Work Education, 25*(7), 723–734.

Duffy, J., Das, C., & Davidson, G. (2013). Service user and carer involvement in role-plays to assess readiness for practice. *Social Work Education, 32*(1), 39–54.

Duncan, N., Prowse, S., Wakeman, C., & Harrison, R. (2003/4). "Feed-forward": Improving students' use of tutors' comments. *University of Wolverhampton, Learning and Teaching Projects 2003/4:*127–132. Retrieved April 13, 2018, from http://wlv.openrepository.com/wlv/bitstream/2436/3778/1/Feed-forward%20pgs%20127-132.pdf

Francis, R. (2013). *The Mid Staffordshire NHS Foundation Trust public inquiry*: London: The Stationary Office.

Health and Care Professions Council. (2014). Service user and carer involvement in education and training programmes. Retrieved September 19, 2017, from http://hpc-uk.org/Assets/documents/10004167SUCstandardwebsiteinformation

Hughes, M. (2013). Enabling learners to think for themselves: Reflections on a community placement. *International Journal of Social Work Education, 32*(2), 213–229.

Hughes, M. (2017). What difference does it make? Findings of an impact study of service user and carer involvement on social work students' subsequent practice. *Social Work Education, 32*(2), 203–216.

Katz, E., Tufford, L., Bogo, M., & Regehr, C. (2014). Illuminating students' pre-practicum conceptual and emotional states: Implications for field education. *Journal of Teaching in Social Work, 34*, 96–108.

Knowles, M. (1990). *The adult learner: A neglected species* (4th ed.). London: Gulf.

Kolb, D. A. (1984). *Experiential learning: Experiences as a source of learning and development*. London: Prentice Hall.

Kostoff, M., Burkhardt, C., Winter, A., & Shrader, S. (2016). Instructional design and assessment: An inter-professional simulation using the SBAR communication tool. *American Journal of Pharmaceutical Education, 80*(9), 57.

Liaw, S. Y., Scherpbier, A., Rethans, J.-J., & Klainin-Yobas, P. (2012). Assessment for simulation learning outcomes: A comparison of knowledge and self-reported confidence with observed clinical performance. *Nurse Education Today, 32*, 35–39.

Logie, C., Bogo, M., Regehr, C., & Regehr, G. (2013). A capital appraisal of the use of standardized client simulations in social work education. *Journal of Social Work Education, 49*, 66–80.

Loomis, J. A. (2016). Expanding the use of simulation in nurse practitioner education: A new model for teaching physical assessment. *Journal for Nurse Practitioners, 12*(4), 151–157.

MacLean, S., Kelly, M., Geddes, F., & Della, P. (2017). Use of simulated patients to develop communication skills in nursing education: An integrative review. *Nursing Education Today, 48*, 90–98.

Manning, S. J., Skiff, D. M., Santiago, L., & Irish, A. (2016). Nursing and social work trauma simulation: Exploring an interprofessional approach. *Clinical Simulation in Nursing, 12*, 555–564.

Mole, L., Scarlett, V., Campbell, M., & Themessl-Huber, M. (2006). Using a simulated chaotic home environment for preparing nursing and social work students for interdisciplinary care delivery in a Scottish context. *Journal of Interprofessional Care, 20*(5), 561–563.

Mooradian, J. K. (2007). Simulated family therapy interviews in clinical social work education. *Journal of Teaching in Social Work, 27*, 89–104.

Naylor, S., Harcus, J., & Elkington, M. (2015). An exploration of service user involvement in the assessment of students. *Radiography, 21*, 269–272.

Nursing and Midwifery Council (NMC). (2017). Education framework: Standards for education and training for all UK providers of nursing and midwifery education. Draft for consultation. Retrieved August 22, 2017, from https://www.nmc.org.uk/globalassets/sitedocuments/edcons/ec4-draft-education-framework--standards-for-education-and-training.pdf

Nimmagadda, J., & Murphy, J. I. (2014). Using simulations to enhance interprofessional competencies for social work and nursing students. *Social Work Education, 33*(4), 539–548.

Olson, M. D., Lewis, M., Rappe, P., & Hartley, S. (2015). Innovations in social work training: A pilot study of interprofessional collaboration using standardized clients. *International Journal of Teaching and Learning in Higher Education, 27*(1), 14–24.

Osborne, V. A., Benner, K., Sprague, D. J., & Cleveland, I. N. (2016). Simulating real life: Enhancing social work education on alcohol screening and brief intervention. *Journal of Social Work Education, 52*(3), 337–346.

Pearson, E., & McLafferty, I. (2011). The use of simulation as a learning approach to non-technical skills awareness in final year student nurses. *Nurse Education in Practice, 11*, 399–405.

Race, P. (2014). *Making learning happen. A guide for post-compulsory education* (3rd ed.). London/California/New Delhi/Singapore: Sage Publications Ltd.

Rhodes, C. A. (2012). User involvement in health and social care education: A concept analysis. *Nurse Education Today, 32*, 185–189.

Skoura-Kirk, E., Backhouse, B., Bennison, G., Cecil, B., Keeler, J., Talbot, D., & Watch, L. (2013). Mark my words! Service user and carer involvement in social work academic assessment. *Social Work Education, 32*(5), 560–575.

Washburn, M., Bordnick, P., & Rizzo, A. (2016). A pilot feasibility study of virtual patient simulation to enhance social work students' brief mental health assessment skills. *Social Work in Health Care, 55*(9), 675–693.

6

Utilising Interprofessional Learning to Engender Employability

M. Coward and A. Rhodes

Introduction

Interprofessional Learning (IPL) has become part of the culture within the School of Health Sciences at the University of Surrey whereby our educational provision extends across a wide range of healthcare professions (Paramedic Practice, Nursing, Midwifery and Operating Department Practitioners) at both undergraduate and postgraduate levels. This shift in culture has not happened overnight and is still evolving through the delivery of our modules. The approaches to taught undergraduate module delivery capture our curriculum philosophy, which will be illuminated further by sharing our experiences of delivering one of our Professional Preparatory modules 'Innovation and Leadership'. Our experiences and application of IPL as a pedagogy has supported an evaluation that has informed our curriculum development. However, to fully appreciate IPL and its impact on learning,

---

M. Coward (✉) • A. Rhodes
University of Surrey, Guildford, UK
e-mail: M.Coward@surrey.ac.uk

© The Author(s) 2018
D. A. Morley (ed.), *Enhancing Employability in Higher Education through Work Based Learning*, https://doi.org/10.1007/978-3-319-75166-5_6

it is worthy of exploration as a concept to establish what the term and its component parts actually mean and its effect on the future employability of students.

Views on Interprofessional Learning

A significant viewpoint from the Centre for Advancement of Interprofessional Education (CAIPE 2002) concluded that the term 'interprofessional' denotes a situation where individuals from different professions utilise knowledge and skills to bring about change and improvement to practice. The term IPE has a multitude of definitions which Barnsteiner et al. (2007) note all encompass the following terms: common learning, shared learning, multiprofessional learning, multiprofessional education, collaborative education, multidisciplinary education and interdisciplinary education. This list should be seen as an enabler for learners to be ready to integrate into a workforce, thus increasing their employability.

Historically, learning within one's own profession has been common place but over time the professions have become aware of pedagogies that generate learning and teaching strategies that are inclusive across all professions. The World Health Organisation (WHO 2010) identified that the pool of healthcare professionals has been diminishing and developed a framework to guide strategies/pedagogies for interprofessional education (IPE). They visualised the development of healthcare workers through IPE to create a 'collaborative practice-ready workforce' which in turn would generate "collaborative practice" leading to "optimal health services" (WHO 2010, p. 18). Leading on from this, Barr and Low (2011) through their work developed insights into values and behaviours that are commensurate with equality, parity and synergistic learning; which have informed our approaches to this pedagogy.

Since 2009, UK Professional Regulators for medicine, nursing and allied health professions have advocated the provision of IPE on all professional preparatory programmes (NMC 2010; GMC 2009; HCPC 2014).

Being cognisant of the Francis report (2013) further highlights the importance of interprofessional working and leadership in assuring the most effective care. The Francis Report (2013) highlighted the devastating impact on the quality of patient care when interprofessional communication and care breaks down. Utilising an interprofessional approach during professional preparation empowers the future workforce to demonstrate their readiness to work in effective ways and has become an essential component of recruitment criteria to enable employers to embed the recommendations from Francis (2013) into their organisations.

The Pedagogy of Interprofessional Learning

The basis of our IPL framework is 'Learning Partnerships' across professions, whereby learning and working together engenders a sharing relationship that can be transferred to any team in any setting. These approaches to learning partnerships prepare our students for the reality of clinical practice where interprofessional approaches ensure safe patient care (Francis 2013; Basit et al. 2015). We would go as far to say that IPL is a pedagogy in its own right, that strives to achieve excellence in care, decision making and is solution focused through connectedness and collaboration. Learning from one another and about one another enables us to reflect on our actions as educators, often with students, in order to evaluate and inform our future educational practice. In doing this, we are evolving our pedagogy through ongoing improvement and development, making it flexible, student centred and patient focussed. This collective approach enhances learning through the application of Bloom's Cognitive Taxonomy (1964), enabling the sharing of learning, understanding, application and effective knowledge acquisition to develop through a structured approach. The application of Bloom (1964) constructively enables transformation within learners, sharing knowledge and generating understanding together. This approach supports the three domains of learning, as described by Bloom (1964): Cognitive (knowledge), Affective (self) and Psychomotor (skills) to be challenged and developed within the interprofessional group. This approach should also mirror the practice setting where professionals work together to enhance the patient experience (NHS 2014).

Through this educational strategy, the interconnection between learning interprofessionally and the application through a practice/theory/practice approach makes the learning journey meaningful, whereby lifelong learning (Jarvis 2006a) becomes more significant and achievable. Supporting students to develop an innovation for practice whilst utilising relevant evidence encourages them to embrace both the practical and the theoretical components of their professional programme. This in turn helps to produce a future workforce of healthcare staff who are able to consider service enhancement and improvement as part of their everyday practice. We believe that in our culture of IPL, criticality and reflectiveness are key elements to develop greater quality improvement and employability, which is reflected in the NMC consultation for the Standards of Proficiency for Registered Nurses (NMC 2017).

Our Adaptation of Interprofessional Learning

At the heart of our curricula, is our students, recognising their diversity but also their contribution to the IPL process and the transformative and experiential journey (Phillipi 2010) that all of our students take. Therefore, IPL is a journey of discovery and engagement across a number of professions leading to the ultimate goal of becoming a healthcare registrant who is employed to work within an interprofessional healthcare team.

Through this learning journey, the analysis, synthesis and evaluation of values, knowledge and behaviours can be undertaken in the context of many professions to discover how roles and responsibilities can form an approach to interprofessional collaboration. Their team working, self-reflection and consideration are paramount to the success of this pedagogy (Bloom 1964).

In order to achieve a learning environment mindful of working collaboratively to ensure best patient outcomes, our philosophical stance within the School of Health Sciences is grounded in humanism (Rogers et al. 2013) built around values (both personal and professional), professional knowledge and behaviour (the ability to learn and apply theory to professional practice) to establish greater inclusivity within the realms of IPL. In addition to this, our philosophy acknowledges the social and collaborative nature of learning and is influenced by the social constructivist's viewpoint described by Dewey (1933), and latterly applied to the health professions by Schön (1987). These key theorists are highlighted and discussed in taught sessions to help students appreciate the roots of reflection within professional education. To acknowledge the students as adult learners, opportunities are given to develop an understanding of the theories that can be utilised and translated into practice. This approach ensures that students are not constrained by models of reflection and develop critical and creative thinking skills to enhance their practice (Coward 2011). These approaches integrated through our curriculum have proven fundamental in supporting students to achieve their learning goals within an interprofessional group and our students are noted for their thoughtful approaches to their clinical practice by mentors.

Supporting the IPL process, students are valued as adult learners (Knowles 1980) and as such humanistic strategies are adopted to support new ways of thinking and deep learning (Moon 2004; Schön 1987; Rolfe et al. 2001). Humanism embraces the individual along with their experience and unique understanding shaped through their life course (Jarvis 2006b). The ideas generated within their interprofessional groups may be challenged by facilitators but students are encouraged to think freely. This approach enables critical thinking rather than constraining them to the ideas of the academic with whom they are working. The facilitators, teaching staff within the school, role model and approach of experiential or discovery learning that enables staff to share their own reflections in order to help students understand how they might learn from their own practice experiences (Dewey 1938; Bolton 2014). Staff therefore openly role model their own success with reflection.

These approaches steer students to the concept of reflection, learning from thoughtful doing, rather than giving them a method of thinking with subheadings, as is offered by so many models of reflection (Coward 2011). These strategies form a meaningful framework that has made our IPL approach worthy of sharing. We believe this approach develops lifelong criticality that can be recontextualised (Bradbury et al. 2010) within any interprofessional team and clinical environment and therefore is essential to future employability.

Introduction to the Innovation and Leadership Module

To contextualise the module in terms of the curriculum, the Innovation and Leadership module is designed to occur in the second year of the BSc programme at a time when students are also studying other profession specific modules and undertaking an elective placement in a clinical area of their choice. The timing of this module is significant, as newly acquired knowledge and experience through the first year and professionally focused knowledge from second year modules, can be applied within the realms of this IPL strategy.

The module runs weekly over the course of three months split between 'whole group' core lectures and learning sets. The core lectures capture the underpinning concepts of leadership but more importantly leadership in the context of team working extending into change management. The learning sets (12–14 in total depending on student numbers) enable smaller group working in interprofessional groups facilitated by an academic member of staff. However, each set is subsequently split further into even smaller interprofessional groups of 6–8 students. Through the core lectures and the learning sets, the students engage in the works of Tuckman (1965) and Belbin (1981) and are asked to undertake a self-assessment of their role within their team (learning set) but to also appreciate and understand how a team functions. Belbin presented team roles and descriptions: Plant, Resource Investigator, Co-ordinator, Shaper, Monitor Evaluator, Team Worker, Implementer, Completer and Specialist. This self-assessment forms an important part of the critical analysis of the IPL learning set and their contribution to the team's effectiveness through an analytical appreciation. The students start to generate a deep understanding of what their role is within this arena and observe the traits of others within the learning set.

The ethos of the module is to encourage students to engage in a unique learning experience, considering their own and other team member's roles leading to self-insight, reflection and ultimately, an awareness of the diversity in interprofessional teams. Through the learning sets students identify an innovation, problem or an area of practice that requires development and/or improvement.

The module encourages reflection and reflexivity (as a pedagogical method and an assessment form), whereby explicit and tacit knowledge (Gulick 2016; Brummell et al. 2016) can be shared, celebrating successes and identifying areas for further enquiry in order to engender deep learning. This approach is deliberate in order to nurture students to develop a critical stance within their professional practice, intrinsically developing their motivation to seek an understanding of complex situations and not become complacent or potentially unsafe. Our approach to reflection involves both staff and students with an aim to deepen everyone's consideration of their professional roles which is worthy of further exploration.

Contemporary Reflection

A non-traditional approach to reflection in healthcare education has been creatively developed within the School to support students to become reflective and thoughtful practitioners. Students are coached in the purposes of reflection, learning from experience (Dewey 1938), developing knowledge from these experiences (Carper 1978) and then applying their knowledge in order to demonstrate sound approaches to their practice (Benner 1984). This reflective approach discourages students from accessing traditional 'models of reflection' but supports them to trust their thinking by being thoughtful. Students are asked to embrace the word 'significant', noting what they see that matters to them in the first instance but to then translate that to develop their practice. Bolton (2010) highlights the need for professionals (and students of the professions) to explore what might be significant and open their eyes, literally to make sense of what is in front of them. In ensuring that they pick up on what they 'notice,' the students are being encouraged to trust their own view of professional practice. This is an attempt in encouraging them to become more independent thinkers with the ability to rationalise their viewpoints and judgements. Rather than waiting for a mentor or educator to ask them to make a change, they will in fact utilise their knowledge and experience in order to consider what might be different. Within this module, students are actively encouraged and supported to trust themselves and speak up, within a safe environment whilst engaging in their learning sets but with consideration to the care setting in which they practice.

From the outset of the module, students are encouraged to keep a formative reflective journal to provide a 'think place' for their experiences but to also form part of their assessment (Moon 2004). The reflective journal element of the module, is seen as enabling them to consider all of their experiences whilst learning, in order for them to 'sort' what may or may not be relevant.

Interprofessional Learning Sets

All students across all professions attend the core lectures within this module but the uniqueness of this IPL strategy is the learning sets. The large group is split into smaller IPL learning sets with a membership reflecting nursing (adult, mental health and child), midwifery, paramedic and operating department practitioner students. The logistics of designing the interprofessional groups is complex but they are viewed positively by students who evaluate the module on completion.

The learning journey through the sets is structured with specific activities to build from the core lectures, thereby applying the concepts of leadership and team working into the experience of their group collaborations. Each week the activities commence with a core lecture topic, ranging from reflective approaches to leadership and management through to service user involvement, service redesign and financial challenges. Through this involvement in the activities, relationships begin to build whereby individuals can share, discuss and pose questions, learning from one another within their varying professional groups. This strategy engenders IPL at all stages, which would not be easy to facilitate in the large group. The distinctiveness of the sets both contextualises and recontextualises existing knowledge and skills utilising learning experiences gained from both theory and practice. Through the learning set, it becomes apparent that the students are able to assimilate a specific skill set that clearly begins to enhance the team working. Through this experience, each set develop an awareness of how each individual's contribution makes the team stronger. Part of the IPL strategy is to keep the learning set membership unchanged throughout the module journey, enabling a peer group to be formed who are able to truly undertake action learning by the end of the module.

Examples from the Innovation and Leadership Module

Having discussed the module structure and learning sets as the main strategy for IPL, we would like to present our experiences.

Student Perceptions

From group to group, initial reactions to the module vary and the need to understand the summative assessment requirements, discussed during the first core lecture, becomes the priority for many students. Although students prioritise assessments, the module team are keen to embed the philosophy of IPL at this early stage. The students are asked to keep a reflective journal as a weekly record of their IPL experiences within their sets which informs the two-part summative assessment based on an innovation in clinical practice. On realising that they may be dependent upon each other, in a group not selected by them, a sense of anxiety is visible in the lecture theatre from the outset. However, the philosophical underpinning for this approach is the need for health care professionals to work in teams.

It is without doubt that the learning sets are an unknown entity for the students but the one thing that assists the groups to settle into their learning sets is the skilled approach taken by the facilitator, generating an atmosphere of value, warmth and security which is an important part of the IPL process. The following excerpts confirm the pedagogical approaches taken within the module action learning sets.

Group A is made up of 8 students. There are 2 adult nursing students, 2 midwifery students, one paramedic student, one ODP student and 2 mental health nursing students. The facilitator for the group (Tilly) is an experienced nurse teacher who is an advocate of reflective learning.

The membership of group A is typical of all IPL sets and as Tilly meets the students within the learning sets for the first time, techniques of group working are applied through sharing ground rules. It is important to recognise at this juncture that for IPL sets, strategies need to be more defined and focused on relationships initially rather than the task.

Group A meet for the first time in a classroom. They are quiet and do not look engaged as Tilly notes on entering the room. The group are asked to introduce one another and share what they feel the purpose of the module might be. There is an air of negativity which Tilly allows, with students saying that they have too many stresses to deal with this now.

To overcome the anxiety and feelings of negativity, humanism and social constructivism are learning theories that are explicitly utilised but in a measured way in order to generate an environment to support learning from and with one another. This safe space ensures students are able to speak freely and critically explore their own and others' views. Whilst this might be challenging it gives an opportunity to demonstrate and utilise the values associated with IP team work and the benefits that brings. The plan of learning for this initial set is designed in time phases of 5–10 minutes with deliberate activities to generate friendliness, communication and security and with the setting of ground rules strives to achieve a value based approach of respect and collaboration. The main aim of this session is to build relationships within the teams.

Tilly recounts a story from her own clinical practice where she sees a situation in patient care which is not ideal. She notices the situation, reflects on it and considers what might be improved. Tilly shares with the group how she expressed her thoughts for improvement with a senior colleague who laughed at her.

However, Tilly was adamant that a service improvement was necessary and would also be beneficial. It is at this point that Tilly realises she has the attention of the group, they are almost frustrated as they share her understanding.

To find an innovation for each individual learning set to work on is very complex and can be quite time consuming as there needs to be effective communication, negotiation, collaboration and respect.

Tilly asks the group to consider what they find to be a problem in practice which they believe they have a solution for? She receives an overwhelming response and then the paramedic in the group states 'it needs to be something that we are all interested in.' Tilly allows the group time to consider this, then the paramedic goes on to say, 'you are all talking about acute settings but I work mostly in the community and that's where your patients all come from.' There is acknowledgement by all that this is the case. One of the mental health nurses suggests that everyone has mentioned record keeping in some shape or form and then poses an idea;

'I came across a lady with dementia recently at home. Her husband was struggling to keep track of how much she was drinking. He kept some plastic drinking bottles and painted them different colours. Every time she drank a glass of water or a cup of tea, he placed a bottle on the mantel piece. It was almost like a game in terms of her seeing success at what her fluid intake was but he was also getting to record her intake to share with the care staff when they came in. Surely that could be used in a busy ward where everyone is so busy. I appreciate as a paramedic that may not be relevant?'

The paramedic students then said, 'well it is, because it would prevent her getting an infection, becoming more confused, falling over and us getting called out. I get that this is important in terms of patient safety.'

It is the role of the facilitator to move between the smaller IPL sets, assessing when there is readiness to fully participate, which effectively commences the generation of team building.

Tilly suggested that the group consider how they might split the work they needed to do in order to undertake background reading to find evidence and policy to support their innovation idea. The paramedic took the lead on this and suggested they work in pairs. She then asked that they establish a 'WhatsApp' group so that they could communicate on their progress.

The key role of monitoring the effectiveness and functioning of the IPL sets rests with the facilitator who may step in to assist the team to refocus when necessary. The facilitators for each IPL set are able to share questions and puzzles on the virtual learning platform, thus enhancing the understanding of all to aid critical enquiry. This supports IPL and also ensures that problems and queries are shared to develop a culture of openness and enquiry.

> *Tilly commended them for working well to establish themselves and agree a project. She also offered that they could contact her should they have any questions during the time prior to them meeting again as an ALS.*

The Emergence of Group Performance and Team Roles

From a facilitator's perspective, it is clear to see that within the early stages of the Innovation and Leadership module, there can be, and sometimes are, particularly difficult situations erupting within the groups that may interfere with group performance. Through an analysis of the works of Tuckman (1965) and Belbin (1981), the groups begin to appreciate the complexities of how groups function. This theory lends itself to their own exploration within the IPL set and encourages deep exploration within the group (Tuckman 1965).

In considering this concept, Tuckman (1965) talked of Forming, Storming, Norming and Performing in his model of group performance and how long each group stays in each stage is dependent on the team members but also the facilitator. The forming stage may take some time but once they are secure, they take themselves through to the storming phase where they discuss and put forward their ideas as to what the innovation could be. It is crucial that the facilitator observes the strength and depth of the storming phase to ensure that the skills of communication, negotiation and delegation are all being utilised by the team appropriately. Through this collaboration, the team enters into the decision-making process and agrees on the innovation that they will be working on. If the decision is not made, the team will lose precious time and will remain in the storming phase. The next time the team meet, they will commence back within the same stage with the inability to move on until a decision has been taken. The start of the module, enables the facilitators to share previous examples of projects undertaken by learning sets. These examples are meant to spark interest, not to be repeated. In most cases, at least one member of the group shows an area of interest in which they wish to explore further the potential for an innovation. Placing this module in year 2 was a strategic curriculum decision as it was hoped that students would have enough clinical experience along with professional voice to drive their ideas forward. Having undertaken this module for several years now, it is evident that this is the case.

The pedagogy of this learning and teaching strategy is not haphazard but is carefully designed to ensure that all teams function steadily, moving from one stage to the next in a timely way rather than labouring within a specific stage, potentially creating conflict and not achieve the elements of the task. If the activity is stalled for whatever reason, the momentum and continuity of the team's function will be delayed which will have an effect on their motivation. Through these observations, Belbin's (1981) work associated with team role theory can be applied by the students to enable them to further understand the mechanisms of their learning set and the characters within it.

By asking students to complete a self-assessment of their team role(s) it becomes clear to see how the roles are being played out during the IPL sets. The students, through this engagement appear to become insightful as to the function of their team, their contribution and through Belbin's (1981) role theory, attribute and measure their support to the process. These elements form part of the students formative and summative assessment requirements for the module. Each week the students meet in their IPL sets, there is a visible warmth, demonstrating the motivation they have to work together and achieve the best possible outcome for their innovation. It is also apparent, that students often feel uncomfortable with their initial observations, feeling that they are being critical to colleagues. However, they start to appreciate that Belbin's team roles are visible in most groups in which they will work, and that all of the roles have an important function in supporting one another to succeed. This supports students to develop an appreciation for the varying roles and see the worth of individuals rather than their personality or work types.

The final taught day of the module, embraces the learning journey that has been undertaken by the whole group and its subgroups. They take it in turn to present their learning set innovation to the rest of the group receiving feedback and evaluation from their peers. This is a meaningful time in which they are able to rationalise their project in respect of relevant policy and evidence.

Student Evaluation of the Innovation and Leadership Module

One group of eight students highlighted that their innovation was well received and was in fact adopted by one of the local NHS trusts on an elderly care ward where it is still being used. This type of innovation is important in demonstrating to students how they can play a part in affecting change which will enhance the care setting.

The influence this module has had on students has been captured within the module evaluation questionnaire whereby the students are asked to offer free form qualitative comments. Example of students' feedback is given below:

> *Having to set up an innovation was helpful in understanding how difficult it can be to work as a team with different opinions and get people motivated to make changes. The module was very interesting.*
>
> *I enjoyed learning about Belbin team roles and found that they were quite accurate.*
>
> *I think the subject matter is very relevant to the job. I will use the principles of team working in my role every day … overall I feel more confident walking into a new team knowing where I fit into most teams.*

The overall feedback from students on the module demonstrates the depth of learning and understanding that has occurred but more importantly the depth of confidence that the students gain from this experience is translated into their clinical practice and team working. It is also significant to note that our practice partners have commended this module approach, noting the ways in which Surrey students consider the solutions to practice challenges.

Conclusion

As the Innovation and Leadership module challenges students to undertake an interprofessional approach to providing a solution to a 'problem' in practice, it encourages students to look for aspects of care which can be improved. The experience of this module demonstrates enhancement of the student experience incorporating concepts of multi-professional peer review and critical thinking.

The knowledge which they gain from one another is seen as valuable to their current and future practice (Carper 1978) and the experience of IPL is in preparation for working towards becoming a health care professional with unique professional knowledge (Benner 1984). Key authors such as Benner (1984) and Carper (1978) considered the impact of experience in nursing generating professional knowledge and expertise in practice and these concepts are worthy of consideration in terms of IPL. Through utilising both experience and knowledge, with reflection, students will start to assemble their own approaches to practice utilising relevant evidence to ensure safe care (Francis 2013).

During the module experience, students are supported by academic staff and their multi-professional group peers to develop contemporaneous approaches that are both novel and creative to support innovation in the practice setting. Within the learning sets, students develop an appreciation of their group and individual skills and qualities relating to team working and leadership across varying fields of practice. The evaluation of the module shows that many students initially struggle with the interprofessional approach taken. However, their comments by the end of the module demonstrate the worth of their IPL and greater insight for the professions with whom they work and study alongside. Some of their understandings come about through their scholarship within the module, such as the exploration of theories relating to teamwork and leadership. The diversity of the multi-professional groups enables challenge and criticality to develop novel approaches which enhance a specific and agreed (by the group) element of practice. This collaboration enables the creation of a clinical innovation to be developed for application in the practice setting.

Learning together and building professional trust enables students to share and explore one another's profession specific knowledge that they have accrued to date in their learning journey. Within this knowledge are the 'nuggets' of practice, described by Benner (1984) as 'maxims.' Maxims are what Benner (1984) defined as areas of knowledge that can only be understood by other 'experts' with a deep understanding also. These maxims will often underpin and determine judgement (Dreyfus 1982) although to the onlooker they may be less apparent. Upon questioning an expert, they would be able to start to give a rationale but further probing would lead them to realise the level of aesthetic knowledge (Carper 1978) or 'craft' that they are utilising in their thinking (Benner 1984). This craft knowledge is visible in students early in their professional learning. Watching them share early maxims within their learning sets shows their understanding and application. The use of reflection within the module further teases out their understanding along with their questions and learning.

If we had one recommendation from our experience, it would be to contact past students who are now qualified to see if this module has and is still having an impact on their ability to affect change through interprofessional team working and the development of clinical innovations.

The ethos of the module is to support students in developing an appreciation for interprofessional learning and decision making by being able to shape their learning journey and develop their team's innovation. The students are very proud of their ability to choose an aspect of care that will enhance the patients' experience and the quality of the patient outcomes. As facilitators of this creative pedagogical approach, we too feel a sense of fulfilment relating to the students' integration in IPL and their achievements. The students remember the IPL sets and often recollect the events of the action learning that took place. This module has shown us that this innovation extends beyond knowledge acquisition to a much deeper development of confidence and interprofessional transferable skills that can be utilised across many situations and clinical environments.

Leading on from this, the confidence that the students gain encourages them to see practice in a new light, not accepting that 'custom and practice' is the only way to deliver care but to individualise meaningful care for each patient offering diversity and equality. The students seem to embrace the transferrable skills that they have developed with the ability to utilise and finely tune conceptual skills such as communication, compassion, courage and the care of differing patients and clients. Strikingly, the students demonstrate a true professional commitment towards their role as a healthcare professional, which is a motivating factor the academic module team.

The intention of our IPL pedagogical approach is to support both facilitators and students to gain insights across their professional groups to enable the analysis of their values and beliefs in respect of their clinical practice approaches. With future curriculum design, our own learning from the approaches taken will inform team considerations to module and programme design, in order to utilise the potential benefits of IPL more broadly across a three-year programme.

References

Barnsteiner, J. H., Disch, J. M., Hall, L., Mayer, D., & Moore, S. M. (2007). Promoting interprofessional education. *Nursing Outlook, 55*(3), 144–150.

Barr, H., & Low, H. (2011). *Principles of interprofessional education*. UK: CAIPE.

Basit, T., Eardley, A., Borup, R., Shah, H., Slack, K., & Hughes, A. (2015). Higher education institutions and work-based learning in the UK: Employer engagement within a tripartite relationship. *Higher Education, 70*(6), 1003–1015.

Belbin, R. M. (1981). *Management teams: Why they succeed or fail*. Oxford: Butterworth Heinemann.

Benner, P. E. (1984). *From novice to expert: Excellence and power in clinical nursing practice*. California: Addison-Wesley Pub. Co.

Bloom, B. (1964). *A handbook of educational objectives—The cognitive domain*. New York: McKay.

Bolton, G. (2010). *Reflective practice writing and professional development* (3rd ed.). London: Sage Publications.

Bradbury, H., Frost, N., Kilminster, S., & Zukas, M. (2010). *Beyond reflective practice: New approaches to professional lifelong learning*. London: Routledge.

Brummell, S. P., Seymour, J., & Higginbottom, G. (2016, May). Cardiopulmonary resuscitation decisions in the emergency department: An ethnography of tacit knowledge in practice. *Social Science and Medicine, 156*, 47–54.

Carper, B. A. (1978). Fundamental patterns of knowing in nursing. *Advances in Nursing Science, 1*(1), 13–24.

Centre for Advancement of Interprofessional Education (CAIPE). (2002). *Interprofessional education: The definition*. UK: CAIPE.

Coward, M. (2011). Does the use of reflective models restrict critical thinking and therefore learning in nurse education. What have we done? *Nurse Education Today, 31*, 883–886.

Dewey, J. (1933). *How we think*. New York: Prometheus Books.

Dewey, J. (1938). *Experience and education*. USA: Macmillan.

Dreyfus, S. E. (1982). Formal models vs. human situational understanding: Inherent limitations on the modelling of business expertise. *Office Technology and People, 1*, 133–155.

Francis, R. (2013). *Report of the Mid Staffordshire NHS Foundation Trust Public Inquiry Volume 1: Analysis of evidence and lessons learned (part 1)*. HC 898-I. London: The Stationery Office.

General Medical Council. (2009). *Tomorrow's doctors*. Manchester: GMC.

Gulick, W. (2016). Relating Polanyi's Tacit Dimension to Social Epistemology: Three Recent Interpretations. *Social Epistemology, 30*(3), 297–325.

Health and Care Professions Council. (2014). *Standards of education and training*. London: Health and Care Professions Council. Retrieved September 16, 2017, from www.hpc-uk.org/aboutregistration/standards/sets/

Jarvis, P. (2006a). Learning practical knowledge. *New Directions for Adult and Continuing Education, 1992*(55), 89–95.

Jarvis, P. (2006b). *Towards a comprehensive theory of human learning*. London: Routledge.

Knowles, M. (1980). *The modern practice of adult education: From pedagogy to andragogy*. Wilton, CT: Association Press.

Moon, J. (2004). *A handbook of reflective and experiential learning*. London: Routledge.

National Health Service. (2014). *NHS five year forward view*. London: HMSO.

Nursing and Midwifery Council. (2010). *Standards for pre-registration nursing education*. London: NMC.

Nursing and Midwifery Council. (2017). *Standards for pre-registration nursing education: Consultation*. London: NMC.

Phillipi, J. (2010). Transformative learning in healthcare. *PAACE Journal of Lifelong Learning, 19*, 39–54.

Rogers, C. R., Lyon, H. C., & Tausch, R. (2013). *On becoming an effective teacher—Person-centered teaching, psychology, philosophy, and dialogues with Carl R. Rogers*. London: Routledge.

Rolfe, G., Freshwater, D., & Jasper, M. (2001). *Critical reflection in nursing and the helping professions: A user's guide*. Basingstoke: Palgrave Macmillan.

Schön, D. A. (1987). *Educating the reflective practitioner*. San Francisco: Jossey-Bass.

Tuckman, B. W. (1965). Developmental sequence in small groups. *Psychological Bulletin, 63*(6), 384.

World Health Organisation. (2010). *Framework for action on interprofessional education and collaborative practice*. Geneva: WHO Press.

Part III

University Strategies to Optimise Students' Learning While in the Work Based Learning Setting

7

Embedding Work Based Learning Opportunities into an Undergraduate Curriculum Through Participation in a Touring Dance Company

C. Childs

Introduction

Securing employment within the dance profession upon graduation is highly competitive and generally statistics that come from surveys such as the Destinations of Leavers from Higher Education (DLHE) reflect a mixed picture based on six-month post-graduation in comparison to other more traditional subject areas, but are still considered an important measurement of employment trends. Creative arts students often take longer to establish their careers with employers who require a track record or portfolio of professional experiences and this group are also reported in Institute of Fiscal Studies/Nuffield Foundation Report (2016) as graduates who attract the lowest earnings. In June 2016, the Department for Education published the first Longitudinal Education Outcome (LEO) dataset which looked at employment and earnings from graduate cohorts in 2008/09, 2010/11 and 2012/13 (DfE 2016a, b).

C. Childs (✉)
University of Chichester, Chichester, UK
e-mail: C.Childs@chi.ac.uk

© The Author(s) 2018
D. A. Morley (ed.), *Enhancing Employability in Higher Education through Work Based Learning*, https://doi.org/10.1007/978-3-319-75166-5_7

Providing opportunities for dance students to gain relevant work based learning (WBL) experiences whilst still studying is becoming essential and will be explored within this chapter and questions whether this approach can positively impact employment progression.

When the subject of dance came into the higher education setting in 1974, The Art of Movement Studio, later to become the Laban Centre for Movement and Dance (LCMD) developed a three year Diploma in Dance Theatre; the focus was on movement studies, and the term 'employability' which has become common place now, was not a central focus. By 1977 the LCMD had validated the first BA Dance Theatre programme awarded by the Council for National Academic Awards. Today, university dance programmes and vocational training centres now include a variety of specific vocationally orientated modules with the emphasis in supporting students into employment, made even more relevant by the responsibility of student debts following the substantial increase in tuition fees to £9000 in 2012. The Quality Assurance Agency Higher Education Review: Themes for 2015–16 highlighted the importance of student employability and stated that this priority "reflects a growth in public interest in the extent to which higher education is providing the professional skills needed by industry and society in general" (QAA 2014, p. 6). The expansion of dance at university level has resulted in over 1175 undergraduate dance degree students completing each year according to the Higher Education Statistics Agency (HESA 2016) in 2015–16. These graduates are from approximately 196 vocational training and university dance courses from fifty-two institutions, giving an indication of the potential employment competition. The Teaching Excellence Framework (Department for Education 2016a, b, pp. 21–22) identified key metrics including employment outcomes and the importance of university programme level preparations such as providing WBL opportunities which was reflected the panel feedback comments to the University of Chichester (UoC) which stated a 'proactive approach to employer engagement including employability skills training embedded in the curriculum which develop highly valued employability skills' (HEFCE 2017). This chapter explores the impact of an embedded learning approach at the UoC to provide BA Dance students with WBL experiences as part of a contemporary dance company. It examines the setting up, learning experiences and reflections of the 2015–16 cohort whilst also drawing on the first year post graduation trends of 2014 and the 2010 dance company destinations to provide a longitudinal study of dance graduates progression and subject specific employment focus linking the transferability of the skills undertaken during their studies. This chapter suggests that by providing students with WBL in external settings, it enables them to deepen their subject knowledge and increase their confidence through a continuous reflective approach that provides a smoother transition into employment in the dance industry. A sample of reflections from individual student project reports suggest a developed metacognitive awareness and these are shared within this chapter to provide further data evidence.

The level six Dance Production (DP) module represents a quarter of the student's final year assessments with the module operating as '3Fall Dance Company' (3Fall). Enabling students to specialise and take greater responsibility in their choices as they progress through their studies, would seem to help the transition into their career choice upon graduation and the research has adopted the following methodology:

Section 1 An overview of the DP module—experiencing real time practice.
Section 2 Dance employment and career progression destinations.
Section 3 Case Study 1—2015–16 3Fall cohort,
Case Study 2—2014–15 3Fall cohort—initial destinations post-graduation,
Case Study 3—2009–10 3Fall cohort—7 years post-graduation.

Section 1—Experiencing Real Time Practice in 3Fall Dance Company

The impact for students when a module has embedded WBL, and the approach of working with students as partners in their own learning with increasing levels of autonomy and independence, is at the heart of the pedagogic philosophy. Healey et al. identify a partnership approach as enabling "a more authentic engagement with the very nature of learning itself, understood as an experiential process of reflection and transformation, in relation to oneself and with others" (2014, p. 17). The initial setting up of the DP module is essential in establishing the culture and working practices; involving students committing to the collaborative creation and touring of a repertoire of dance works and self-motivation for the individual's personal and professional development when dealing in public facing situations. The three discipline areas—performers, administrators and technicians are co-dependent in this process, although it can take time to develop the necessary specialist, technical, communication and transferable skills. These attributes were identified in the Higher Education Academy (HEA) Framework for Embedding Employability in Higher Education (HEA 2015) based on Cole and Tibby's (2013) 'Defining and developing your approach to employability'. The student learning is divided to include the creation and collaboration with professional choreographers to create an evening repertoire of dance; undertaking performance bookings and working to the contracts set out by the theatre venue, delivering teaching workshops booked by the venue, adapting to different lighting rigs and theatre crews to prepare the stage and undertaking special projects, such as a residency to create a new work for a less experienced school dance group to perform providing a valuable performance opportunity, knowledge transfer and learning experience for all.

Working to a brief within 3Fall involves the tutor commissioning choreographers to make suitable works for touring to public audiences, overseeing and troubleshooting throughout the year and giving guidance to consolidate and improve the learning from one situation to the next. Hereafter, the remaining works that make up the repertoire are decided in discussion with the administration team. This can be a pressurised situation and dance students need resilience and maturity to be able to respond to feedback, alongside developing self-refinement and the perfecting of individuals own technical, expressive, communication and performance skills. This execution through on-going discussion, reflective practice and rehearsals in the studio/theatre setting are essential and as Policastro and Gardner (2010) state "creativity is not solely as the product of an individual mind, but rather as the result of a dynamic interaction among the creative 'individual', the 'domain' in which he or she works, and the set of judges (or field) that assesses the quality of work(s) that have been executed" (in Sternberg 2010, p. 214). The teaching approach is based on tutor facilitation and empowering students to take responsibilities with problem-solving to manage challenging situations, effective communication and through 'learning by doing' but having the space to make mistakes.

The three specialisations of performers, administrators and theatre technicians have technical and artistic elements to master and the initial learning period is spent exploring and honing skills such as learning/creating new choreography, devising appropriate publicity and marketing material following a photo shoot and developing lighting designs with the choreographers. Each sub-team develops their independence and identity with specialist roles emerging alongside team and company roles. As the module progresses, the aim is to give students increased levels of autonomy and independence where possible, with the students working alongside the tutors to develop their skills in selecting, refining and perfecting in each of the specialist areas. Empowering students with confidence in their skills set is essential to undertake whilst in the learning environment, but to take them out of their comfort zone in order to make the transition to employment more manageable having worked with an externally focussed framework.

The setting up of the module starts in the previous academic year when students audition for the performer's role or apply through a curriculum vitae for the administrator's and technician's roles. Auditioning is an example of a real situation for assessing and selecting potential dance applicants and this process is essential preparation for future experiences. The audition instantly brings in a competitive element because similar to a real job application, numbers are limited. This formal audition/interview process sets out the expectations and as a result if selected there is the sense of achievement that is similar to securing a job.

The working practices of the module draws on David Kolb's Experiential Learning Model (1984) to analyse in more detail the creative process and application to the DP module experience. This exploration interest initially formed part of a wider programme level study entitled 'Dance Map—The Employability Journey: A Toolkit for Mapping Employability

Journeys' (Childs and Clegg 2016) and was developed as part of the Higher Education Academy Strategic Enhancement Programme. Kolb (2015, p. 18) identified what he describes as the contemporary applications of experiential learning theory, and specifically relevant to this chapter, experiential education is described as 'on-the-job training/learning'. Kolb also broadly categories artistic practitioners such as performers and technicians within the divergent learners section (Kolb 2015, p. 184) in the diagram entitled 'The Structure of Careers shown in relation to the Structure of Learning Knowledge and Fields of Inquiry' in four areas of learning—Divergent, Assimilative, Convergent and Accommodative. Kolb offers a hierarchical categorisation with the 'artist' at the pinnacle. Interestingly though, this approach takes time to embed into the working process and the externally facing nature of the dancer's role such as receiving 'feedback' through the applause from the audiences, can make their role appear to have a prominence and links to Kolb's reference to the 'artist'. In addition, the learning experience is also about generic and transferable skills and these less tangible qualities, once described as 'soft skills', are not always recognised with the same importance by the students until much later in the reflective process.

Engaging dance students to utilise their creative and interdisciplinary skills is part of the everyday studio based practice but coupling this with developing confidence and resilience in new settings, alongside taking on new responsibilities and leadership roles is a chance for students to bring together the components that prepare them for employment. As Barnes states in her article entitled *Graduate Salaries and new Challenges for the Arts, Humanities and Social Sciences*, 'Arts, humanities and social sciences creates graduates who are well equipped to deal with the challenges we face today: to analyse and evaluate evidence; to describe and contextualise, pointing out and unravelling complexity; to be resilient, adaptable and flexible, with an ability to navigate change' (2017). The importance placed on developing and honing discipline specific skills such as mastering and executing technical dance, runs alongside the freedom to develop new ideas and new ways of moving conveyed through choreographic concepts or themes that are important to the individual, the choreographer and ultimately communicated with the audience. This links more closely with a dialogic learning approach which "in experiential learning fully immersing oneself (internal), with bodily, emotional and cognitive awareness in the activity (external), creates the greatest potential for learning to happen" (Desmond and Jowitt 2012, p. 223). Technical dance considerations include lighting, stage management, sound, health and safety, producing workable documentation for cues as well as liaising with choreographers, to develop the scenography wanted by the different choreographers, are the challenges faced by the technicians. Dance performance training is about holistically nurturing the whole dancer to become a physical and articulate practitioner and "attending to somatic experience allows the whole person to be included in the learning process, not just the cognitive aspect of the learner" (ibid 2012, p. 225). This dialogical experiential learning approach enables the sharing of co-creating in the devising, interactions when performing and informs teaching pupils in a school whilst working to professional standards.

Figure 7.1 draws on Kolb's original 1984 model (later Kolb refers to the development of levels of integrative complexity (2015)) whilst representing the cyclical dance students' learning journey and works from the outside in with the individual learners (outer circle—the creative process) through increased autonomy (middle circle—refining craft/touring) to independence (inner circle—repetition of practice-led methodology) as a reflective practitioner. This connects the student engagement of planning/rehearsing/repeating/refining reflecting the concrete creative experience of engaging directly with professional choreographers and theatre venues and a further layer of analysing/reflective observations/sharing and group planning to develop a critical understanding. Application of knowledge to new situations and implementing the studio learning in the new theatre context, run in parallel to maintaining and enhancing technical and interpretive skills. Developing independence for improvement, and maintenance of fitness and technique/building on each performance in relation to performance skills and communication with the audience, empowers students with greater autonomy, enhance student's ability to reflect; to deepen/perfect subject knowledge and the sharing of embodied knowledge with others through teaching and performing.

Working alongside professional dance artists, lighting designers, arts administrators specialising in marketing and promotion, is providing real 'work experience' with the module aim 'to build a repertory of dance

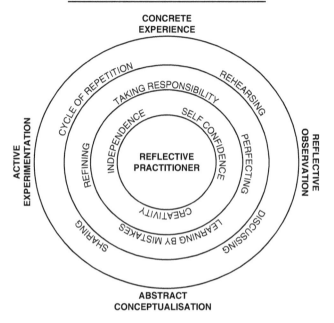

Fig. 7.1 The development and three stages of the student learning experience © c.childs

works, tour the work to a variety of different venues and experience the choreographic and performance process in action within a professional context' (UoC 2016). In 'Teaching the Whole Dancer', Daniels (2009, p. 9) refers to the learner-centred pedagogical approach where:

> Learner-centred education shifts the class focus from what the teacher knows to what the student understands, valuing the student's personal awareness and discoveries. It encourages active learning supported by self-reflection, accompanied by the self-cueing and self-direction essential to technical progress.

Within the learning cycle, the timeframe is divided into the creative process, the touring to theatres and schools/college venues and the workshop teaching commitments and then the reflective period before students hand in their paper (see Table 7.1). This has to be a fully budgeted

Table 7.1 3Fall Dance Company 2015–16 WBL schedule

Type of WBL	Duration	No of events	Assessment
Creative studio-based process with professional choreographers (group work)	Semester 1 for 5 hours per week + 2 weeks everyday 10–5 (September to December)	Three professional works by Filip van Huffel, Carrie Whitaker, Cai Tomos + four student choreographies	Process feedback from choreographers
Public dance performances (90 minute duration)	Semester 2 (January to mid-February)	13 across nine counties	Assessed by tutors in final two performances
Teaching and choreographing 1. Teaching workshops in schools/colleges 2. Residency, creating a new dance work on young groups	Semester 2 (January to mid-February)	10 workshops (operating in teams of 5) Two residencies	Tutor observations and on-going feedback
Individual reflective summary	Semester 2		Project Report

operation whereby the income provided by undertaking the performances and teaching balances the costs of travel, accommodation, costumes and much more. The role of managing this is taken by the administration team who work with the university finance department.

The creative process period, when the repertoire is devised and rehearsed, culminates in a technical rehearsal week bringing together the whole company. Enabling students to work with professional choreographers in an intensive rehearsal environment replicates the working processes of a professional company. In addition, there is the added pressure of wanting to impress the choreographer by interpreting the style and nuances of the piece, being judged on how creatively a student responds to given tasks to develop phrase material and then there is the attitude of the individual whilst working that can draw the choreographer to 'take notice' of the approach and professionalism that is being shown by the student. Students work with three professional choreographers and therefore have to be able to respond to different challenges each time. Four months into the process, the administrators will have secured all, or most of the theatre or school/college bookings, through liaising directly with clients, negotiating fees and setting dates and arrangements in places, and bringing this all together is a rewarding part of the process. The major transition of the work based model is in full flow and the importance shifts to the quality of the rehearsing, refining and perfecting, as shown in Fig. 7.1 in preparing for the touring the show. To reach this stage requires the administration team to have organised all of the transport arrangements, accommodation, publicity, programmes, website creation, ticketing, liaison with venues, arranging content for workshop teaching, formal contracts and a full workable touring schedule. Simplistically from the dancer's perspective, this might sound like once the show is ready, then it is just a case of moving from venue to venue, but the reality is very different with problem solving required on a daily basis. These challenges include having to adapt to the different performance spaces—size of space, type of floor, audience proximity; coping with injuries and having to adjust the repertoire which may require new partnering or groupings, group dynamics and dealing with working in close proximity over intense time periods, and sudden changes in arrangements.

The WBL goes beyond the theatre space and into the educational and teaching environment with the delivery of workshops to varying aged groups of usually young people. With this element, comes further opportunities to develop communication of specific dance subject knowledge and skills, and students here develop professionalism required in leadership and teamwork strategies. The combination of transferable and subject specific skills also consolidates the student's own subject knowledge through the planning process. Here, the role of the tutor is one of observer, supporter and facilitator.

> Subject matter experts, using the modes of reflective observation and abstract conceptualization, help learners organise and connect their reflection to the knowledge base of the subject matter.
> (Kolb 2015, p. 303)

The intense nature of the experience and regular practice, results in students increasing skill levels. One students commented that having to understudy a new part at short notice due to an injury made her realise *"that when working in the professional environment quick decisions need to be made and with the experience behind me I now feel confident to do this in the future if I am required"* (student A, 2016). Another stated that *"the practical elements have trained me to work faster and to be able to adapt to creative tasks quickly which I believe will enhance my capability in audition situations and generally in the professional environment"* (student B, 2016).

Following the final performances, there is a period of time to reflect on what has been achieved before students are required to formally draw these thoughts together in a reflective paper. Providing head-space often results in students identifying growth areas that they hadn't previously considered. One reflective paper commented *"this experience changed my perceptions of teaching students, it has made me look forward to pursuing a career in this sector and I feel that if I did not take the opportunity to perform in the company, these opportunities would not have arisen"* (student C, 2016).

Section 2—Dance Employment and Career Progression Destinations

Initially, upon graduation the more likely route to subject specific employment in the dance sector is through freelance, or self-employed work (DCMS 2014, p. 10), and what is now increasingly referred to as having a 'portfolio' career whereby several jobs are undertaken requiring a range of different skills that can be applied to varying situations. Typically, this might include a short contract on a performance project as well as some dance teaching.

The focus of employability (Yorke and Knight 2006) recognises the positive effects of having undertaken work experience and, whilst developing skills and knowledge within a specialist vocational subject, being able to recognise the experiences to then reflect, articulate and communicate these to future employment situations will place students at an advantage in securing relevant employment. Graduates from artistic practice-based programmes have much to offer employment settings having experienced working in interdisciplinary and creative projects, using arts specific and dance subject knowledge, leadership and group work. The process therefore within the DP module is to develop students' understanding and transferability of learning, who can communicate these skills, qualities and attributes when required either as in a curriculum vitae, at an audition or interview and ultimately then adapt these skills to new environments and work settings.

'Building a Creative Nation: The Next Generation' questions what it means to have a 'T-shaped' skills set and highlights "within the creative industries there may be a further dimension to both the wide ranging knowledge and the deep specialist capabilities" (Creative and Cultural Skills 2015, p. 28). Students are considered to be employable because they possess the necessary combination of broad based transferrable skills alongside the essential deep and specific subject knowledge. Acknowledging both these areas is essential whilst still studying and reflecting upon the experiences that enables students to see the achievements and learning in a meaningful way. Creativity is not always easy to quantify in a written form and the reflective paper that accompanies this module process is aimed to assist students in the articulation process.

Section 3—Case Studies

The following section provides case studies as further evidence of the impact and outcomes for the graduate destinations from three cohorts who have undertaken WBL in the DP module spanning from 2010 to 2016. The breadth of dance career destinations can be wide ranging and include dance performers, teachers within primary, secondary as well as post 16 training, choreographers, arts administrators, theatre technician, dance movement psychotherapists, and producers (see Childs and Clegg Fig. 8: Dance employment destinations 2016, p. 63). The case studies show the shifting patterns that occur from the initial period immediately after graduation, the work trends and further study necessary in order to establish professional dance careers. A positive observation is most students who engaged with the WBL module are still working within the dance industry with only a small number having moved away from dance completely. The information in this section only gives an indication, but still demonstrates the shift patterns over time and, in particular, the current trend for the continuation of higher level study over seeking work straight after graduating that is indicated.

Case Study 1—3Fall Dance Company 2015–16

This company comprised of fifteen dancers, four technicians and four administrators. There were two tutors whose role was to oversee the artistic and technical facilitation and guidance. Gathering data from these groups was undertaken through a written reflective paper submitted by all students. The paper required them to 'reflect on their experiences of the creative, choreographic, teaching, technical or administrative processes and how it has enabled them to enhance their future employment opportunities within the dance/arts sector'. Students could alternatively select to respond to the 'working to professional standards in the undergraduate 3Fall Dance Company'. This enabled reflections on the process of examples that put them directly into real working situations and the benefits and learning from this.

Working with a Professional Choreographer

The 2015–16 company worked with three professional choreographer including Filip Van Huffel. Van Huffel is a contemporary dance choreographer from Belgium who created a new dance work that was entitled 'Below the Radar'. Placing students in a new environment with a choreographer that they respect resulted in their work ethic increasing. The students' perspective of working with Van Huffel, resulted in comments such as *"this choreographer didn't know our backgrounds … it meant that the company had to be on its best behaviour, no 'marking' the movement in rehearsals or questioning/talking back to the choreographer"* (student D, 2016). This apprehension quickly changes as relationships are built and learning approaches are adopted and everyone become that bit more comfortable. The approach, dialogue and creative reciprocity between the company and the choreographer supports the continuous interactions that Albert Bandura (1986) refers to within his social learning theory in relation to memory and retention. Van Huffel would, for example, start the day with a company class and students recognised this practice in a different way to undertaking a normal contemporary technique class because it was seen as a preparation for the all-day rehearsal ahead. The experience developed a strong rapport and working relationship within the group that would later be reflected in the stage performances. Company class also engages the dancers in the stylistic qualities that are explored creatively in the choreography and becomes embedded into student's performance memory. Another student commented that *"Huffel looked for rigour and drive in the movement vocabulary and this helped me explore my capabilities as a dancer and pushed me beyond my 'thought' ability"* (student E, 2016).

Facilitating students to teach in schools/colleges enables students to apply knowledge acquired in the module and others areas of their studies but also develop new knowledge and experiences. An example of this is being able to think 'on the spot' and to work with the skills of the pupils in front of the students. One student commented that *"it is hands on experience that can be directly applied to later jobs"* (student C, 2016) and as Kolb states "knowledge is created through the transformation of experience" (1984, p. 41).

Figure 7.2 provides the employment and further study data for the 3Fall company graduates and is an insight into the immediate destinations that students enter upon graduation which include a range of professional, part-time/full-time work with the majority, 30%, progressing onto higher level study.

Case Study 2—3Fall Dance Company 2014–15

Two years post-graduation and the picture looks quite different. Firstly, in Fig. 7.3, already 35% have completed post graduate training and have entered the labour market. This would suggest that a higher level qualification is beneficial in enabling graduates to make a smoother transition to enter the profession, such as 29% who undertook a specialist PGCE Dance were now in full time dance teaching posts. Dance teaching is

Embedding Work Based Learning Opportunities... 127

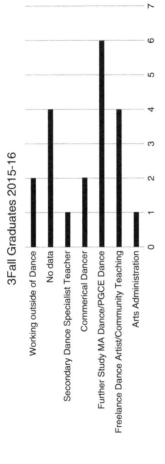

Fig. 7.2 2015–16 3Fall Dance graduate employment and further study

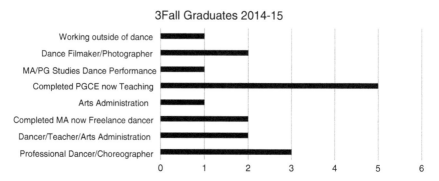

Fig. 7.3 2014–15 3Fall Dance graduate employment

more stable than the 12% who graduated from MA Dance programmes training in performance and choreography, who are now establishing themselves in the profession as freelance dance artists or who have a portfolio career combining areas such as teaching, performing and choreographing. These statistics would seem to support the LEO data giving a clearer representation of the value of undertaking subject specific undergraduate study than the six month post-graduation DLHE findings.

Case Study 3—3Fall Dance Company 2009–10

Taking a longer range subject specific approach a stage further, Fig. 7.4 gives an insight into the employment and career development of dance graduates seven years on from graduation. This information gives a snapshot of the longer term career progression developments.

In Fig. 7.4 the data reveals that 22% of the graduate group are freelance dance artists and teachers who have successful portfolio career. These professionals have worked with renowned choreographers such as Akram Khan, Shobana Jeyasingh, have received Arts Council funding to make work and/or have worked for key organisations such as the English National Ballet and Dance Umbrella. This group are now in their late twenties and the gender balance within dance is still predominately female and although not considered within this study, starting a family can be an interruption or obstacle to the trajectory of a woman's career.

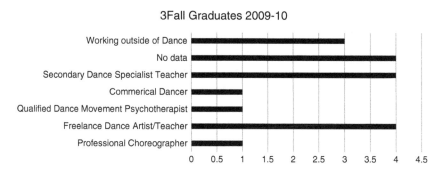

Fig. 7.4 2009–10 Dance graduate employment

The range of career destinations represent performing, teaching, choreographing as well as established freelance portfolio career profiles in identifying potential areas for career progression with 28% employed within professional teaching or qualified dance movement psychotherapist roles. To achieve the status of a professional choreographer can have a very slow trajectory but one of the graduates from this cohort has achieved an international reputation as a choreographer. What is also evident is that this group appear to now have moved beyond post graduate studies and the more recent trend to obtain a higher level of qualification soon after completing a BA, is still more favourable.

Conclusion

Through the case studies undertaken, the initial questions and evidence gathering has given an indication of the value of WBL in relation to supporting a dance graduate to progress into professional roles within the field of dance. By providing WBL opportunities within the final year of the BA Dance programme, student are able to engage in real time practice, reflect and consolidate their career aspiration in a more efficient way, which students are then able to build upon more quickly as they move onto seeking relevant employment within the dance industry. The WBL experience appears to enable the student to have the confidence to make decisions more quickly about the direction that they do want to take and an example of this, is a student who might have thought that they wanted a career as a dance performer but having undertaken the intense training and touring realises that this is not for them, this refocussing is more time efficient. All students will have experienced resilience, achievement and shared concrete experiences and the data indicates that the majority are working within the dance sector rather than general employment. The impact of embedding WBL opportunities into the curriculum are enhanced when the experience is credited and valued as part of their studies. Reflections from individuals are sometimes only fully realised when observers, such as audience members at a theatre performance or a peer commenting in class, gives feedback stating a noticeable improvement in a performer or in their dance technique. One student reflection highlighted having a 'good work ethic' and that at rehearsals, punctuality and working to tight deadlines was an attribute that it takes to work in the dance industry and that this was at the heart of her learning experience.

WBL, when embedded within the curriculum and within this dance context, provides a stepping stone to enabling students to be part of a collectively shared outcome; the engagement, reflection and alignment with professional values and standards whilst honing specific dance skills that works. When WBL is relevant and authentic to the discipline the positive outcomes can go beyond the individual benefits to enhance the programme's reputation. It is hard to definitively prove that there is a correlation between undertaking WBL and how students perceive their studies and success, but the knock on effect would appear to influence areas such as the National Student Survey (NSS). In the 2016 NSS optional bank questions on careers, students were asked if the programme had improved the student's career prospects and if there had been help and advice for career choices and further study—the UoC Dance department scored 98% for this section and achieved a 100% overall student satisfaction rating for 2015 and 2016. Enhancing the mechanisms to provide detailed departmental alumni tracking systems would enhance the longitudinal data further, as currently the data provided by LEO is grouped into generic areas with dance sitting within the Creative Arts and Design subjects. A further study would be to increase the level of analysis to include data from all graduates from the years analysed.

This chapter has explored how taking dance students out of the traditional module format to experience working patterns akin to a professional company schedule; and exposing them, with a support system, to physical and mental challenges in sometimes unfamiliar settings, can be a successful and rewarding learning experience. Facilitating networking with professional dance artists, choreographers and theatre venues embodies both the process and final products and this model within a contemporary dance company setting provides students with a necessary preparation. "Knowledge is created through the transformation of experience" (Kolb 1984, p. 41) and it is the value of the experiences, the integration and application of knowledge that helps to prepare students for the realistic challenges of their future dance careers.

References

Bandura, A. (1986). *Social foundations of thought and action: A social cognitive theory.* Prentice-Hall, Inc.

Barnes, H. (2017). *Graduate salaries and new challenges for the arts, humanities and social sciences.* Retrieved September 19, 2017, from http://www.wonkhe.com/blogs/graduate-salaries-and-new-challenges-for-the-arts-humanities-and-social-sciences

Childs, C., & Clegg, A. (2016). *Dance map—The employability journey.* Higher Education Academy. Retrieved September 19, 2017, from https://www.heacademy.ac.uk/resource/dance-map-employability-journey

Cole, D., & Tibby, M. (2013). *Defining and developing your approach to employability.* Higher Education Academy.

Creative and Cultural Skills. (2015). *Building a creative nation: The next decade.* Creative and Cultural Skills.

Daniels, K. (2009). Teaching the whole dancer, synthesizing pedagogy, anatomy, and psychology. *The IADMS Bulletin for Teachers, 1*(1), 8–10.

Department for Culture, Media and Sport. (2014). *Creative industries economic estimates.* London: DCMS.

Department of Education. (2016a). *Teaching Excellence Framework: Year two specification.* Department of Education. Retrieved June 20, 2017, from https://www.gov.uk/government/publications/teaching-excellence-framework-year-2-specification

Department of Education. (2016b). *Employment and earnings outcomes of higher education graduates: Experimental data from the longitudinal education outcomes (LEO) dataset.* Department of Education Official Statistics SFR36/2016 [Online]. Retrieved June 26, 2017, from https://www.gov.uk/government/uploads/system/uploads/attachment_data/file/543794/SFR36-2016_main_text_LEO.pdf

Desmond, B., & Jowitt, A (2012). Stepping into the unknown: Dialogical experiential learning. *Journal of Management Development, 31*(3), 221–230. Retrieved August 2, 2017, from https://doi.org/10.1108/02621711211208853

Healey, M., Flint, A., & Harrington, K. (2014). *Engagement through partnership: Students as partners in learning and teaching in higher education.* York: The Higher Education Academy.

Higher Education Academy. (2015). *The framework for embedding employability in higher education.* Higher Education Academy.

Higher Education Funding Council for England. (2017). *University of Chichester Teaching Excellence Framework 2 statement of findings.* HEFCE.

Higher Education Statistics Agency. (2016). Retrieved September 19, 2017, from http://www.hesa.ac.uk/data-anda-analysis/students

Institute of Fiscal Studies. (2016). *What and where you study matter for graduate earnings—But so does parents' income.* Retrieved August 24, 2017, from https://www.ifs.org.uk/uploads/publications/pr/graduate_earnings_130416.pdf

Kolb, D. A. (1984). *Experiential learning: Experience as the source of learning and development.* Pearson Education Ltd.

Kolb, D. A. (2015). *Experiential learning: Experience as the source of learning and development* (2nd ed.). Pearson Education Ltd.

Policastro, E., & Gardner, H. (2010). From case studies to robust generalisations: An approach to the study of creativity. In R. J. Sternberg (Ed.), *Handbook of creativity.* Cambridge University Press.

Quality Assurance Agency. (2014). *Higher education review: Themes for 2016–16.* Gloucester: The Quality Assurance Agency for Higher Education.

University of Chichester BA Dance Programme Handbook. (2016). Module descriptor for dance production. Retrieved from www.chi.ac.uk/dance

Yorke, M., & Knight, P.T. (2006). *Embedding employability into the curriculum.* Learning and Employability Series 1, No 3. York: ESECT and the Generic Centre, Learning and Teaching Support Network.

8

Student Experience of Real-Time Management of Peer Working Groups During Field Trips

Dawn A. Morley, A. Diaz, D. Blake, G. Burger, T. Dando, S. Gibbon, and K. Rickard

Introduction

A field trip is a signature pedagogy (Shulman 2005) of disciplines such as geography and ecology. It presents opportunities not only for application of knowledge and technical competencies but for deep socio constructivist learning (Wenger 1998) seen as highly relevant to employability readiness (Arrowsmith et al. 2011). During June 2015, these principles were further tested by the Student Environment Research Teams (SERTs) model of partnership work between students, academic staff and practitioners whereby five undergraduate ecology students undertook the roles of peer group leaders on a ten-day field trip organised collaboratively between a consortium of four UK universities, the National Trust and the Royal Society for the Protection of Birds (RSPB). The chapter draws on

D. A. Morley (✉)
Department of Higher Education, University of Surrey, Guildford, UK
e-mail: morleydawn@yahoo.co.uk

A. Diaz • D. Blake • G. Burger • T. Dando • S. Gibbon • K. Rickard
Bournemouth University, Poole, UK

© The Author(s) 2018
D. A. Morley (ed.), *Enhancing Employability in Higher Education through Work Based Learning*, https://doi.org/10.1007/978-3-319-75166-5_8

this field trip as an example of peer collaborative learning and one that presented the five student team leaders with the authentic experience of real- time fieldwork management.

The similarity of the characteristics of the fieldwork teams to Wenger's definition of 'communities of the practice' (1998) provided an evaluative lens for the trip. Student team leaders were interviewed, and also submitted reflective statements six months following the completion of the fieldtrip. The nature of their learning and progression during the trip, and their perceptions of their 'learning gain' (BIS 2016) going forward into employment and lifelong learning, are explored.

The student group leaders are all co-authors of this chapter.

The Transformative Nature of Students' Learning on Field Trips and Learning Gain for Employability

With the increased focus on both equitable and economic pedagogy to support the students' experience in higher education, traditional fieldwork is under scrutiny as an accepted element of environmental science curricula.

The assumptions that fieldwork is a positive and essential learning element of geography, earth and environmental science degree courses is scrutinised by Boyle et al.'s (2007) study of 300 UK based HE students in a survey of their pre and post field trip responses. By questioning students' changes in their affective domain; their emotions, feeling and values, Boyle et al. (2007) hypothesise for a link between fieldwork and an improved affective domain with a subsequently deeper learning approach. Scott et al. (2006) dispute the effect of field work on enhanced grades and course criticality against alternative learning approaches. However, their comparison of lecturers' views of field work with students concur with Boyle et al. (2007) where great value is placed on the social aspect of fieldwork although students also identify greater benefits of authentic learning and transferable skills.

Arrowsmith et al. (2011) argue that the identification of students' personal attributes is integral to preparation for employability. Like other disciplines, the nature of work based learning refocuses learning on a socio constructivist, process approach that may not be prioritised in more traditional, product led curricula. Whalley et al. (2011) highlight the importance of this social dimension for geographers' preparation for the twenty-first century and reposition fieldwork as an active research setting where students can work with academics in partnership. This is the very ethos supported by the SERTs approach.

Hill et al. (2016) highlight the case of fieldwork as an example of a "borderland" space where previous SERTs teams have had their learning disrupted, and therefore challenged by the impact of the fieldwork experience. The difference in the learning environment with that of academia; including the dissolution of known teaching structures such as power differences between lecturer and student, places students in a liminal space. Students are encouraged to become "border crossers" (Hill et al. 2016, p. 378) and this encouragement towards explicit, transformational learning is a common strategy of many lecturers, across multi disciplines, who have viewed the impressive effect of placement learning on student development (Morley et al. 2017).

The removal of traditional university barriers to education can create pedagogic possibility and increased student advancement (Hill et al. 2016). Wenger (2012) also identified the impact of the exceptional, and novel, placement learning experience where students are 'helicoptered to the top of the hill'. This requires a nuanced balance between challenge and support for these exceptional learning experiences to reach their potential for students (Eraut 2007) for they can carry learning risk as well as possibility.

Communities of Practice as an Evaluative Tool for Monitoring Students' Professional Identity on Fieldtrips

> Communities of practice are groups of people who share a concern, a set of problems, or a passion about a topic, and who deepen their knowledge and expertise in this area by interacting on an ongoing basis. (Wenger et al. 2002, p. 4)

Wenger's (1998) community of practice model has a significant contribution to make to the ongoing debate highlighted by Hill et al. (2016) as to how graduate attributes for employability are embedded in higher education curricula. Communities of practice draw on the social nature of learning and the positive effects of learning through team collaboration already identified in the pedagogy of fieldwork (Scott et al. 2006; Boyle et al. 2007).

Lave and Wenger (1991) challenged the then dominant discourse that learning was an individual activity and Wenger's subsequent community of practice theory (1998) reasoned that "the sharing of practice in a likeminded but unique professional group advanced both the learning and professional identity of group members" (Morley 2016, p. 161). This was accomplished through the critical aspects of 'mutual engagement', 'joint enterprise' and 'shared repertoire'. Mutual engagement allowed learners access to the community of practice before they began functioning with other members through joint enterprise. This was promoted by a shared repertoire of common language and artefacts related to their group.

Wenger's model presents the potential for a strong sense of student agency to develop for the student on placement, and in this case a fieldtrip, as they become part of a work based group that has a common purpose but must accommodate different levels of experience to be successful. Through working and learning together, each member can develop his or her own professional identity. Wenger recognised that communities of practice can arise organically within an organisation. It is this very lack of structure that gives students the opportunity to individualise their own learning towards employability and reach their individual potential through interaction with others (Vygotsky 1962; Goltz et al. 2008). Aguilar and Krasny (2011), in their application of the community of practice framework to an after school environmental educational programme, found that students' understanding of learning through participation, membership and identity formation was unique to each individual environmental club.

Student Environment Research Teams (SERTs)

SERTs are an established learning system, created at Bournemouth University, that provide opportunities for students, academic staff and professional practitioners to co-create new research and understanding (http://www.cocreate4science.org/serts/). SERTs are co-curricular and students participate either as volunteers or as part of a short placement. The ethos of SERTs is that they offer students the opportunity to gain leadership and team work skills within a strong peer-supported learning culture. SERTs foster employability by enabling student to enhance and evidence their gain in crucially demanded soft skills such as communication, commitment, time-management, decision-making and flexibility as well develop their subject specific skills, knowledge and experience.

The Purbeck SERT-NET was a cross-university network of 25 student volunteers who collaborated with academic researchers and professional practitioners in the National Trust and RSPB to co-create ecological surveillance and new research knowledge on how best to manage heathland for wildlife. It ran for ten days during July 2015 and the students came from four HEIs; Oxford Brookes, University of the West of England, University of Gloucestershire and Bournemouth University. Five of the students from Bournemouth University were student team leaders who each led four other students as a team. All student team leaders were second year students studying for a BSc in Ecology and Wildlife Conservation and the other students were studying for degrees in the broad area of environmental conservation and geography at BSc and MSc level. The five resulting teams were each composed of students from all four institutions. The students worked together within their teams throughout a ten-day residential field trip where they also organised data entry and practical logistics such as shopping and cooking rotas. More details on this SERT are available in this short video: https://www.youtube.com/watch?v=VpqiajOLgjk.

Data Collection from the SERTs Fieldtrip

At the end of the fieldtrip the group leaders volunteered to take part in telephone interviews conducted by a researcher from outside of their faculty. They contributed a further written reflection about their longitudinal experience of being a team leader six months afterwards.

The categories of Wenger's community of practice theory; mutual engagement, joint enterprise and shared repertoire informed the unstructured questions that student group leaders were asked during their telephone interviews. The group leaders were asked to comment on how the student groups were formed (mutual engagement) and how the groups functioned (joint enterprise and shared repertoire) with the identification of their own role in this process. Group leaders were finally asked to write a short reflective piece commenting on the effect of their group leadership six months following the completion of the fieldtrip.

Data Analysis from Immediately After the Fieldtrip

The transcripts of the student group leader telephone interviews were categorised per the three stages highlighted by Wenger's (1998) community of practice theory.

Mutual Engagement

Being Set Up as a Credible Leader

From a fieldwork perspective, it was important that students were set up as credible leaders within their groups so that the groups performed both effectively and accurately when undertaking their fieldwork surveys. The training offered to student group leaders on how to conduct surveys proved crucial to group leader's confidence and credibility. The team leaders had a full day in the field with two academic group leaders and a PhD student before the fieldwork began. It was here that student leaders became familiar with identification and species found in the habitats they were investigating. Although academics were not at hand to aid student group leaders during the identification process with students during the surveying, student leaders were given tools, such as an identification sheet, to aid students in the classification of species and identifications of samples were checked with academics in the evenings.

The training that students received contextualised their knowledge so they were prepared to educate the other students to a wider educational level.

Although it wasn't a task our group was doing themselves we could use that knowledge to explain why we were doing it and how it would be used in research (B)

The student team leaders articulated that they needed to be able to contribute skills that were unique to the group so the group could begin to function as a working unit.

I felt quite confident when I got my group for the first time I could explain the methods we were using so I think the training stuff worked really well (D)

… So we knew the methodology quite well, this helped me a lot in being able to support my team in the time period before we were all at the same level, which wasn't long at all (C)

One important aspect of giving credible leadership to the student leaders was that the rest of the student group were interested in how they had achieved their leadership position. In some ways, the student leaders themselves became role models for other students even though they were sometimes at a less advanced level in their own courses.

[They] didn't quite realise that I was only at the end of my second year. They were really interested in how I had go into the management of the SERT and asked me how they could get involved …how they could do it and they asked me about the volunteering I had done (E)

Realising the Nuances of Group Management

Student leaders found themselves in the position of managing teams who were often more experienced than themselves.

I was slightly nervous about whether [graduates and masters students] would take me seriously seeing I was under their educational level. However, they really respected my decisions or came to me with help or advice and because I was a manager in that situation they didn't really see that educational difference or age gap (E)

But, by having a mix of experience within the group, student team leaders quickly recognised the learning that they could take from other students for the mutual benefit of the surveying.

> *They then ended up helping me because I had never done that sort of thing before … so in that way it was great because they were teaching me that I something that I could relay on to the rest of the group. It was amazing to have that extra skill that they could teach me (E)*

By leading a peer group the student leaders equalised the power dynamics usually present between academic and student; the team leaders recognised the skills that they could learn from other students and appreciated the patience of peers who were protective of their leader as one of their group. The subtleties of group management therefore became real for student leaders.

> *I was trying to show myself to be not in charge because we were all equal but show that I knew what I was doing but at the same time trying to learn with them and so that was quite an interesting dynamic that I hadn't experienced before…. over the course of the two weeks that really helped the dynamic of our group as we were all pushing each other on and we actually learnt quite a lot together (D)*

> *I definitely learnt that if you tell your team everything, that you know then they know where they stand as well whereas if you keep them in the dark they will get frustrated. As long as you tell them you don't know then they were "ok, we will wait until you do" (E)*

The group leader also learnt the nuances of differentiating learning within the group; by the end the group leaders had enjoyed the process of the group's development by carefully balancing those students who needed more initial assistance against those students who were confident to work independently.

> *They contributed quite a lot and they didn't take long to get the hang of it and because we went through it together as a whole group team at first they got to grips with it quite quickly. I didn't let the two who knew what they were doing take over, I made sure the other two inputted and helped out and by the end of the ten days they were so confident and it was so great to see (E)*

Three group leaders commented on this as an effect on the quality and the efficiency of the collecting data; having an expert in the group also increased the quality of the work. By the end of the fieldtrip student leaders could identify how the induction process could be improved upon to increase awareness and information exchange prior to the field trip. The diversity of strangers that student leaders had to work with was found challenging rather than the diversity of knowledge or skills.

A team building exercise as a group would have been useful before we were out in the field (B)

Joint Enterprise

Making the Groups More Effective

Following the initial socialisation period student groups developed strategies for their group to work and learn effectively. Students formed strong bonds and a group identity. Student groups were drawn together though the work and were demanding greater autonomy and control of their work processes. Some student leaders took responsibility for the more complex or less desirable tasks asking one person to help.

Cross university groups added to the experience and the richness of the group learning.

… You meet people from different areas they have been all taught differently, different so you can see how they contrast… (B)

It gave a good perspective on how the different courses are taught throughout the UK and we all learnt new identification skills from each other. (B)

Everyone contributed fairly equally in different ways with different strengths and weaknesses but after the first couple of days when everyone was finding their role in the group and bonding and stuff it was really good that everyone got on with it and really good that we got on really well. (D)

Some student teams responded well to the responsibility and autonomy and were suggesting ways that this could be extended.

Debrief the team leaders and then we would go on and debrief everyone else in our individual team. It would work more smoothly. (E)

We always walked to our sites and once we had done the sites we would be waiting for one of them to pick us up… later on we were all given our sites just at the beginning of the day and we all navigated ourselves there. We all enjoyed it more when we were trusted to get on with the job (D)

Experiencing Authentic Management Issues

Some of the challenges of leadership included injury, personality differences or an attitude that did not fit with the group.

Student leaders encouraged students to keep active and participating in the group with the realisation that tolerance was needed as students worked at different speeds. Tiredness and motivation in the heat were common experiences for all the group leaders.

You need the whole team support to gather all the data information and also if one person is sitting down on their phone they automatically separate themselves from the team and don't feel part of the team. (E)

Towards the end of the project when people were very tired, we had to keep momentum and motivation. (C)

The placement replicated the real world of work with issues ranging from the length of the day, working in heat and managing issues back at base. Student group leaders needed the ability to manage the two environments of the fieldwork and the domestic management of their student team.

The management of tasks such as shopping and cooking was part of the group processes where team leaders blended more equally with their groups. The dynamics altered and student leader peer support was found to be helpful.

My biggest stress of the week was less the fieldwork but more the management at the base with the logistics in terms of food but then you are dealing with not just the team but the whole of the group. Your team get to know you and who you are and how you work and you build up this dynamic. (E)

Although it was quite challenging doing both at times I appreciated the confidence [the academic group leader] gave us in managing the base logistics as it gave us insight into what it is like to run a whole project. It's not just surveying but also food and accommodation and back at base arguments. That confidence helped us group together and push each other up. (E)

Looking Forward into the World of Work

External speakers drawn from the conservation groups were *"inspirational" (B)* although student team leaders sometimes had to give up these opportunities as they oversaw buying food and shopping. The talks allowed students to appreciate what could be their future professional journey but also the wider context of conservation work.

What they were doing and the extra knowledge when we were out in the field helped us understand that what we were doing had value and helped keep our motivations up, inspiring us (C)

[The academic leader] asked her to give a bit of a talk about her life and how she got where she was. I think out of both of the parts she did it was the bit about her life was really important and really useful because she told us all to travel and volunteer as much as possible so I think volunteering is a really good way to get a job in conservation. She went through the stages of how she got to where she was to doing a PhD … It was really interesting to get an idea of how people can progress to that type of level and the jobs that she had had along the way so it's nice to see that there are .. that you don't just have to get one job and stay in that job for life that there are loads of different jobs that you can go to related to the degree so that was useful.

Data Collection Six Months After the Fieldtrip

Student group leaders were asked to contribute a written reflection six months after the completion of the SERTs fieldwork trip to further ascertain the value of this experience on their longitudinal development.

Application of Skills to Final Year Academic Work

Two student group leaders identified how the SERTs experience had assisted their academic development in the following university year as it "*helped to create a platform for me to build and expand on*" *(E)*.

> *The skills I acquired by undertaking and helping to run the research project helped me to efficiently plan, test and collect data for my dissertation, giving me reliable results with very little problems, which I am now currently analysing and evaluating. (E)*

> *Being involved in research project from a managerial sense helped me to understand the logistical challenges and questions that need to be addressed regarding my own research for my final year Independent Research Project. (D)*

Professional Networking

Three of the student group leaders identified that networking with peers, academics and outside organisations made "*me more confident to approach them for help and questions*" *(B)*.

> *By talking to them now and on the project, I have been able to seek extra advice and guidance for future career opportunities which has helped me to developed ideas for what I want to do once I graduate. (E)*

Despite seeing the importance of networking two group leaders expressed disappointment that they hadn't managed to keep in contact with their groups on social media.

Leadership and Managerial Skills

Student group leaders could articulate the leadership and managerial skills that they had learnt "*such as problem solving, time management and strong communication skills*" *(E)*.

They discussed the heightened self confidence that they had gained thus:

I am now far happier to put myself forward to take charge of groups and drive my own progression as a leader, rather than sitting back and letting others take the lead...Being put in a situation with different people, with different motivations and skill levels was a challenge, and the thing I struggled most with on the SERT; finding ways of getting a group of unique personalities who work in different ways, working together and feeling part of the team. (D)

which, in turn, had deepened leader's sense of work readiness.

Fieldwork Skills

Student group leaders felt that their surveying methods had been enhanced so they could be undertaken *"reliably and without hesitation in the future" (E)* with the *"ability to write a report and skills based surveying skills ... having the experience of doing the SERTs I was then a level up when it came to writing reports and identification" (B).*

By leading a student team a *"greater understanding of the amount of work and organisation involved in running a project from start to finish, as well as some of the risks that could be involved" (A)* had been learnt. The participation but *"having to explain others to understand the methods and identification played a big part in my own personal learning" (D).*

Confidence in Applying for Further Positions

Six months following the SERTs fieldtrip four students had used their SERT management experience to gain further positions on paid internships, volunteering and positions on the student union committee.

Without the practical and survey skills gained from this SERT I am not sure I would have applied for the position. (E)

I feel more at ease with the prospect of starting work with a new team of people upon graduation (E)

…For this position I was able to use [the academic leader's] evaluation of my own performance as a reference as well as the skills I had gained. (D)

I feel I have been able to take that into my new role making me more understanding of others needs and trying to find a way of working that everyone can participate within. The regular feedback we received as leaders on the SERT was invaluable in that sense, as it allowed me to take the advice on board and critically look at my own strengths and weaknesses as a leader and then take it away and apply it to a new role. (D)

Inspiration for the Subject of Conservation

One student highlighted their renewed inspiration for a career in conservation following the SERTs trip.

Conclusion

The mutual learning and working experienced by the SERTs student groups was typical of the communities of practice model (Wenger 1998) whereby a common goal united the groups while simultaneously advancing their own professional identities. Unusually, the common duality of 'newcomer' and 'old timer' found in communities of practice (Wenger 1998) was not so apparent as student groups were peer led with different levels of experience emerging during the fieldwork experience. For the purposes of this chapter, data collection reflected solely that of the student group leaders who believed their work readiness and employability skills were substantially advanced during the fieldwork trip by an authentic experience of managing a field work group.

Using the stages of Wenger's community of practice theory proved an effective structure to analyse student group leader's experience of the value of their ten-day peer management on their work readiness. By using Wenger's structure student group leaders focused their interview responses on the nuances of the induction of their groups (mutual engagement) against the skills required to make these groups functioning survey groups (joint enterprise). Results demonstrated important differences between the preparation and support student group leaders required for their role at these two different stages of group formation. The effect of working with students from other universities, who were unfamiliar to student leaders, coupled with the management of both the fieldwork and domestic duties, gave student leaders a wider and richer base of expertise that theorists such as Klein (1998) see as essential to the development of professional expertise.

Both management stages exposed a disseminated leadership model whereby student group leaders were the managerial bridge between the SERTs academic leaders and the rest of the students.

The middle person really helps as there is a domino effect of information or pyramid effect. [The academic leaders] needed that middle person [the student group leaders] in there dealing with such a big group of people. (E)

In this way student leaders experienced an authentic exposure to authority and management but one that was supported by both the academic team and the students within their group. Although Lave and Wenger's (1991) theory of legitimate peripheral participation discuss how newcomers are afforded some protection as they journey to full professional status at the centre of a community of practice, it was felt that student group leaders went beyond a conventional learner's role. By adopting a disseminated model of leadership, that distanced itself from the impositional methods traditionally faced by students at university (Fryer 2011), the greater equalisation of power differences between students and academics aided the developmental potential of the work based learning into future employability. The student group leaders' role, as an important bridge between the community of practice of their own fieldwork group and the community of practice of their academic leaders, put them in the influential position of 'brokers' (Wenger 1998). This enhanced learning position as facilitators of communities of practice, as opposed to participators, gave student group leaders a greater experience of the real world learning of fieldwork management.

Student leaders benefitted from the experience of genuine autonomy running their groups

> *I think it was a good thing to let it happen naturally so people could take their positions and then just making sure everyone had a role doing something so no one is on the periphery that everyone is involved and everyone has a role in whatever site you go to. (D)*

but mechanisms were put in place to support student leaders to be both credible to their groups and effective in carrying out surveying. The survey preparation student group leaders undertook before the fieldtrip gave them access to unique skills that were required by their groups to function. Once operational the use of tools such as the ID charts (what Wenger would term 'reification' where participation is enhanced by written artefacts) and daily debriefings supported students through their disseminated leadership role. The management skills that student group leaders subsequently commented on were highly nuanced as they learnt to capitalise on their groups' skills while motivating them through different stages of learning and even weather conditions.

As well as achieving more immediate management skills, the timely nature of established professional experts speaking to the student groups in the evenings, gave the student leaders an opportunity to be inspired for their own professional trajectories. These are equally acknowledged by Wenger (1998) as a strong contributor to future professional development and the strength of the SERTs experience was that both were achieved together in the immersive ten-day leadership experience that student leaders undertook.

By the time of student group leader's reflection six months after the SERTs field trip student leaders could articulate how this experience had added to their future employability and skills, such as professional networking, that would allow them to achieve this.

Recommendations

SERTs peer leadership demonstrated the impact of a standalone, immersive work based learning opportunity on student leaders' skills, attitude and aspirations for their future employability. The 'Goldilocks effect' was significant to this experience where student leaders attained just the right amount of supported leadership responsibility against the authentic challenges that they faced. This concurs with Eraut's (2007) recommendation that work based learning needs to have the right mixture of challenge and support to be impactful on students' learning.

The effect of student leaders discussing their learning experiences and writing a reflection for the purposes of this research, gave student leaders an additional opportunity to make their work based learning explicit. It is unknown whether this had any effect on student leaders' ability to articulate their work readiness but it is recommended that immersive experiences such as these are consolidated with tools, or an event, that give students this opportunity. The ten SERTs, which have run since 2015, have been able to adopt these recommendations easily because each involved smaller teams of students from a range of courses at Bournemouth university. This has enabled establishment of pre-SERT meetings where each student selects a leadership role for one or more components of all stages of the SERT. This has greatly enhanced the integration of each SERT as a community and the engagement and learning of all members. Students also write a reflection on what they have gained through their SERT experience.

References

Aguilar, O. M., & Krasny, M. E. (2011). Using the communities of practice framework to examine an after-school environmental education program for Hispanic youth. *Environmental Education Research, 17*(2), 217–233.

Arrowsmith, C., Bagoly-Simo, P., Finchum, A., Oda, K., & Pawson, E. (2011). Student employability and its implications for geography curricula and learning practices. *Journal of Geography in Higher Education, 35*(3), 365–377.

Boyle, A., Maguire, S., Martin, A., Milsom, C., Nash, R., Rawlinson, S., et al. (2007). Fieldwork is good: The student perception and the affective domain. *Journal of Geography in Higher Education, 31*(2), 299–317.

Department of Business, Innovation and Skills. (2016). *Success as a knowledge economy: Teaching excellence, social mobility and student choice*. London.

Eraut, M. (2007). Learning from other people in the workplace. *Oxford Review of Education, 33*(4), 403–422.

Fryer, M. (2011). Facilitative leadership: Drawing on Jurgen Habermas' model of ideal speech to propose a less impositional way to lead. *Organization, 19*(1), 25–43.

Goltz, S. M., Hietapelto, A. B., Reinsch, R. W., & Tyrell, S. K. (2008). Teaching teamwork and problem solving concurrently. *Journal of Management Education, 32*(5), 541–562.

Hill, J., Thomas, G., Diaz, A., & Simm, D. (2016). Borderland spaces for learning partnership: Opportunities, benefits and challenges. *Journal of Geography in Higher Education, 40*(3), 375–393.

Hill, J., Walkington, H., & France, D. (2016). Graduate attributes: Implications for higher education and policy. *Journal of Geography in Higher Education, 40*(2), 155–163.

Klein, G. (1998). *Sources of power: How people make decisions.* Cambridge and London: The MIT Press.

Lave, J., & Wenger, E. (1991). *Situated learning: Legitimate peripheral participation.* New York: Cambridge University Press.

Morley, D. A. (2016). Applying Wenger's communities of practice theory to placement learning'. *Nurse Education Today, 39*(April), 161–162.

Morley, D. A., Archer, L., Burgess, M., Curran, D., Milligan, V., & Williams, D. (2017). A panel discussion—The impact of students' placements. In *ExCiTes 2017 Teaching and Learning Conference*. Guildford, UK: University of Surrey.

Scott, I., Fuller, I., & Gaskin, S. (2006). Life without fieldwork: Some lecturers' perceptions of geography and environmental science fieldwork. *Journal of Geography in Higher Education, 30*(1), 161–171.

Shulman, L. (2005). Signature pedagogies in the professions. *Daedalus, 134,* 52–59.

Vygotsky, L. (1962). *Thought and language.* Cambridge, MA: MIT Press.

Wenger, E. (1998). *Communities of practice: Learning, meaning and identity.* New York: Cambridge University Press.

Wenger, E. (2012). Social learning theory and healthcare education. In *Contemporary issues in clinical education.* London: Institute of Education.

Wenger, E., McDermott, R., & Snyder, W. (2002). *Cultivating communities of practice: A guide to managing knowledge.* Boston, MA and London: Harvard Business School and McGraw-Hill Distributor.

Whalley, W. B., Saunders, A., Lewis, R. A., Buenemann, M., & Sutton, P. C. (2011). Curriculum development: Producing geographers for the 21st century. *Journal of Geography in Higher Education, 35*(3), 379–393.

Part IV

Supporting and Supervising Work Based Learning

9

Building Students' Emotional Resilience Through Placement Coaching and Mentoring

S. Eccles and V. Renaud

Introduction

Many Higher Education Institutions (HEIs) in the UK now offer undergraduate students the opportunity to undertake a work placement as part of their degree, some of which are a built-in requirement of a sandwich degree (up to twelve months in industry) and others are shorter and/or optional. As Brooks and Youngson (2016) noted, the overarching purpose of work placements is to enhance the graduate employability of students through developing their skills, knowledge and ability. In addition, several studies (e.g. Bullock et al. 2009; Gomez et al. 2004; Mansfield 2011) have suggested that placement students perform better academically in their final year and achieve higher final degree outcomes than non-placement students. The placement experience also provides 'learning gain' for students when seeking graduate employment through the

---

S. Eccles (✉) • V. Renaud
Bournemouth University, Poole, UK
e-mail: seccles@bournemouth.ac.uk

© The Author(s) 2018
D. A. Morley (ed.), *Enhancing Employability in Higher Education through Work Based Learning*, https://doi.org/10.1007/978-3-319-75166-5_9

demonstration and evidencing of relevant skills, experience and attributes (Brooks and Youngson 2016). However, there is an increasing awareness that the benefits students derive from placements go beyond enhanced employability and academic achievement. Eden (2014, p. 268) argued that graduate employability should be "about developing a whole, employable person who integrates skills, qualities, values and relationships—what has been called "graduateness"—with a personal history through the embodied experience of work".

This chapter explores how this 'whole employable person' can be supported and developed through coaching and mentoring by a Placement Development Advisor (PDA), with a particular focus on the emotional resilience that students need to successfully transition into, through and out of a sandwich year placement. Using a case study from the Faculty of Media and Communication at Bournemouth University in the south of England, we will explore how students can develop the level of flexibility, confidence and knowledge required to become successful advertising and marketing professionals. Implications for practice at institution and placement level are discussed.

Emotional Resilience

Emotional resilience is the ability to adapt to and overcome stressful situations or crises. Stein et al. (2009, p. 900) defined emotional resilience as "the ability to maintain healthy and stable levels of psychological functioning in the wake of stress and trauma". Grant and Kinman (2014, p. 24) noted that resilience is the ability "to 'recover' from adversity, react appropriately or 'bounce back' when life presents challenges". They argue that emotional resilience, rather than being an innate or fixed characteristic, should be developed through carefully targeted interventions. The more emotional resilience a student develops, the more likely they are to be able to adapt to and cope with stress and life changes, whether major or minor. Within the work placement, this ability to adapt and cope becomes even more evident as students strive to maximise the opportunities and learning that a placement year can offer.

There have been studies exploring emotional resilience and the student placement experience—particularly in relation to health and social care students who are often faced with additional emotional and stress-related challenges (Grant and Kinman 2014; Foster and McKenzie 2012; Freshwater and Stickley 2004). It is clear that supporting students to understand and develop their ability to 'bounce back' will help them in the everyday challenges they face, as well as those that are more stressful or demanding. Resilience in the workplace requires the development of additional characteristics—including good support networks, self-awareness, social confidence and reflective practice (Grant and Kinman 2014)—as students learn to adapt to the demands of full-time employment whilst still within the higher education system.

There are also links between emotional intelligence and learning. Ellstrom (2001) noted that work based learning can not only positively benefit the organisation through enhanced productivity, innovation and competitiveness, but also promote healthier working conditions and reduce stress at an individual level. He argued that such learning may be adaptive (where aspects of the work-learning situation are 'given'—prescribed and non-negotiable) or developmental (where there are fewer 'givens', rules or previous experiences to rely on). For placement students, there are likely to be opportunities for both modes of learning; understanding and demonstrating competencies in routine problem solving through adaptive learning but also developing their ability to use their own knowledge and creative skills to resolve new or unfamiliar problems and question or challenge existing routines or practices through developmental learning. He concluded that "the learning processes and outcomes of different people placed in the same task or job with the same learning potential will be expected to differ based on their personal learning readiness" (Ellstrom 2001, p. 432). Developing the emotional resilience to manage some of the stresses and challenges of work based learning can be supported through, for example, 'train-the-trainers', classroom- or computer-based resilience-building programmes. However, as Vanhove et al. (2016, p. 278) noted, "programmes employing a one-to-one delivery format (e.g. coaching) were most effective" in identifying and supporting employees' needs and stressors.

Coaching and Mentoring to Strengthen Emotional Resilience

The emotional resilience of placement students is best strengthened through purposeful interventions which focus on a range of competencies. This, we argue, can be supported by coaching and mentoring by the PDA and enhanced through, for example, the use of reflective log books or diaries, supervision and supported experiential learning. Barnett and O'Mahony (2008) suggest that mentoring tends to be a longer-term opportunity for reciprocal learning and sharing of experience and ideas "where one person provides individual support and challenge to another" (Bush 2013, p. 244). Coaching tends to be more short term and focuses on developing specific skills although, as Bush (2013) acknowledges, the two are often used interchangeably.

Gyllensten and Palmer (2007) explored effective coaching within the workplace and noted that two key criteria of successful coaching were transparency and trust. Building a trusting relationship between coachee and coach reduced the impact of power relations and strengthened issues around confidentiality. Explaining the process, purpose and theories around coaching created greater transparency and this, together with trust ensured a strong and productive relationship between the coachee and coach.

Coaching and mentoring for HE students is increasingly seen as an important means of encouraging greater reflections and exploring future possibilities. The literature indicates, for example, that peer coaching amongst students can have a positive impact on their academic performance (Andreanoff 2016). Mentoring by experienced placement supervisors or line managers can be "a facilitating process to support the professional growth of individuals" (Barnet and O'Mahony 2013, p. 260) and help equip students with the professional knowledge and skills required. What is less understood is the impact on work placement students coached by a PDA—a non-academic member of their university with a commitment to supporting students in their professional, cognitive, career and adult development whilst on work placement.

The remainder of this chapter presents a case study of the experiences of media and communications students into, through and out of their placements, demonstrating how a planned and personalised package of coaching and mentoring develops the levels of emotional resilience required by students to adapt to a work/life balance and cope with the challenges this presents. In particular, the impact of the four dimensions noted by Bush (2013) that link content-focused programmes (i.e. academic studies) and process-rich activities (i.e. work experience) to PDA coaching and mentoring will be explored. These dimensions include: linking practice to the learning situation, focusing on personalised learning needs, supporting active learning and ensuring effective support.

Placement Support in Practice

For students at Bournemouth University, the PDA serves as the primary link between the student, university and placement supervisor during students' 40-week work placement. Whilst placement supervisors can provide the tacit knowledge and mentoring to engage and develop the placement student from a practitioner perspective, they are not always equipped to help students make the links between their theoretical knowledge and how this impacts on media and communication practice. The PDA mentors the students to encourage formal and informal employability development over the course of their placement and coaches them around specific individual issues or problems. The students discussed here are on marketing and advertising undergraduate programmes. Their placements range from international companies and advertising agencies to national media and marketing companies. The competition for graduate entry to such organisations is high. Graduates who have had a meaningful placement experience that has enabled them to develop the knowledge, skills and ability to understand and contribute to company goals and values are likely to be more confident in applying to, and being interviewed for, roles in these organisations.

Bournemouth University has designated PDAs who visit each student whilst on placement. Each visit consists of objective planning, short and long term goal planning, and other key topics to encourage the student towards greater self-empowerment. This also includes a joint discussion with their company supervisor. To ensure a thorough and consistent approach, standardised documentation is used (the Placement Review Form) and this provides the basis for individualised coaching and mentoring.

The PDA serves as the main point of contact from the university to the student during their placement year. Serving as an independent coach/mentor, each student receives two official placement reviews; the first review in the first 6 months of the placement, and the second in the latter part of the placement. These visits enable students to discuss and reflect on their performance, and make the links between the theoretical elements of their academic studies and industry standards. Where necessary, additional contact is made via email, Skype or telephone.

The topics discussed and recorded are:

1. First Placement Review: (a) skills development: skills sheet, top skills for employers, transferable skills sheet and personal audit, (b) SMART objectives, (c) GROW model of coaching
2. Second Placement Review: leaving placement checklist, CV and the STAR (Situation, Task, Action, Result) analysis, interview skills and questions
3. Post Reviews and Pre Final Year

The GROW (Goals, Reality, Options, Will) model of coaching, developed by Whitmore (2009), is used by the PDAs in group workshops and individual reviews. As part of the first placement review, it helps students to reflect on, be aware of and develop resilience strategies. This increased awareness of self during placement year plays a vital role in current and future student resilience.

Tensions and Challenges

However, whilst we know that the PDA/student relationship over the placement year has a positive impact on developing students' resilience (both in the workplace and subsequently), there are also potential tensions which need to be taken into account and overcome. Such tensions tend to arise as a consequence of misunderstandings, misperceptions and personal issues rather than a lack of formal planning or procedures.

Conflicts of Interest

A perceived conflict of interest between the key stakeholders (the university, employer and student) can arise when a student recruited for a specific role (and therefore with specific expectations as to what that may entail) is not given opportunities to fulfil these expectations—therefore not meeting the learning objectives required from the placement experience. The employer, in striving to meet their own business strategies and goals, may be unaware of the limitations of the placement experience they are providing or even, occasionally, unwilling to provide the breadth of experiences that students require. At the same time, the University has a commitment to ensure that students have the opportunities and experiences to ensure that the learning objectives are met. The PDA has a critical role in negotiating through situations such as this, either through directly intervening with the employer or through encouraging the student to find additional work experience during the summertime to add to their overall learning from industry. One of the most common examples is when a marketing or advertising student spends their placement experience working 'in house', and then seeks out additional work experience at an agency, and vice versa. This experience of both environments is ideal in setting the student up with the necessary knowledge, skills and confidence to help them identify what they want to do following graduation.

> *I didn't know how to deal with the situation at my placement* [a large international mass media company]. *My PDA helped me to explore and define the options and the best way forward. I appreciated that she didn't tell me what to do but instead helped me find the solution myself. This support helped impact my placement year in a positive way. While I'm sure things would have potentially gotten better between my supervisor and myself, it wasn't a guarantee and therefore having my PDA support me was the best solution. Regarding placement students from other universities, most did not receive a face-to-face visit which I think helped to develop the relationship.*
>
> (BA Advertising student)

Competing Interests

Another tension that a PDA often encounters is that of an inner conflict within the student. While the student may be working in a programme-related placement environment, their passions may be in another area. It is through the coaching interaction, where the focus is on the empowerment and wellbeing of the student, that various options can be discussed and explored. The PDA's ability to be an independent, mentoring coach can be rewarding for both PDA and student; the PDA is able to focus on the needs of the student whilst the student is able to identify and vocalise where they would like to be in an ideal situation. This then helps them to clarify steps and actions going forward. An example of this is the PDA working with a marketing student who had expressed a keen interest in equestrian events at her second Placement Review. Through discussing her 'dream job', they were able to identify a local equestrian centre which the student later approached for additional work experience following her official placement. At the beginning of the following academic year, the PDA was struck by the student's increased confidence and general excitement for her future as a direct result of this work experience. She had met all the 'official' requirements of her placement but at the same time, through the PDA coaching, had been able to articulate and action an aspiration she had not previously thought possible.

> *I do think the placement year has been a positive learning experience, although my placement turned negative it has helped me learn about people and the type of businesses I would not like to work in in the future. It has made me a stronger person and I now feel I have the skills to be able to adapt to any working environment.*
>
> (BA Advertising student)

Navigating Between Education and Employment Environments

A common tension is when the PDA's expectations of the student's awareness do not match where the student is actually at, regarding emotional resilience within the workplace environment. While students spend the first two years of their academic course on campus learning how to navigate within the academic context and with their peers in this 'new environment', the sandwich placement experience represents the first time they have had to navigate the professional landscape. The role of the PDA is to help the student integrate into their work environment as quickly as possible. It is not uncommon for students who are very talented academically (and have immersed themselves in their studies) to find it challenging to adjust to the workplace environment. They often find it difficult initially to understand and adhere to deadlines, observe workplace etiquette, integrate into team projects and self-manage key workplace tasks. While these students have had the emotional resilience to navigate within the academic context on campus, they are less able to cope with workplace requirements. Here, the PDA role as a mentoring coach, is crucial to the student so they can develop the skills, knowledge and self-awareness to make this transition. As one PDA commented, *"we are impartial coaching mentors, in that some questions are open and others are more directly related to action, and we have the experience to realise when to use different questioning approaches most effectively"*.

There are, perhaps inevitably, tensions and issues at a personal, educational and work placement level that arise. The approach of coaching and mentoring by the PDA allows these to be aired, discussed and resolved.

Well, because of the placement reviews and the support I received, I understood the purpose of the placement year and I started to enjoy it. So I think, for me, it was definitely a positive learning experience in every aspect of my life as I now think more like a grown up, working person. I have improved my skills through by meeting all the goals and objectives I had for my placement year. I am now more open, confident and responsible. I know how to make a good impression in a working place, how to be professional and I am more career orientated. Most importantly I know what I am going to do when I graduate, I've already set up goals and objectives, and I know I'm going to be ok. I have always been insecure and never really believed in my abilities. Now I know I have potential, so I guess this is the area I made most progress in.
(BA Marketing Communications student)

Reflecting on her role as a PDA, one colleague commented:

We are impartial coaching mentors, in that some questions are open and others are more directly related to action. While previously we have indirectly used the GROW Model, we have incorporated the model into our placement reviews this year (2017–18). Students greatly value the relationship they have with us during the placement year. Going forward, we want to develop the support for students' pre-placement and post-placement so that there is even greater synergy between their transition into higher education, their placement experiences and graduate employability.

Evaluation

Evaluation of the effectiveness of coaching and mentoring placement students focuses around the following four broad areas:

(a) How was the intervention delivered? *(process)*
(b) What difference did it make? *(impact)*
(c) How did it work? *(mechanisms)*
(d) Was it worth it? *(economic and personal benefits)*

Students' experiences and evaluations are gained through the institutional Annual Placement Survey and Placement Progress Forms, as well as through informal interactions and student podcasts, where the impact of coaching and mentoring, as part of the placement support offered to students by the PDA, can be seen. Employers are able to formally feedback at each review, through institutional questionnaires and informally. This results in a range of qualitative and quantitative data—some very specific to the individual student, placement and employer and others providing an overview of the process, impact and benefits of placements in general and placement support in particular.

When asked to reflect back on their placement experience, students are able to rate and comment on some of the key issues. Implicit in their comments is evidence of their increased emotional resilience to some of the stressful and challenging situations they have faced as well as the impact the relationship with their PDA made.

The Process

The process of incorporating coaching and mentoring into placement support is straightforward. The PDAs, as part of their own professional development, are able to undertake in-house training on coaching and mentoring, so have the skills and ability to 'ask the right questions at the right time'. In many cases, interventions with students will be part of planned reviews but where necessary, the PDA will follow up with a telephone or Skype conversation. Feedback from students indicates that face-to-face visits are often felt to be the most beneficial, especially when they can be followed up with an email or telephone conversation where necessary. Skype or telephone reviews are easier for students to manage from a time management perspective and often easier to slot into their working calendar and can be particularly effective once the rapport and trust has been built up between the student and PDA through face-to-face contact. Because coaching and mentoring are integrated into the review process, there is a seamless shift between these and the more structured monitoring requirements.

The end-of-placement student questionnaire is an opportunity for students to comment on statements about their experience. As the questionnaire is anonymous, it is not possible to attribute each response to individual students, but the following comments were made:

(a) I felt supported by the University for having my PDA there with me as we spoke to my supervisor:

This three-way conversation in person was really helpful.
My supervisor commented on how helpful and thorough the review process was.

(b) The PDA helped me through a difficult time:

Through this process I feel better prepared when I next encounter something similar.
I felt like they were an independent coaching mentor, a refreshing change from an academic who would only tow the University line.

> *I felt the PDA was really there for me, listening to me and understanding what I was saying. They actually 'heard' me and was there asking me questions helping me be the best I could be.*

(c) I knew the PDA was always there for me:

> *I knew if I needed to speak to my PDA, I could send her an email and we could speak right away.*
>
> *During my placement year my PDA was unbelievably supportive and very helpful. She would go above and beyond her means to ensure I was okay and supporting me through leaving my placement. There would be times when we would speak late at night and even on bank holidays when I had a concern. I had a very disruptive end to my placement and she was the person that kept me positive and professional.*

Impact

There is existing institutional data that can be scrutinised to identify the academic progress and graduate destinations of placement students. From this, we know that our placement students tend to perform better academically in their final year, as noted above. Understanding how their emotional resilience has developed is less easy to ascertain from these data. However, the effectiveness of the intervention by the PDA in particular can be observed at an individual student level through, for example, their completed Placement Log Book and end-of-placement reflections. Some of the most powerful feedback can come from podcasts and interviews that these students are asked to provide in their final year, where their reflections and commentary about their individual 'journeys' highlight the importance of practitioner mentoring and PDA coaching and mentoring in building their emotional resilience and confidence. It is also worth noting, however, that when questioned, many students do not have a clear idea about what emotional resilience actually is. They can (and do) articulate increases in confidence, motivation, problem solving and developing the skills and experience to fit into and cope with the everyday demands of working in a competitive industry. There is, therefore, a need to ensure that the language used in initiatives such as these is shared, explicit and fully understood by all parties.

Comments from the student questionnaire include:

(a) Focus the rest of my placement for my future career:

The PDA helped me think and explore on how to best make use of my time on placement, regarding identifying what I wanted to get out of it based on real life job descriptions to then help me steer the rest of my placement.

(b) Identify additional opportunities for both personal and professional growth:

The PDA helped me think of new opportunities and possibilities I had never thought of, regarding the summertime following my placement, final year, and post-graduation aspirations.

Feedback from employers acknowledges the approach taken by Bournemouth University in supporting placement students:

The BU PDA system is the best by far amongst universities in the way that students are supported.
The holistic approach taken by the PDA for the placement year was excellent; not only was the 'here and now' discussed, but also the 'future'.
It is obvious that the University really cares about their students.

Feedback from an employer (sports industry), who is a BU PR graduate who went on a 40 week sandwich placement himself:

What is your idea of emotional resilience?
For me, it is managing life's disappointments etc., in a way that does not negatively affect one's long-term existence. That's an incredibly difficult thing to do but can be helped if an individual is able to compartmentalise elements of their life. That sounds quite robotic but I think an ordered mind allows for sound decisions.

When thinking back, do you think your placement year affected it in any way; how?

Yes, absolutely. Ostensibly because I was faced with new tasks that took me outside of my comfort zone. Predominantly, it exposes you to the manger-employee relationship, which provides different challenges to the lecturer-student one. By nature, someone can only become resilient if they have been challenged in some way.

Thinking about the support and relationship you had with your PDA, did that engagement help you? Do you feel that it helped your emotional resilience at that stage? How?

Undoubtedly so. As in life generally, having a support network around you gives you a feeling of greater security. Pertinently, because my PDA was so vested in my development I felt I was achieving even more.

How did the whole placement experience, so on the 40 week placement in industry and the link with your PDA, affect you for your final year?

I would like to think that it brought even greater professionalism to my studies. I tried to take the structure of a working day into the unstructured 'down time' that university can give. Again as in life generally, if you're returning to a scenario with even greater experience you should be better equipped to deal with all the variables.

If you did not have the support of your PDA, do you think you would have developed the same both personally and professionally?

The role of the PDA is vital. They provide an outlet for students who are at a particularly unique stage of their careers. The development might have been the same but would likely have taken longer and been achieved with less self-confidence.

Now that you are a supervisor, how do you see the process from that angle? Do you feel that the support given to BU students on placement is positive?

Having recruited students from a range of universities I can say—in the absence of all bias, of course!—that the support offered to BU students from the University is second-to-none. It is an holistic approach, which is consistent over the course of the entire year and beyond.

Do you think that the system still promotes, and has the impact, on emotional resilience?

Yes. The PDA's forensic monitoring of placement year students means that opportunities to talk about the good, and not so good, parts of the year are discussed regularly. This means that opportunities to review emotional resilience are plentiful, which otherwise would likely not be the case.

Mechanisms

Bush (2013) discussed the need for effective personal development. Although he was specifically exploring this in the context of education leadership, his argument that a holistic approach to combining content-focused programmes with process-rich activities is a useful way of understanding how coaching and mentoring can, as part of the overall student placement experience, support students in drawing links between their academic studies and work experience. It is clear from the comments by students noted above that the support of the PDA encourages them to reflect on their experiences and share these reflections with the PDA in order to make links between their academic and professional knowledge. By focusing on personalised learning needs, the PDA can support active learning where the student can make sense of the new knowledge and skills they are gaining. The effective support to enable this to happen comes through the development of a trusting and transparent relationship between the student, the PDA and the placement supervisor.

Benefits

A key benefit of this approach to supporting placement students is how it strengthens their emotional resilience. Whilst students may not necessarily articulate it in these terms, they do highlight their enhanced awareness of and ability to adapt to and cope with stress and life changes, whether major or minor. Hammond (2004, p. 560) noted: 'Greater self-understanding and independence are potentially empowering and have positive implications…[although]… personal development can lead to conflict and difficulty because it 'challenges the status quo' … Understanding one's situation within a wider context can put personal difficulties into a perspective that makes them easier to cope with.'

We argue in this chapter that using the PDA, as a non-academic member of their university, to coach and support placement students provides a different type of relationship that they may have with their lecturers. As Chepchieng et al. (2006) commented, students often view lecturers as role models that inform and support their learning and academic progress. However, the PDA is able to act as a 'bridge' between their academic studies and placement experiences, thus enabling open discussions around the challenges and concerns that students can face. This in turn, enhances students' abilities to reflect on, discuss and develop the emotional resilience that will not only allow them to fully engage with and benefit from their placement experience, but also provide them with the skills and self-awareness to cope with stresses and life changes in the future.

From an institutional perspective, one of the benefits of using PDAs as coaches and mentors is that it aligns with their other responsibilities around monitoring and recording student progress. In many respects, PDAs are not being asked to do anything additional, but asked to do it differently—the topics discussed with the student are likely to be similar in all situations but the way questions are posed and responded to changes this interaction from fact-finding or monitoring to facilitating person-, problem- and solution-focused conversations (Barnett and O'Mahony 2008). The combination of written progress reports, discussions with placement supervisors and interviews with students provides a rich insight into the progress the student is making, their successes and challenges, as well as identifying areas for further development. The standardised documentation provides a framework for capturing the work students are undertaking, their progress, alignment with learning outcomes and personal reflections. Face-to-face discussions explore these areas in more depth and can reveal areas that require additional scrutiny or support. We argue that it is the combination of these two approaches that enables the PDA and student to reveal and focus on areas requiring bespoke coaching and mentoring input.

This approach to supporting placement students in building their emotional resilience requires little additional institutional financial support apart from the initial training of PDAs, with ongoing input from experienced PDAs, which in practice is usually resource-neutral as it is integrated into individual workloads. The initial training benefits from being 'on-the-job' and consists of a holistic programme with information and support from various services on campus such as Student Affairs, Counselling

Service, Careers Service. The GROW coaching model is discussed and explained between the experienced and new PDAs, with experiential learning taking place when the new PDA observes a placement review taking place between an experienced PDA and student. The new PDA is quite often encouraged to contribute to the review and reflections on the exercise are discussed following the review. The link between old and new PDAs continues as they have regular catch-ups to discuss the self-reflections the new PDA may have on their role and experience of conducting reviews. This relationship reflects that of a mentor as the experienced member supports the inexperienced member.

The value to individual students can be seen through not only some of the expected positive outcomes of placement experience (such as improved academic performance in final year) but also through their increased confidence, self-awareness and ability to cope with and manage the stresses and pressure of work.

Implications for Practice and Placement Support

This chapter has outlined how coaching and mentoring placement students by their PDA can build their emotional resilience as an integral element of their overall placement experience. It supports the views of, for example, Eden (2014) that 'employability' should extend beyond knowledge, skills and attributes to embrace the whole person, providing them with the ability to cope with the range of stresses and life changes they will face in order to succeed in future. This is supported by initiatives by professional organisations, such as the recent study undertaken by Baird and Palmer and presented at a GTI Breakfast News conference on HE students and mental health in November 2017.

At institutional level, the interventions to support this are both resource based—having appropriately trained staff in place—and policy driven—ensuring that there is institutional commitment to further and fully enhance a 'whole person' approach to the placement experience and student employability. The introduction of the Teaching Excellence Framework in the UK (QAA 2017) highlights the need to support students not only towards graduate employability, but also in terms of retention and academic success. 'Student resilience' is gaining more recognition as a key factor in ensuring that students can learn and gain from their time at university. A key theme emerging in relation to placements is how to best support students with their transition from a 'student mind-set' to a 'professional mind-set'. Recommended interventions include the implementation of an embedded professional practice unit into the curriculum, Placement Peer Assisted Learning (PPAL) initiatives where returning final year students work with second year students in the preparation for their sandwich placement experience, and raising awareness of entrepreneurial skills, including that of learning from 'failure'.

Cascading this down to programme or faculty level, there needs to be a greater awareness of emotional resilience and how students can understand, reflect on and build this as they prepare for, go through and emerge from their placement experience. Increasingly, this is likely to be through curriculum-based initiatives, PPAL and greater integration of placement opportunities and experiences into the wider student experience.

Our argument is that a successful placement experience for students, which builds and develops the emotional resilience they will need to become successful and confident graduates, requires face-to-face interventions by an experienced member of staff from their university. Such interventions incorporate coaching and mentoring as part of a structured but individualised review to allow these students to understand, benchmark and develop their ability to rise to and cope with the challenges faced not only whilst on placement, but as employable graduates in the future. Importantly, the PDAs recognise that: "student resilience cannot be embraced nor tackled with a one-size-fits-all approach; interventions, initiatives and ideas are vast, both in terms of scope and number" (ASET 2017, n.p.).

Developing a process which has institutional coherence and congruence, yet has the flexibility and personalised approach to provide individualised coaching and mentoring through PDA interventions, is an important step forward in building placements students' emotional resilience to manage the present and plan for the future.

References

Andreanoff, J. (2016). The impact of a peer coaching programme on the academic performance of undergraduate programmes: A mixed methods study. *Journal of Learning Development in Higher Education,* (10). Retrieved September 3, 2017, from http://www.aldinhe.ac.uk/ojs/index.php?journal=jldhe&page=article&op=view&path%5B%5D=358

ASET. (2017). Student resilience. ASET Viewpoints. Retrieved January 12, 2018, from http://www.asetonline.org/wp-content/uploads/2017/09/9-ASET-Viewpoints-Student-Resilience.pdf

Baird, A., & Palmer, D. (2017, November 23). The Fear Factor. GTI Breakfast News Conference, *How well do we do mental well-being?* London, UK. Retrieved January 14, 2018, from https://www.slideshare.net/TARGETjobs89/gti-breakfast-news-23-november-how-well-do-we-do-mental-wellbeing-82587799

Barnett, B. G., & O'Mahony, G. R. (2008). Mentoring and coaching programs for the professional development of school leaders. In J. Lumby (Ed.), *International handbook on the preparation and development of school leaders* (pp. 232–262). New York and London: Routledge.

Brooks, R., & Youngson, P. (2016). Undergraduate work placements: An analysis of the effects on career progression. *Studies in Higher Education, 41*(9), 1563–1578.

Bullock, K., Gould, V., Hejmadi, M., & Lock, G. (2009). Work placement experience: Should I stay or should I go? *Higher Education Research & Development, 28*(5), 481–494.

Bush, T. (2013). Leadership development. In C. Wise, P. Bradshaw, & M. Cartwright (Eds.), *Leading professional practice in education* (pp. 240–254). London: Sage Publications Ltd.

Chepchieng, M. C., Mbugua, S. N., & Kariuki, M. W. (2006). University students' perception of lecturer-student relationships: A comparative study of public and private universities in Kenya. *Educational Research and Reviews, 1*(3), 80–84.

Eden, S. (2014). Out of the comfort zone: Enhancing work-based learning about employability through student reflection on work placements. *Journal of Geography in Higher Education, 38*(2), 266–276.

Ellstrom, P.-E. (2001). Integrating learning and work: Problems and prospects. *Human Resource Development Quarterly, 12*(4), 421–435.

Foster, K., & McKenzie, H. (2012). Educational approaches to enhance emotional intelligence. In J. Hurley & P. Linsley (Eds.), *Emotional intelligence in health and social care: A guide for improving human relationships*. London: Radcliffe Publishing.

Freshwater, D., & Stickley, T. (2004). The heart of the art: Emotional intelligence in nurse education. *Nursing Inquiry, 11*(2), 92–98.

Gomez, S., Lush, D., & Clements, M. (2004). Work placements enhance the academic performance of bioscience undergraduates. *Journal of Vocational Education and Training, 56*(3), 373–385.

Grant, L., & Kinman, G. (2014). Emotional resilience in the helping professions and how it can be enhanced. *Health and Social Care Education, 3*(1), 23–34.

Gyllensten, K., & Palmer, S. (2007). The coaching relationship: An interpretative phenomenological analysis. *International Coaching Psychology Review, 2*(2), 168–177.

Hammond, C. (2004). Impacts of lifelong learning upon emotional resilience, psychological and mental health: Fieldwork evidence. *Oxford Review of Education, 30*(4), 551–568.

Mansfield, R. (2011). The effect of placement experience upon final year results for surveying degree programmes. *Studies in Higher Education, 36*(8), 939–953.

QAA, Quality Assurance Agency. (2017). *Teaching Excellence Framework*. Retrieved October 5, 2017, from http://www.qaa.ac.uk/assuring-standards-and-quality/teaching-excellence-framework

Stein, M. B., Campbell-Sills, L., & Gelernter, J. (2009). Genetic variation in 5HTTLPR is associated with emotional resilience. *American Journal of Medical Genetics, 150B*(7), 900–906.

Vanhove, A., Herian, M., Perez, A., Harms, P., & Lester, P. (2016). Can resilience be developed at work? A meta-analytical review of resilience-building programme effectiveness. *Journal of Occupational and Organizational Psychology, 89*, 278–307.

Whitmore, J. (2009). *Coaching for performance: GROWing human potential and purpose: The principles and practice of coaching and leadership. People skills for professionals* (4th ed.). Boston: Nicholas Brealey.

10

The 'Ebb and Flow' of Student Learning on Placement

Dawn A. Morley

Introduction

There is a rise in interest in work based learning as part of student choice at subject level in the UK (DOE 2017) but there remains an absence of specific guidance on how to best support higher education students learning on placement. An alternative HE experience in England, the degree apprenticeship, underlies the continued focus by policy in securing placement experiences for students without stipulating the type of support that is required at the 'coal face' of work based learning. Policy documents (UUK 2016), that urge universities to enter into partnership agreements with both employers and FE colleges to plug skills shortages, are noticeably lacking in their appreciation of the unique qualities of work based learning and how best to support students in this setting (Morley 2017a). Unfortunately, this is not unusual as placements have predominantly been an enriching 'add on' to the real business of

D. A. Morley (✉)
Department of Higher Education, University of Surrey, Guildford, UK
e-mail: morleydawn@yahoo.co.uk

© The Author(s) 2018
D. A. Morley (ed.), *Enhancing Employability in Higher Education through Work Based Learning*, https://doi.org/10.1007/978-3-319-75166-5_10

academic learning in more traditional university programmes. Support initiatives, such as that described in Chap. 9, are a rare appreciation of the importance of this role.

Undergraduate nursing programmes currently support a 50:50 split between practice learning in clinical placements and the theory delivered at universities. Vocational degrees, such as this, provide an interesting case study as to how students can be supported in the practice environment by an appreciation of how students really learn on placement and how hidden resources can be utilised more explicitly for practice learning. During 2013–2015 a professional doctorate research study (Morley 2015) conducted a grounded theory study of 21 first year student nurses on their first placement to discover how they learnt 'at work' and the strategies they enlisted to be successful work based learners.

Literature Review

Many theorists advocate that a novice, working closely with an expert, is more likely to have their learning strengthened and enabled. Vygotsky (1962), theorised that cognitive development arose from social situations. Students developed beyond their individual potential, the 'zone of proximal development', when additional guidance from an expert took a learner to a more advanced level. This is seen in traditional master-apprenticeships (Morley 2017b) but also in learning as part of a wider professional community (Wenger 1998), or as a distributed apprenticeship between several colleagues (Eraut 2007), clients (Eraut 2004) and peers. Crucial to the apprentice's journey is the social context of their learning where the learner's developing professional identity is determined by their social interaction, and application of their accumulating practice skills, with members of their own work communities (Lave and Wenger 1991; Wenger 1998).

Although practice assessment for student nurses was placed under the mandatory new role of a 'mentor', a registered nurse with additional responsibility for the students' practice learning in 2004 (NMC 2004), research indicates that this significant sole supervisor's role is fraught by difficulty. The Shape of the Caring review (Raising the Bar) (Willis 2015), highlighted the significant variation in the quality of mentorship that student nurses experienced. It was found that mentors were sometimes burdened by their supervisory responsibilities which were both under resourced, and unrecognised, leading to the current review of the role (NMC 2017).

In the UK, with the demise of nursing leadership roles in practice learning (O'Driscoll et al. 2010), and the rise of the mentors' unique status as the lynchpin in students' practice learning, (Gray and Smith 1999, 2000; Myall et al. 2008; O'Driscoll et al. 2010) the mentors' role became highly significant. Helping students to adjust to the realities of practice (Gray and Smith 2000; Myall et al. 2008), challenging their theoretical knowledge in a new context to enhance critical thinking (Spouse 2001) and acting as influential role models (Gray and Smith 2000) were recognised as important parts of the mentors' role. Like in other disciplines, the quality of the mentor relationship also effected explicit support of learning, such as feedback, as well as influencing the motivation, self-efficacy and confidence of the student (Spouse 2001; Bradbury-Jones et al. 2011a).

Although the student nurses in Gray and Smith's (2000) study were able to articulate the optimum characteristics of mentors the research lacked detail on how these characteristics impacted on students' practice learning strategies. The significance of role modelling was also identified by Gray and Smith (2000), Myall et al. (2008) and Davis (2006) but there remained a lack of specific data on how students learnt from professional experts.

Although mentors were aware of the significance of their learning role they also admitted that increased clinical workload affected the support and learning experience they provided (Gray and Smith 2000; Myall et al. 2008) to students. Despite students' supernumerary status Bradbury-Jones et al. (2007) found that student nurses were excluded from learning opportunities to meet workforce demands. The culmination of both mentors and students being busy with clinical work meant that they risked to work separately and, by remaining at the lower end of the professional decision making hierarchy, students nurses received a fragmented version of the work of their future professional roles (Holland 1999; Gray and Smith 1999; Cope et al. 2000). Third year students

(Gray and Smith 1999) recognised a division between the care work associated with unqualified care staff, the health care assistant, and the duties of the qualified nurse and gravitated towards higher status work associated with the latter.

> If [the student] had been left to wander around the ward talking to patients, or had been given mundane activities that had kept her busy and out of the mentor's way, she would have missed out on learning the artistry and the science of caring …that her mentor could teach her. (Spouse 2001, p. 23)

Displaying characteristics of helplessness and dependence led students to be labelled by permanent staff as not meeting the criteria of the clinical setting (Allan et al. 2011). If students worked in a supportive environment they began to learn the nuances of 'negotiating voice' (Bradbury-Jones et al. 2011b) and Allan et al. (2011) found that third year students began to recognise and adapt to the politics of placement learning.

Levett-Jones and Lathlean (2009) found that the degree of conformity of 18 third year students in an Australian mixed method study varied according to their sense of 'belongingness' on placement. In those situations, where belongingness was not met, (Levett-Jones and Lathlean 2008) students were more likely to be subsumed into the workforce in their attempt to fit in. With their self-imposed invisibility student nurses' learning needs were compromised. They did not have the confidence to develop critical thinking beyond asking rudimentary questions in an atmosphere where they were fearful of making mistakes. Argyris and Schön (1974) term this as a compromise between 'espoused theories' and the 'theories in use' used in practice.

The placement ethos, and the particular support of the mentor (Levett-Jones and Lathlean 2009; Bradbury-Jones et al. 2011a, b) emerged as critical factors in students' adherence to their personal and taught values of nursing. Ellstrom (2011) made the distinction between an 'enabling' and 'constraining' learning environment whereby the structures in practice impacted on how easily a student could move between 'adaptive' (skills acquisition) and 'developmental' (professional critique) learning. A constraining working environment could prioritise adaptive learning, or be detrimental to the development of both, with students displaying the attributes of acquiescence. Although the prioritisation of adaptive or developmental learning may naturally and appropriately occur during their learning, students needed encouragement to be able to question what and how they are being taught.

Barriers to learning were erected when mentors displayed behaviour akin to bullying (Bradbury-Jones et al. 2011a) or overprotected students leaving them predominantly to observe, do unwanted work and have insufficient feedback (Gray and Smith 2000).

Some student nurses recognised the constraints of their mentor's role and realised that their own learning could be compromised with their mentor's dual responsibility for clinical management as well as mentorship. Students also reported incorporating other staff into their learning to increase the range and opportunity of their practice learning experiences. Students who showed attributes of self-direction and, who were able to capitalise on learning opportunities outside of an exclusive learning relationship with their mentor, were seen as more likely to have successful mentoring relationships (O'Driscoll et al. 2010).

Eraut (2007) identified a clinical learning culture for the trained nurses in his study where 'helpful others', other than designated mentors and including patients themselves, contributed significantly to the learning in the workplace. The growing occupation of health care assistants has been found to contribute a hidden but significant amount of time to student nurse practice learning (Hasson et al. 2013).

Focus on the Novice Practice Learning Experience

For the purposes of the research a particular focus was taken on the practice learning experiences of first year students on their first clinical placement; situated three months after the beginning of their adult nursing degree. The literature review highlighted both their vulnerabilities and the lack of research undertaken with first year students (Andrew et al. 2009; Grealish and Ranse 2009). It was felt that the issues identified in the literature review could have a particularly detrimental effect on student nurses at the beginning of their practice learning but what this effect was, was under researched.

The first year student nurses, studying at the university site for the research, undertook an induction day prior to placement and were given guidelines on the number of learning outcomes to achieve from their practice assessment tool during their six weeks of practice. They were recommended to contact their mentor prior to placement but apart from these similarities each clinical setting had a different approach to their support of students.

Research Design

Following approval from a faculty ethics committee, twenty-one first year adult nursing students (three male and nineteen female) of mixed age, previous care experience and academic background volunteered from three separate cohorts of first year adult nursing students from one UK University. This meant participants entered their first clinical placement at different times and this was compatible with the cumulative data collection and analysis of the constant comparative method used in the socio constructivist grounded theory method (Charmaz 2006) for this research.

Procedures were followed to gain informed consent from participants. It was hoped that a clear explanation of the research would help to equalize power differences that may exist between the participants and the researcher, who was a lecturer in the same academic institution, and encourage full and open participation by the student (Guba and Lincoln 2005). The nature of the researcher-participant role can be a complex one and the dual role of the researcher from the outset had to revisited and negotiated as the research unfolded.

Students undertook individual unstructured interviews twice during data collection and analysis (January–November 2013); the first was conducted via the telephone mid placement and the second face to face once students had returned to university after the placement was over.

Data collection and analysis followed the different coding stages of the grounded theory process. As particular categories emerged theoretical sampling was pursued in order to gain further data that only pertained to the particular learning experiences of the emerged categories. Using Charmaz's (2006) approach the researcher's background was less about bias and more positively positioned as a possible influence on the interpretation through her own background and experience.

The final categories of the study were validated by two focus groups of participants before the categories were viewed as saturated and that there was no further data to add. An overarching theory of 'learning to be a professional' emerged as the final stage of the grounded theory approach.

Results

In the clinical setting, the student participants learnt in a predominantly unstructured learning environment where learning opportunities could occur randomly as a shift progressed. Some students' learning proved to be of better quality than their peers and students could isolate different aspects of the management of their learning that were key to successful practice learning.

The Experience of Learning in Practice

There is a lack of clarity on the role of a first-year student nurse on their first placement experience; *"some of them weren't sure if that was a nurses' role or more of a healthcare role that they were doing" (13, end of placement interview)*. Quite often the mentor was viewed as a protector of students' learning interests, as well as a facilitator of their learning, and, without this particular level of support, the student was at risk of being buffeted by the adversities of practice. This included instances of horizontal bullying by permanent staff, being directed to work with no link to students' learning and being made to feel unwelcome in practice.

Students displayed a strong desire to find a useful role on placement where they felt occupied and did not experience a sense of 'placement drift'. This could occur undertaking activities not linked to their learning, but ones that promoted students' self-worth and sense of independence. On their first placement students preferred to be occupied *"I'm *not someone who likes to just stand and observe" (1, end of placement interview)* and *"I don't want to be one of those people who have to keep asking stuff" (15, mid placement interview)*. Students did not identify observing and questioning practice as components of learning in practice and fell into the characteristics of 'keeping busy'. Students needed active encouragement and permission to be a learner in a purposeful manner. Not having these learning skills scaffolded for them meant students saw the observation of care work negatively; as a period of inactivity where learning stopped.

With respect to both learning, and the setting up of a learning experience, the first year student was unable to effectively negotiate their learning on their own. The relationship with their mentor was crucial to being both challenged and nurtured in their practice learning. It was identified by students that, in the absence of the mentor, they undertook personal care with health care assistants, *"they're easier to access" (19, mid placement interview)*, particularly in residential and nursing home settings where students were asked to work with senior care staff. Although students were content to be looked after by health care assistants in their initial induction period they became dissatisfied if they felt they continued to work as a 'health care assistant' as the placement continued.

> *I'm just left with the care assistants washing and some of the care assistants can do the blood sugar monitoring machine and I asked if I can have a go and I'm not allowed 'cos I'm not trained and it feels like some of the things I can't do so I can't be left on my own sometimes unless it's like just basic washing. It feels like, I want to learn more …. (9, end of placement interview)*

For students, the richest learning experiences occurred when they were challenged beyond their first-year role. Emergency situations, such as a cardiac arrest of a patient, allowed students immediate access to the vast potential of a real-life learning situation. Without exception participants were supported emotionally and the clinical incident was deconstructed by the trained nurses involved into discussion points for learning. Students, as a result, felt more confident of their future role if the same emergency situation occurred again.

> ... It was sort of exhilarating but actually reflecting on it with my mentor I think it all sort of came up and it was a bit like scary. She sort of pulled me aside and said, 'How do you think that went?' which was good because I wasn't going to really talk about it but it was good that she brought it up. (5, end of placement interview)

The Experience of Working and Learning with a Mentor

Finding time with their mentor became a constant management issue for students. Night shifts afforded greater access but during the day the availability of the mentor became more organic and opportunistic. Students, most satisfied with their practice learning, intensively shadowed their mentor through the majority of their work with the student 'dropping away' from their shadowing role when an alternative clinical need arose. This could occur when the mentor required personal or professional space to perform their clinical role on their own, or when an alternative learning opportunity was created for the student.

> Initially I'd obviously stay with her but then if another opportunity came up she was pretty fine to let me go; she often set up learning opportunities. We'd go off with other team members and she was fine with that and I just joined her back on, but on quite a few of the days I was with her the whole of the time which was good. (5, end of placement interview)

The success of this mentorship model was dependent on the student being able to 'ebb and flow' their contact time with their mentor against the rhythm of their mentors' clinical work needs or the students' own alternative learning opportunities. Students and mentors thus managed time together, and time apart, and this required a mutually understood approach by both mentor and student and effective communication between the two. Some students became so attuned to this style of supervision that they developed a sixth sense of when it was inappropriate to stay with their mentor. Alternatively, the mentor explicitly directed the student to a different activity when they became busy. This was seen as acceptable by student and mentor and was clearly managed. This could also be accompanied by a clear arrangement as to when the supervisory relationship would resume at a given time or during a given activity.

The 'ebb and flow' approach used the possible fluidity of the students' role to release the mentors' time spent supervising when there was an increased clinical demand on the mentors' time. However, whilst working with their mentor, students had the opportunity to experience the registered nurse role in its entirety and became party to the subtleties and complexity of professional judgements that their mentors made. Students were, therefore, at the heart of professional decision making rather than being directed away to smaller nursing tasks where they were unable to view the multitude of ongoing judgements made by the nurse in charge. Importantly, students were required to communicate with their mentor frequently in an ongoing discussion of work priorities and care decisions. This created a rich and dynamic learning environment that was constructed through an effective professional relationship between student and mentor.

With the 'ebb and flow' model of mentorship an additional positive was that the students' 'need to be useful' was addressed as the mentor continually directed the student to tasks either with them or away from them. This included opportunities to work with other staff or to follow patients on their journeys to other departments and specialists.

In contrast to the 'ebb and flow' model of mentorship, supervision also occurred in alternative ways. One student eloquently described 'grab and go' situations where students were quickly summoned to see a particular procedure, such as a wound dressing or an injection, which was thought to be of benefit to their learning. These learning situations, like many within the practice setting, were unplanned and relied on the learner being available and ready to take the learning opportunity offered.

> *I would have been too scared to do it, but because she was like 'you can do it, I'll do it, I'll show you, I'm not going to let you go wrong or anything and then I want you to do it and see if you can do it, is that alright?' (11, end of placement interview).*

Students were given the confidence to 'give the procedure a go' and could feel a sense of achievement afterwards. However, if students were hurried into completing a new competence without having the opportunity to be assessed, or building on their initial experience, their learning retention and potential development was weakened.

The most popular mentors challenged students' depth of learning and had an approachable learning style. These mentors saw the importance of quizzing students through 'grab and go' opportunities so students felt they had not only achieved the procedure but also had a critical knowledge of the underlying rationale. This learning required mentors to go 'beyond the procedure' challenging students to reach a higher level of learning and becoming increasingly proactive as a learner.

Every time I go to do something he specifically knows that I've done it before rather than explaining it to me he'll get me to explain it to him to make sure I've taken it in. (17, end of placement interview)

Discussion

The research found that although student participants were meant to be supernumerary on placement their mentors were part of the placement management team so the supervision of learning could be compromised through workforce pressures. Mentors either prioritised clinical work, or attempted to build 'work around' supervisory solutions, so students could be supported at the same time. One of these included students undertaking personal care with health care assistants; often viewed as a poor alternative to working with a qualified nurse particularly if this arrangement was prolonged. Participants valued the learning they could achieve with their mentor and sometimes begrudged time spent 'working as a health care assistant'.

'Ebb and flow' mentorship modelled a successful method of continually balancing the work and learning commitments of the mentor with their student. Significantly, students were party to the clinical decision made by their mentor with a reduction in the fragmented end tasks of the decision-making process that Melia's (1984, 1987) student nurses received. The recognised difficulties of bringing all the disparate parts of professional practice into a whole (Benner 1984; Eraut 2004) could therefore be embodied in the practice of one person who the student worked closely with. By observing the work of an expert in action, participants enjoyed the rare opportunity for a more holistic view on professional practice. The 'ebb and flow' model therefore addressed two issues of Melia's study; greater exposure to expert decision making and a bridging of the theory—practice gap through constant coaching and observation of how registered nurses manage and work.

The subtleties and complexities of the registered nurse role were viewed at close proximity on placement, and participants learnt from and were often truly inspired to emulate their mentor. Students were genuinely awed when they saw examples of professional expertise akin to the tacit knowledge or the connoisseurship of professional practice identified by Polanyi (1962). Arguably the 'ebb and flow' model could be one vehicle for moving students through the novice to expert stages identified by Benner (1984) although it remains highly dependent on students having consistent, quality learning time with their mentor. Allan et al. (2011) identified this type of learning intimacy as 'sponsorship'.

The professional sponsorship identified in the research emphasised the building of a professional identity dependent on a deeper socialisation to practice through interaction with more experienced 'old timers' (Wenger 1998). Some participants connected their own professional ambitions to the professional journey already undertaken by their mentor; what Wenger (1998) termed a 'paradigmatic trajectory', and this inspiration was particularly important to male and mature participants when their mentors came from the same demographic. The opportunity to work, and be supported beyond the usual boundaries for first year learners, was particularly inspirational for students as they experienced their future professional selves (Wenger 2012).

Participants described how mentors and other staff, such as health care assistants, tried to create one off 'grab and go' learning opportunities for students as a learning opportunity arose. Although higher level metacognitive skills could be lacking, the strategy provided achievement of specific practical skills or competencies. In clinical situations, where mentors rarely undertook personal care, working with health care assistants sometimes provided the only opportunity for students to practice these skills.

Conclusion

The disparity of learning experience described by study participants indicated that student nurses required sponsorship to negotiate and fulfil the potential of their practice learning on their first placement. The first-year placement took on significance as the first staging post in the formation of a professional identity that, if compromised, could affect student nurses' practice learning and the confidence they felt moving forward.

Like Eraut (2004) this study showed that the structuring of practice learning was influential to students' progress. Poor allocation to inappropriate tasks, or supervisors, eroded the potential for situated learning to occur (Lave and Wenger 1991). Gherardi et al. (1998) introduced the concept of 'situated curriculum' in an ethnographic study of Italian construction site managers. Patterns of learning were naturally aligned to work opportunities providing an organic but logical sequence to development that were neither linear nor progressive.

It was found that if first year student nurses worked closely with a professional expert, usually their mentor, they were more likely to gain an appreciation of the many facets that make up the whole of professional practice through their close involvement in the day to day work of a registered nurse. This included the complex and political nuances of a registered nurses' work that are often implicit within their role and difficult to isolate. As commented by Dreyfus and Dreyfus (1986, p. 30), "an expert's skill has become so much part of him that he need to be no more aware of it than his own body", and thus teaching these 'embodied' aspects of professional practice are a particularly challenging aspect of work based learning.

Benner (1984, 2001), informed by the work of Dreyfus and Dreyfus, found that a nurse moved between five stages of competence as they developed from novice to expert. Although criticised for the lack of explanation of how a nurse progresses through the different developmental stages (Altmann 2007) Benner's work recognised that practice learning could be both implicit and explicit. The risk to learning was when it was obscured by work processes where learning was not made explicit enough for students to recognise and action (Benner 1984; Eraut 2000, 2004).

Benner (1984) believed that the skilled pattern recognition of experts could be taught, rather than being incidental, and the learning emphasis should be placed on the whole of practice and not the isolation of the component skills. Mentorship systems, such as the 'ebb and flow' model, ensure that students are continually assisted in their focus on their professional learning despite the busyness of the placement environment.

Figure 10.1 provides an overview of the 'ebb and flow' model of mentorship. First year students are placed on the side of the diagram where the learning role dominates but work in partnership with health care assistants (who have a dominant working role) and the mentor (who bridges both learning and working). If the student spends the majority of their time with the health care assistant, they work and learn at a 'tasks and specific work' level and are at the farthest point away from the professional decision making of the mentor. If the student learns and works consistently with the mentor, using a collaborative 'ebb and flow' model, they are more likely to be party to the whole of professional practice rather than the fragmented or 'grab and go' parts of clinical roles. By following the 'ebb and flow' model of mentorship students are at the epicentre of professional decision making, rather than on the periphery, but also have the chance to move to alternative learning if the opportunity arises.

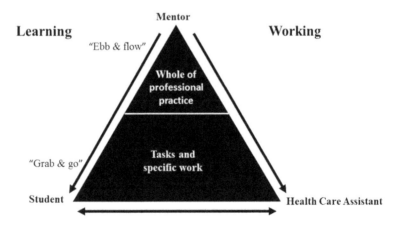

Fig. 10.1 Student nurse learning in practice

For most higher education students, at the beginning of their placement learning, it is sometimes difficult to progress beyond the novice stage of learning where their performance is halting and fragmented (Benner 1984). By successfully working with experienced personnel the vision of expertise and the illusive nature of tacit learning can be more easily isolated for students' learning.

The research findings exposed the 'ebb and flow' mentorship model as a recognisable and simple model of clinical support that could be transferrable to other disciplines beyond health care. The accommodation of students' learning needs, with the workforce requirements of the placement, provided a way for students to work and learn in early professional sponsorship with their mentor. Likewise, more obscured areas of supervision, such as that provided by health care assistants or 'helpful others' (Eraut 2007), was revealed more fully in the context of the research.

By making higher education placement experience more explicit to students as 'learning' the work on placement has the potential to more positively contribute to students' development. The significant amount of time all levels of staff spend with students needs to be converted into valuable and recognised learning for it to be acceptable to students. The 'ebb and flow' model has the potential to be extended into a social model of learning with named individuals contributing to students' learning when novices are not working with their main supervisor. Creatively using existing resources for placement learning, also transmits the important message to all levels of the organisation that everyone has a responsibility to settle and educate students on their placement experience.

Opportunities to consolidate learning, such as students' use of reflective models or having formal reviews, were not built into this research with the risk that students' learning was lost in the busyness of practice. It would seem timely to address whether both supervisors, and other possible facilitators of placement learning, are being prepared sufficiently to support students in the idiosyncrasies of learning in practice. The 'ebb and flow' model highlighted the success of a coaching style of supervision that responded to the fluidity and the opportunistic nature of this particular learning environment.

References

Allan, H. T., Smith, P., & Driscoll, M. (2011). Experiences of supernumerary status and the hidden curriculum in nursing: A new twist in the theory-practice gap? *Journal of Clinical Nursing, 20*(5–6), 847.

Altmann, T. K. (2007). An evaluation of the seminal work of Patricia Benner: Theory or philosophy? *Contemporary Nurse, 25*(1–2), 114–123.

Andrew, N., McGuinness, C., Reid, G., & Corcoran, T. (2009). Greater than the sum of its parts: Transition into the first year of undergraduate nursing. *Nurse Education in Practice, 9*, 13–21.

Argyris, C., & Schön, D. (1974). *Theory in practice: Increasing professional effectiveness*. San Francisco: Jossey Bass.

Benner, P. (1984). *From novice to expert: Excellence and power in clinical nursing practice*. California: Addison-Wesley Publishing Company.

Benner, P. (2001). *From novice to expert: Excellence and power in clinical nursing practice*. Vol. Commemorative Edition. Upper Saddle River, NJ: Prentice Hall Health.

Bradbury-Jones, C., Sambrook, S., & Irvine, F. (2007). The meaning of empowerment for nursing students: A critical incident study. *Journal of Advanced Nursing, 59*(4), 342–351.

Bradbury-Jones, C., Sambrook, S., & Irvine, F. (2011a). Empowerment and being valued: A phenomenological study of nursing students' experience of clinical practice. *Nurse Education Today, 31*, 368–372.

Bradbury-Jones, C., Sambrook, S., & Irvine, F. (2011b). Nursing students and the issue of voice: A qualitative study. *Nurse Education Today, 31*, 628–632.

Charmaz, K. (2006). *Constructing grounded theory*. London, Thousand Oaks, and New Delhi: Sage Publications.

Cope, P., Cuthbertson, P., & Stoddart, B. (2000). Situated learning in the practice placement. *Journal of Advanced Nursing, 31*(4), 850–856.

Davis, J. (2006). The Importance of the community of practice in identity development. *The Internet Journal of Allied Health Sciences and Practice, 4*(3), 1–8.

Department of Education. (2017). *Teaching Excellence Framework: Subject-level pilot specification*. Retrieved August 14, 2017, from https://www.gov.uk/government/publications/teaching-excellence-framework-subject-level-pilot-specification

Dreyfus, H. L., & Dreyfus, S. E. (1986). *Mind over machine*. New York: Macmillan.

Ellstrom, P.-E. (2011). Informal learning at work: Conditions, processes and logics. In M. Malloch, L. Cairns, K. Evans, & B. O'Connor (Eds.), *The Sage handbook of workplace learning* (pp. 105–119). London, California, New Delhi, and Singapore: Sage.

Eraut, M. (2000). Non-formal learning and tacit knowledge in professional work. *British Journal of Educational Psychology, 70*, 113–136.

Eraut, M. (2004). Informal learning in the workplace. *Studies in Continuing Education, 26*(2), 247–273.

Eraut, M. (2007). Learning from other people in the workplace. *Oxford Review of Education, 33*(4), 403–422.

Gherardi, S., Nicolini, D., & Odella, F. (1998). Toward a social understanding of how people learn in organisations: The notion of situated curriculum. *Management Learning, 29*, 273–297.

Gray, M., & Smith, L. N. (1999). The professional socialisation of diploma of higher education in nursing students (Project 2000): A longitudinal study. *Journal of Advanced Nursing, 29*(3), 639–647.

Gray, M. A., & Smith, L. N. (2000). The qualities of an effective mentor from the student nurse's perspective: Findings from a longitudinal qualitative study. *Journal of Advanced Nursing, 32*, 1542–1549.

Grealish, L., & Ranse, K. (2009). An exploratory study of first year nursing students' learning in the clinical workplace. *Contemporary Nurse, 33*(1), 80–92.

Guba, E. G., & Lincoln, Y. S. (2005). Paradigmatic controversies, contradictions and emerging confluences. In N. K. Denzin & Y. S. Lincoln (Eds.), *The Sage handbook of qualitative research* (pp. 191–215). Thousand Oaks, London, and New Delhi: Sage.

Hasson, F., McKenna, H. P., & Keeney, S. (2013). Perceptions of the unregistered healthcare worker's role in pre-registration student nurses' clinical training. *Journal of Advanced Nursing, 69*(7), 1618–1629.

Holland, K. (1999). A journey to becoming: The student nurse in transition. *Journal of Advanced Nursing, 29*(1), 229–236.

Lave, J., & Wenger, E. (1991). *Situated learning: Legitimate peripheral participation*. New York: Cambridge University Press.

Levett-Jones, T., & Lathlean, J. (2008). Belongingness: A prerequisite for nursing students' clinical learning. *Nurse Education Today, 8*, 103–111.

Levett-Jones, T., & Lathlean, J. (2009). "Don't rock the boat': Nursing students' experience of conformity and compliance. *Nurse Education Today, 29*, 342–349.

Melia, K. M. (1984). Student nurses' construction of occupational socialisation. *Sociology of Health and Illness, 6*(2), 132–151.

Melia, K. M. (1987). *Learning and working: The occupational socialisation of nurses.* London: Tavistock Publications.

Morley, D. (2017a, August 5). Degree apprenticeships are a ray of light in a gloomy sector. *Times Higher Education.* Retrieved August 15, 2017, from https://www.timeshighereducation.com/blog/degree-apprenticeships-are-ray-light-gloomy-sector

Morley, D. (2017b, August 15). Is apprenticeship learning a thing of the past? *FE News.* Retrieved August 15, 2017, from https://www.fenews.co.uk/featured-article/14619-is-apprenticeship-learning-a-thing-of-the-past

Morley, D. A. (2015). *A grounded theory study exploring first year student nurses' learning in practice.* Doctor in Professional Practice, Bournemouth.

Myall, M., Levett-Jones, T., & Lathlean, J. (2008). Mentorship in contemporary practice: The experiences of nursing students and practice mentors. *Journal of Clinical Nursing, 17,* 1834–1842.

NMC. (2004). *Standards of proficiency for pre-registration nursing education.* London: NMC.

Nursing and Midwifery Council. (2017). *Draft for consultation: Standards for proficiency for registered nurses.* London: NMC.

O'Driscoll, M. F., Allan, H. T., & Smith, P. A. (2010). Still looking for leadership—Who is responsible for student nurses' learning in practice? *Nurse Education Today, 30*(3), 212–217.

Polanyi, M. (1962). *Personal knowledge: Towards a post-critical philosophy.* London: Routledge and Kegan Paul.

Spouse, J. (2001). Bridging theory and practice in the supervisory relationship: A sociocultural perspective. *Journal of Advanced Nursing, 33*(4), 512–530.

Universities UK. (2016). *The future growth of degree apprenticeships.* Universities UK Publications.

Vygotsky, L. (1962). *Thought and language.* Cambridge, MA: MIT Press.

Wenger, E. (1998). *Communities of practice: Learning, meaning and identity.* New York: Cambridge University Press.

Wenger, E. (2012). Social learning theory and healthcare education. In HEA (Ed.), *Contemporary issues in clinical education.* London: Institute of Education.

Willis, G. (2015). *Raising the bar: Shape of caring: A review of the future education and training of registered nurses and care assistants.* London: Health Education England.

Part V

Using the University Experience for Work Based Learning for Future Employability

11

The Role of the Student Ambassador and Its Contribution to Developing Employability Skills: A Creation of Outward Facing Work Roles

H. Baker and K. Sela

Introduction

Universities recognise that a number of students with the ability to progress to higher education still do not do so. It has been widely documented that specific groups in higher education are under-represented. These under-represented groups, often called Widening Participation (WP) students, include those from disadvantaged backgrounds, those with disabilities, care leavers, young carers, mature learners, black minority ethnic (BME) students or those whose parents have no parental history of higher education or are in non-professional occupations. Students from these groups may find barriers to participating in higher education. These barriers offer possible reasons why students from these groups are less likely to progress to higher education. Data shows that the most disadvantaged 20% of young people are 6.8 times less likely to attend a selective university than the most disadvantaged 20% (OFFA

H. Baker (✉) • K. Sela
University of Surrey, Guildford, UK
e-mail: h.baker@surrey.ac.uk

2015). In 2014/15, 33% of pupils eligible for free school meals and 36% of disadvantaged pupils achieved at least 5 A*- C GCSEs (or equivalent) grades, including English and Mathematics, compared to 60% and 64% of non-disadvantaged pupils (DOE 2015). In addition, research on graduate outcomes indicates that while more disadvantaged young people are in higher education than ever before, the gap between the non-continuation rates of the most advantaged and most disadvantaged students has widened in the past year and graduates from disadvantaged and under-represented groups have significant differences in employment outcomes (HEFCE 2015).

Like many other institutions, the University of Surrey annually submits an Access Agreement to the Office of Fair Access (OFFA), an independent public body whose role is to monitor and safeguard fair access to higher education on an annual basis. The University of Surrey's Access Agreement provides official documentation of our commitment to the access, progression and success of under-represented groups in higher education.

The University of Surrey is focused on increasing the participation of under-represented groups in higher education, and supporting the success and progression of these students throughout their student lifecycle. The Department of Widening Participation and Outreach plays a significant role in raising aspirations, awareness of HE and attainment of young people under-represented in HE. Working with state maintained primary schools, secondary schools and colleges in and around Surrey we offer a coherent and sustained programme of events for widening participation students from Years 5 to 13 (ages 10–18) as well as parents and carers, teachers and mature learners. These events offer information, advice and guidance about university and educational pathways as well as subject sessions to motivate, inform and inspire students. Our aim is to minimise barriers and support progression and participation for those who are capable of benefitting from the experience. In 2016/17, 11,933 students were involved in outreach activities run by the department with 1945 parents and carers and 355 teachers also attending activities.

In order to run this number of events the department relies heavily on the outstanding work and support of our widening participation student ambassadors. This requires ambassadors who are capable and confident in their role and the work of the department which requires effective training and investment.

The Student Ambassador

Student ambassadors work in a variety of roles within universities, from marketing and student recruitment to Widening Participation and Outreach (WP&O). The role of the WP student ambassador is a unique opportunity that allows students to experience work based learning in the context of the university itself where they are an integral part of the Department of Widening Participation and Outreach at the university whilst both learning and working as an ambassador. For many student ambassadors their work with the department has influenced their career choice and some have expressed a desire to work in widening participation and outreach, go into teaching, or work with young people after graduation.

Student ambassadors play an essential role in supporting the work of Widening Participation and Outreach Departments to raise the aspirations of students from groups that are under-represented in higher education and help them successfully make the transition to university. The role of student ambassadors at the University of Surrey is as varied as the outreach events and activities the department run. These can include supervising week long overnight residential summer schools at the university, to mentoring individual students, delivering inspiring whole school assemblies in schools and colleges to providing information to parents and carers; helping them feel more confident in supporting and advising their child's decision about future educational pathways.

Ambassadors are expected to represent the university at outreach activities, showing enthusiasm for their subject area and experience of higher education, however their responsibilities go much further than this due to the variety of their work. Student ambassadors' work with students aged 10–18 as well as mature learners, parents/carers, teachers, university academics, external companies and members of the Widening Participation and Outreach Department and must vary their approach according to the group they are working with.

The ability to communicate to a wide variety of audiences through different mediums is one of the most important attributes of student ambassadors as they are often required to deliver informative and inspirational talks and presentations to different groups. Student ambassadors are key to the success of outreach activities and events and their ability to relate to different groups, particularly young people, and communicate advanced concepts is central to the success of their role. A large proportion of ambassadors' work comprises facilitating activities and responding to unexpected situations at events. Ambassadors, therefore, need to have the ability to encourage and motivate groups and individuals, negotiating and influencing without overly contributing to the task. Their ability to manage groups and identify which approach should be taken with each individual is critical in order for those individuals to feel valued and benefit from the outreach work of the department.

Observation and student feedback show many ambassadors benefit from undertaking this type of flexible paid work and their confidence in their own abilities increases as a result:

Being an ambassador has had incredible effect on my confidence and personal skills. While preparing for my placement year I have been able to use the skills I have learnt from leading campus tours and other events put on by the university outreach team during my interviews as well as gaining important and impressive details for my CV.
(WP student ambassador—BSc Maths, Female, June 2017)

I have become more confident, especially from the Year 9 Surrey Skills Fair as I had to be really mature. I think we are benefiting the next generation absolutely because we encourage so many young people to think about university and their futures and help them aspire to do something more than just leave school and get a job. My Ambassador role has made me think twice about my own career options.
(WP student ambassador—BMs Music, Female, June 2017)

Despite this, there is a distinct lack of research and literature on student ambassadors (Ylonen 2010). Existing research examines the student ambassador role within other contexts such as recruitment (Rhodes et al. 2006), mentoring (Colley 2003) or how young people use student ambassadors to make decisions about higher education (Gartland and Paczuska 2007). Very little research has been undertaken on the impact this work has on the ambassadors themselves to discover whether it helps them with their programme of study, personal development or employability. Austin and Hatt (2005) looked at the effect of employing university students for widening participation outreach activities and found that students benefitted from increased confidence and self-esteem. Ambassadors also felt the role had helped develop their transferable and employability skills which would contribute to their Curriculum Vitae (CV) and future employment.

Employability skills and graduate employability rates are increasingly becoming an important part of many university degrees to meet the demand for higher-level skills required by employers (Universities UK 2015). Furthermore, a key feature of university marketing campaigns, with a number of prestigious university rankings such as The Guardian League Table and The Times Good University Guide include graduate employability as a benchmark of success. Although the success and progression of WP students is a priority for many institutions evidence shows that there are differences in employment outcomes for disadvantaged students (Universities UK 2016). Britton et al. (2016) found considerable variation in graduate earnings could be explained by parental income, students from families with higher household income have average earnings which are around 25% more than those from lower income families. One reason for this might be that WP students could be less likely to complete a placement year possibly due to financial, personal or home pressures (Greenbank and Hepworth 2008; Mountford-Zimdars et al. 2015). These are significant findings as research indicates that sandwich placements and work experience are associated with a higher probability of progressing to further study or employment (HEFCE 2015). To further emphasise the importance of this in the context of this paper, 79% of the WP student ambassadors who undertook initial training in 2016/17 identified as coming from a widening participation background. The relevance and value of widening participation departments providing opportunities for students to undertake employment during their studies, that help to develop their transferable skills for progress to the workplace, is therefore vital. The following section outlines the core initial training that WP student ambassadors receive before they start their work with the department and the additional training they are offered throughout their work to support their progression both during and after university.

Training, Development and Reflection

The role of the ambassadors is pivotal to the work of the department. As well as preparing these students for their work as a student ambassador, we are committed to facilitating their personal and professional development in order to support them throughout their studies and on to further education or employment, particularly as such a high number of them identify as coming from a WP background. The Department of Widening Participation and Outreach have worked with ambassadors to create a training programme that not only prepares them for their role with the department, but also to further their personal and professional development. This programme consists of an initial compulsory comprehensive training day, followed by continued observation, feedback and self-reflection as well as annual refresher training and optional continual professional development sessions.

Recruitment for ambassadors takes place at the beginning of each academic year. Students who have applied and been shortlisted are required to attend an interview and complete an enhanced Disclosure and Barring Service (DBS) check for their work with children. Students who successfully complete both these stages attend a compulsory initial Saturday training session. This training consists of multiple activity based workshops which aim to give students a comprehensive understanding of WP and the role of the student ambassador. The training aims to establish an internal support network, develop new and existing skills such as presentation and communication skills, facilitation, group management and self-reflection skills and give them an understanding of their role in safeguarding and child protection. It also aims to build students' confidence to support and deliver WP activities.

Our ambassadors are considered an extension of the department and their ideas and opinions are valued. After each activity the student ambassadors are required to complete an evaluation, the level of detail dependant on the type of activity they were involved in, but the aim of the evaluation is to find out from their perspective what went well and what could be improved and to explore their development through the event. From evaluation of training, and our end of year ambassador survey, together with anecdotal feedback from events and observation by staff, we have been able to develop further training sessions and CPD sessions based on the ambassador needs and the requirements of their developing roles.

One such session was a Vocal Confidence workshop which was developed and delivered with a member of staff from the Guildford School of Acting. The workshop aimed to change the way student ambassadors presented themselves vocally in all situations, from working in small groups of young people to large, mixed audiences. It focused on students' breathing, posture, pitch, volume and body language. All ambassadors who attended found it to be beneficial to their role and felt it would help them to be a more effective ambassador. They also commented on how it had "*improved their self-confidence*".

Another session developed based on ambassador feedback was Additional Needs Training. During 2016/17 the number of young people with a disability, particularly those with Autism Spectrum Disorder (ASD) attending our events has increased. Feedback from ambassadors indicated they wanted further training to enable them to better support these students' needs. As a result, a session was developed with a member of staff from Additional Learning Support at the university which focused on the support and adjustments that could be made at events to ensure inclusivity. All ambassadors who attended felt the training has given them a better understanding of the skills needed to support young people with a disability and felt confident in their ability to apply those skills during WP activities.

Finally, through discussion with ambassadors during events it became apparent not all student ambassadors were able to see how their work, and the skills developed as an ambassador, could be used on their CV and those that did, struggled to effectively communicate the skills and experience they had accumulated. This led us to develop an Articulating Experience training session with the Department of Careers and

Employability. The workshop concentrated on how ambassadors could effectively articulate the valuable skills and experiences they have gained from their role to future employers and focused on CV writing and interview skills. Ambassadors who attended found the session *"really useful"* all agreeing that it had helped them to identify skills they used and developed as an ambassador. One student also commented on the timing of the training being beneficial as it ran at the beginning of the year when they had started to look for graduate employment.

Half of the 35 ambassadors who responded to the end of year survey took part in additional training which was introduced in the 2015/16 academic year. Over 53% of ambassadors took part in vocal confidence training and others have participated in training to learn how to support students with a range of disabilities, how to develop and deliver a workshop and articulating their own experiences for future progression.

Methodology

A mixed method approach was taken, collecting data from in-depth interviews and questionnaires. Quantitative and qualitative data collected through an end of year survey (2017) and interviews with our current student ambassador cohort paints a picture of the impact the role of the WP student ambassador has on development and employability. Survey data included open ended questions exploring the general impact that student ambassadors felt the role had on them, what skills they had learnt and how their training had helped to prepare them for their role. Survey data was collected at the end of each year from 2014/15. The student ambassador survey was run for the third year in 2016/17 and was sent online using Bristol Online Survey (BOS) survey tool to all 152 ambassadors that were registered with the department, a total of 35 students (23%) completed the survey. The relatively low response rate may have been due to the timing of the survey which took place at the end of the academic year.

Gender: 17% Male; 83% Female.
Ethnicity: 86% White; 14% Black Minority Ethnic (BME).

Year of study: 9% Year 1; 57% Year 2; 17% Year 3; 14% Year 4; 3% PTY Year.
No. of years working as a SA: 40% 1 Year; 34% 2 Years; 14% 3 Years; 11% 4 Years.
Faculty: 46% Arts & Social Science; 43% Health & Medical Science; 11% Engineering & Physical Science.

In addition to the survey data, three case studies were carried out with student ambassadors who had worked for the department for more than three years and were leaving the role as they were graduating. In-depth interviews were carried out with the ambassadors and a narrative approach was taken to data collection and this approach enabled a richer understanding of how ambassadors constructed their time as an ambassador and development of employability skills. Each of the ambassadors highlighted some of the best and most varied examples of how the student ambassador role had benefitted students' own learning within a work setting, employability and career direction. Pseudonyms have been used for participants who took part in case studies.

The Department of Widening Participation and Outreach has received ethical approval for all WP activities which includes the evaluation and research of WP student ambassadors.

Findings and Analysis

End of Year Ambassador Survey June 2017

In the end of year survey, over 50% of students said that they had taken part in six or more activities during the year. 37% had taken part in 3–5 activities and 11% had taken part in 1–2 activities. Students who had taken part in the greatest number of activities were more likely to say that the skills they had developed as an ambassador would help their future employability (Table 11.1).

Students who had worked as an ambassador in an IAG (Information, Advice and Guidance) event, a Residential Summer School Programme, acted as a student mentor or participated in a campus visit were most

Table 11.1 Activities participated in and future employability

Do you think the skills you have gained as a WP student ambassador will help your employability?	1–2 activities	3–5 activities	6 or more activities
Yes	9%	37%	51%
No	3%	0%	0%

likely to say that the skills they had gained would help with their future employability.

Initial ambassador training is central to ambassadors being able to carry out their role effectively and over 97% ambassadors who completed the end of year survey said that the training prepared them well for their future role as an ambassador. Ambassadors were asked whether they thought their role had an impact on their own development and 62% said it had a "*significant*" impact on their development. An increase in self-confidence was talked about by ambassadors, particularly in relation to giving presentations and their general communication skills. One student described how they are now more able to communicate to "*suit the audience*" they are speaking to. Another student said that they now feel more "*capable to handle any situation*" and of "*talking to anyone*" as a result of their work.

Ambassadors were asked whether their role had helped to develop their skills and they told us that their communication, team working, interpersonal and public speaking skills had increased. Ambassadors described a variety of ways that they would be able to use the skills to prepare them for their future employability, with one student saying that the interpersonal skills they had gained from their work would give them "*an idea of what to expect when entering a work place*". One student said that she would be able to "*draw upon*" the wide range of experiences she had gained as an ambassador when "*applying to work in schools*". The ability to adapt and deal with a range of situations was also mentioned and one student said that their experience as an ambassador would be "*relevant in my future career*". Some ambassadors felt that their role had helped them to decide on their own future career pathway with one saying it had made them realise that "*working with young people is what I want to do in the future*".

Case Studies

Rebecca is studying for a BSc in Chemistry with a Professional Training Year (PTY). Rebecca has worked with the Widening Participation Department for almost two and a half years and during her first year worked in a shop but stopped this to become a student ambassador, working with both the WP and Marketing team. Rebecca found out about the scheme from her flat mate, felt she identified with the WP students we work with and wanted to help other students in a similar situation.

John is studying for an MSc in Civil Engineering and has worked with the Widening Participation and Outreach Department as a student ambassador for two and a half years. During his second year at university he had worked for a local youth club with troubled children who ended up moving and he felt he wanted to look for a similar type of work to do alongside his studies. Being a student ambassador provided flexibility around his studies and provided a break from having his head 'buried in a text book'. His own experience as a WP student was a key motivation to work in the department being the first generation in his family to go to university.

Robert is studying Law (LLB) degree and has been working as a WP student ambassador for four years. He was attracted to the role as he had a strong sense of education being for everyone and wanted to make a difference. As soon as he saw the poster advertising the role he knew immediately he wanted to apply.

Working Towards Employability

It's helped me develop desirable skills required for within any job role Its also given me more confidence in my own ability and thus will encourage me to heighten my aspirations.

Rebecca described how in her interview for her professional training Year (PTY) the employer was interested in her role as a student ambassador and wanted to know more about what her work had involved. She felt that she was able to demonstrate a range of skills that she had developed through her work as an ambassador and that these were particularly helpful in being offered the placement:

> *They picked up on my CV straight away that I'd been a student ambassador and were asking 'what did it entail, what did you do'? And when I explained they were really interested because it shows such a huge range of skills and different things that lots of other people on my degree haven't done.*

Rebecca describes what the additional benefit might be for the company of having a student with experience of outreach work as the company also had a commitment to providing outreach work to students at open days for example. During the year she was asked to run a family event for young people at a local school and was able to use the skills she had developed through her ambassador work, particularly her knowledge of delivering activities to a wide range of students from different age groups and with different abilities.

John was able to demonstrate the work he had done as a student ambassador to help contribute to achieving his Institute of Civil Engineers (ICE) accreditation to get professional chartership. He is very clear that his role as a student ambassador had put him ahead of other candidates when applying for his current position.

> *I got a long list of events that I did that I could use as evidence for my CPD for my ICE accreditation which helps me get my professional chartership. … If it was a tie up between me and another candidate I'd put money on that being me because I had that experience.*

Similar to Rebecca, John's employer was very interested in his ambassador work during the interview as both could demonstrate that they had done a substantial amount of work during the period of time they had worked for the department. The outreach work that John had done was particularly important within civil engineering as they are required to run outreach activities with schools in science, technology, engineering and mathematics (STEM) and he was able to talk about the design and delivery of activity that he has been involved with as an ambassador an experience he thinks other candidates may not have had.

More than likely they haven't had that experience before I know I wouldn't have any problems doing that, standing up in front of that school or designing and delivering an activity.

Robert worked at a large law firm during his PTY in the area of medical negligence. He describes the interview process being highly competitive and, similar to Rebecca, says that they were particularly interested in his role as an ambassador during his time at university and how important this was in a competitive market for placements:

The particular placement was really, really competitive. The fact that at my interview they spent so long talking about my WP role probably indicates that it set me aside.

Each of the students experienced an interview which drew on the skills they had developed during their work as a student ambassador and the type of experience they could bring to the role.

Learning on the Job

It provides a unique and relevant wealth of experience for me to draw upon when applying to work It has also provided experience that I consider vital for career growth.

Residential summer schools are a large part of the work that the department delivers and student ambassadors play an integral part to supporting the event and ensuring that the weeks run smoothly. Additional training is offered to current ambassadors specifically to help prepare them for their enhanced role during the programme that also involves them in supervising students in Year 12 who are not much younger than many of them. John described how much he learnt about group dynamics which bought to life what he had learnt about in lectures:

Summer schools were a big learning for both students and ambassadors, general time keeping, logistics, getting people to the right place at the right time.

Because of the diverse range of activities ambassadors are required to work, they gain significant experience managing a range of different situations. Learning how to interact and get the best of students of different ages has been particularly helpful for Rebecca who is thinking of going into teaching as a result of her experience as an ambassador. She describes how she is able to assess the level of student engagement and ability which will benefit her as she plans to start a teacher training once she finishes her degree:

I can go into a room now and assess different students and how they engage with things whereas that's something that comes later normally to a lot of trainee teachers and I've developed the skills to help those that are struggling and those who are higher achieving because we work with such a range of people.

Some of the skills that ambassadors have developed during their work are more generally related to their chosen career path. For example, Robert talks about his ability to communicate well with groups of people and present will be particularly transferable in his planned future career working as a lawyer.

Building Skills

Being an ambassador has pushed me out of comfort zone, making me more confident about public speaking and enhancing my communication skills.

Developing confidence in dealing with different people, whether students, teachers or other departmental staff was a key developmental part of the ambassador role. During their work placements, some ambassadors experienced particularly challenging situations. John described having to communicate the company's plans for a site to local residents that was particularly difficult and how he managed to present himself in a calm professional manner which drew on his experiences of his work as an ambassador.

Working Flexibly

A big one was flexibility, if coursework was low I could work more events and if I was a bit stretched I could work fewer events.

When students have a busy schedule of lectures and work to complete, the flexibility that the role can offer is vital to them which Rebecca describes:

It is really flexible and it's an easy job to have when you're at university because you're not committing to 30 hours a week or 10 hours a week, you just sign up for the events and hours you want to work … it's just a really easy option to have a job and actually be able to work alongside your studies.

Thinking Ahead

Being a WP student ambassador has actually made me realise that WP work and working with young people is what I love and want to do in the future after my degree.

John has high aspirations to work in a senior role as a civil engineer. Working as an ambassador has given him a strong sense of how he wants to engage with widening participation students to raise their expectations to go into higher education:

I want to be high up in the company and when I'm in that role it will benefit me as well because I will be able to appreciate the importance of WP…. I'll be pushing WP because I've seen the benefits of it first hand.

Rebecca's ambassador work with school groups and young people helped to direct her towards teaching in the future. She said that before becoming an ambassador she was not sure what she was going to do when she graduated:

I would have been a bit stuck if I hadn't done this because I wouldn't have known what to do come July when I finish so it has really helped me.

The Wider Impact

> *It's made me so much more confident, comfortable with myself my WP work has brought me out of my shell, means I'm happy I feel proud to be a Surrey student ambassador, gives me a sense of purpose.*

As well as getting paid for their work, students enjoy their roles and all three ambassadors talked about it in very positive ways. Rebecca said that it contributed to her enjoyment of the university experience:

> *It's been my favourite part of university being a student ambassador, I sign up for pretty much every job that comes through and then I'm like oh I probably shouldn't be working quite as much as I am, but it's been such a great part of university life.*

Because of their enjoyment of their ambassador role, sometimes it was hard to balance this with their studies. John describes how doing the work improved the quality of his time at university:

> *It was like Christmas when you get the job email list, especially when my degree was so full on! I didn't expect I'd ever want to put WP over my degree because I'm so focussed on my degree. It gave me a better quality of life, you saw the difference in me.*

Being a student ambassador also added an additional motivation for John to do well in his studies as he had a strong sense of representing the university in his role which also meant that he wanted to do well and be a good role model for students:

> *It made me want to get top marks in everything I did. You want to be a true ambassador and role model.*

Throughout their time as student ambassadors staff from the Department of Widening Participation and Outreach have observed a significant change, the most striking in Rebecca and Robert.

When Robert started as an ambassador he said he felt shy and lacking in confidence. His development over the years, most noticeably his self-confidence, has led him to become one of our most trusted ambassadors, contributing significantly to numerous events and taking on additional responsibilities. His work and opinions are highly valued by the team. This year he received the Student Ambassador Spirit Award. This award recognises Robert's understanding and commitment to WP and his ability to engage and empower students of all ages, capabilities and backgrounds.

Rebecca was able to develop her self-confidence and the department helped her to step out of her comfort zone in a supported, safe environment. Now she is confident talking to anyone; students, parents/carers, teachers and university staff. She has delivered whole school assemblies to hundreds of students and worked as lead ambassador for our residential summer schools. In addition, when we learned Rebecca was interested in becoming a teacher we were able to support her in designing and delivering her own chemistry taster days which have been extremely successful and helped her develop key skills she will need as a teacher. This year she received the Widening Participation Contribution Award for her work with the department.

Rebecca graduated from her BSc Chemistry degree with a First Class degree. She has been accepted on a School Direct PGCE teacher training qualification to teach secondary school chemistry. She is keen to develop links between the department and her new school to support their WP student cohort.

John graduated with a First Class MEng in Civil Engineering and is currently employed by one of the UK's largest house builders. He is working towards achieving his ICE chartership and is raising the awareness of outreach within his new company. He has already delivered a number of STEM activities in schools and has returned to support the University's WP activities representing his new company as alumni.

Robert graduated from his Bachelor of Law LLB with First Class Honours. He received the highest marks in his cohort in Medical Law and Ethics. He is currently deciding whether to continue to become a solicitor or pursue a career in Widening Participation.

Conclusion

The widening participation student ambassador role offers a unique opportunity for students to practice work based learning in a professional but safe environment rich in development opportunities, support and new experiences within a university department. Ambassadors delivering IAG sessions, subject specific taster workshops, residential summer schools and acting as student mentors, develop their employability skills which can influence their career direction.

To ensure the continuation of experience between our ambassador cohorts through placement year and graduation, we are developing a first-year ambassador peering mentoring programme where we pair experienced ambassadors to act as role models to newly trained ambassadors. This pairing will allow new ambassadors to settle in to their roles, reflect on their work and develop a more diverse support network, particularly important for students from specific or less represented backgrounds. It will also further develop experienced ambassadors' employability skills and ensure their skills and experience are passed on.

Not only does the work of the student ambassador offer a valuable development opportunity it also helps to raise the aspirations and attainment of the disadvantaged students they work with. By acting as a positive role model for these students and motivating them through their early education, ambassadors become more motivated and committed to their own learning and degree programme, increasing their feelings of belonging and pride in the University and their role.

References

Austin, M., & Hatt, S. (2005). The Messengers are the message: A study of the effects of employing higher education students to work with school students. *Widening Participation and Lifelong Learning, 7*(1), 1–8.

Britton, J., Dearden, L., Shephard, N., & Vignoles, A. (2016). *How English domiciled graduate earnings vary with gender, institution attended, subject and socio-economic background*. IFS.

Colley, H. (2003). Engagement mentoring for 'disaffected' youth: A new model of mentoring for social inclusion. *British Educational Research Journal, 29*(4), 521–542.

Department for Education. (2015). *GCSE and equivalent attainment by pupil characteristics, 2013 to 2014 (Revised)*.

Gartland, C., & Paczuska, A. (2007). Student ambassador, trust and HE choices. *Journal of Access Policy and Practice, 4*(2), 108–133.

Greenbank, P., & Hepworth, S. (2008). *Working class students and the career decision-making process: A qualitative study*. Edge Hill University Report for HECSU.

Higher Education Funding Council England. (2015). *Differences in employment outcomes: Equality and diversity characteristics*. HEFCE.

Mountford-Zimdars, A., Sabri, D., Moore, J., Sanders, J., Jones, S., & Higham, L. (2015). *Causes of differences in student outcomes*. London: HEFCE.

Office for Fair Access. (2015). *Strategic plan 2015–2020*. OFFA.

Rhodes, S., Sherwin, C., & Smith, L. (2006). The role of student ambassadors in university recruitment. *Nursing Standard, 20*(34), 44.

Universities UK. (2015). *Supply and demand for higher-level skills*. Universities UK.

Universities UK. (2016). *Working in partnership: Enabling social mobility in higher education*. Universities UK.

Ylonen, A. (2010). The role of student ambassadors in higher education: An uneasy association between autonomy and accountability. *Journal of Further and Higher Education, 34*(1), 97–104.

12

Enhancing Psychology Students' Employability Through 'Practice to Theory' Learning Following a Professional Training Year

N. Winstone and R. Avery

Introduction

Due to their positive impact on student employability, Professional Training Years (PTY), or 'Sandwich' placements, are an increasingly common component of UK degree programmes. In these schemes, students complete the first two years of their degree at university, spend their third year in the workplace, and return to university to complete their final year of study. A Sandwich placement, or PTY, represents one form of work-integrated learning with the potential to enhance a student's readiness for work (Drysdale et al. 2016). In comparison to peers who did not undertake a PTY, evidence supports that students who undertake a PTY have superior transferable skills (Wilton 2012), a higher likelihood of

---

N. Winstone (✉)
University of Surrey, Guildford, UK
e-mail: N.Winstone@surrey.ac.uk

R. Avery
Caterham School, Caterham, UK

obtaining a graduate level job (Brooks and Youngson 2016), a better sense of career direction (Reddy and Moores 2006), and higher starting salaries (Brooks and Youngson 2016).

Enhancing their students' employment outcomes holds high stakes for Higher Education Institutions (HEIs). The numbers of graduates entering employment, highly-skilled employment and further study (as measured by the Destinations of Leavers of Higher Education survey; DLHE) are key metrics within the Teaching Excellence Framework (TEF Year 2 DfE 2016), as well as influencing positioning in many influential League Tables. Beyond employment, employability is also represented in the TEF, where an institution can argue within their narrative how their curriculum and pedagogic practices support the development of graduate-level skills and attitudes in students. For example, reference SO2 in the TEF Assessment Criteria characterises the extent to which "students acquire knowledge, skills and attributes that are valued by employers and that enhance their personal and/or professional lives" (DfE 2016, p. 22). In their narratives, HEIs are encouraged to document the impact of any initiatives they have developed that are aimed at graduate employability. This qualitative account is important, as "employability is not only about getting that first job. It's beyond that simple measurement of employment" (Norton 2016, p. 2).

Whilst engaging in a period of work experience through a PTY or Sandwich Placement can directly influence the chances of a student gaining employment once they graduate, it can also have a significant impact on the development of skills and attributes that might support future employability. There is substantial evidence that students who undertake a PTY gain higher marks in the final year of their degree than their counterparts who do not undertake professional training (e.g. Brooks and Youngson 2016; Crawford and Wang 2016; Gomez et al. 2004; Reddy and Moores 2006). This is not simply because high calibre students are more likely to choose to undertake a PTY in the first place (Jones et al. 2017); instead, evidence suggests that undertaking a PTY enhances a student's 'horizon for learning' (Clark and Zukas 2016).

The improved academic performance of those students who have undertaken a PTY suggests that the impact of placement learning on employability and career outcomes may be mediated by learning environments, instructional design, and learning opportunities in the final year of study. Whilst students can deploy skills learned from their PTY in final year learning (Auburn 2007), there is scope for placement learning to enhance students' capacity to learn new material. However, academic staff might not facilitate opportunities for students to implement placement experiences, and students often struggle to return to study following a PTY, with some feeling alienated from education (Auburn 2007).

The final year of study is a critical platform for placement work experience to deliver its impact on employability and work success. Whilst on placement, students have the opportunity to apply theory to practice, by observing how course content applies to real-world contexts. However, once students return to their university studies, they have the opportunity to apply practice to theory; that is, they can interpret new course content in the light of their own practical experiences. For example, Schambach and Dirks (2002) suggest that internship experiences enable students to gain a deeper understanding of coursework requirements when they return to study (Schambach and Dirks 2002). In addition, Evans et al. (2010) stress that it is through viewing our knowledge and understanding of concepts in different environments, such as in both practice and academic settings, that conceptual change can occur as knowledge is 'recontextualised'. Thus, a key challenge for educators wishing to enhance students' employability is seeking opportunities to embed both 'practice to theory' and 'theory to practice' learning within curriculum-specific modules.

To achieve this aim, educators can deploy learning and teaching strategies that require learners to engage with activities closely aligned with real-world experiences. In so doing, learners have the opportunity to draw upon their placement experiences, but also to engage with curriculum content in ways akin to how they would use that knowledge within the workplace. Such pedagogic techniques, with the shared characteristic of involving "fuzzy problems that are set in and/or mimic the real world" (Gray et al. 2013, p. 39), include action learning (e.g. Lizzio and Wilson 2004), problem-based learning (e.g. Yew and Goh 2016), authentic learning (e.g. Herrington et al. 2014), and reality-based learning (Smith and Van Doren 2004).

Reality-based learning (RBL; Smith and Van Doren 2004) offers a useful theoretical framework to inform pedagogic design that draws upon prior experience, and transfers learning to new contexts. In this sense, it is a useful framework for capitalising on both the 'theory to practice' and 'practice to theory' learning that sandwich placements/PTY afford. RBL draws upon active and experiential learning, and presents a four-point framework to guide the design of learning activities (Smith and Van Doren 2004):

Principle 1: Learning activities should focus on the knowledge, skills and attitudes (KSAs) to be acquired by students;
Principle 2: Students are co-responsible for learning through their participation in active learning;
Principle 3: Learning draws upon the prior experiences students bring to the classroom, through experiential learning;
Principle 4: Learning develops transferable skills and experiences.

We operationalised this model within two Level 6 Psychology Modules ('Psychology and Education' and 'Work and Organisational Psychology') by focusing on three pedagogic elements: authentic activities, authentic assessment, and reflection, all of which aligned with the four-point RBL framework of Smith and Van Doren (2004). These elements drew upon students' PTY experiences, embedding 'practice to theory' learning within the curriculum. We evaluated the impact of the intervention by assessing students' preparedness for work and employability mind-set at the start and end of the module.

Background to the Intervention

Within class time, we employed authentic activities directed towards active and experiential learning (Principles 2 and 3). Importantly, these activities were designed to mimic the kinds of situations students might be faced with in the workplace (Principle 4), and to require students to think and act like professional psychologists (Principle 1). For example, a common activity involved using case studies to 'diagnose' an issue in the workplace or the classroom, and to make recommendations. As a form of problem-based learning, case studies using real or simulated cases enable students to gain deep understanding of topic material (Burns and Chopra 2017), and can be used within class teaching, leading to enhanced problem-solving skills, enhanced confidence, superior long-term retention of conceptual knowledge (Hung et al. 2008), and stronger academic motivation (Hmelo-Silver 2004). Activities that involve experiential elements seem to result in stronger longer-term retention of knowledge because they are more memorable and meaningful (Elam and Spotts 2004). Such an approach represents "an exciting approach to facilitate experiential learning, where life situations can be transported to classroom contexts for learning, analysis and appraisal, reflection, and application" (Rambruth and Daniel 2011, p. 40).

Students also completed guided reflection tasks, which encouraged them to bring their PTY experience to the fore prior to learning activities (Principle 3), surface their existing assumptions and perspectives, and revisit these after the learning activity to examine how these might have changed, and to consider how their learning might inform their future practice in the workplace (Principle 4). This is an important dimension of RBL, as "reflection is widely acknowledged in literature as a means to enable the learner to extend their learning experiences beyond the classroom by giving them a meaning and place in the bigger picture" (Ashford-Rowe et al. 2014, p. 208). The ability to reflect on practice and experience is also one of the desired KSAs for a Psychology graduate (Principle 1). In many work based learning programmes, reflection is used to "create practitioners for whom it is the "norm" to continuously reflect, plan and develop" (Helyer 2015, p. 18).

Beyond classroom activities, our approach also supported reality-based learning through the use of authentic assessments, recognising that "students should be given tasks that develop and test the skills and practices that they will need in their future careers - tasks that mirror professional practice and test more than just rote memorisation" (James and Casidy 2018, p. 1; Principles 1–4). In designing these assessments, we drew upon the concept of 'proximity', where the assessment task undertaken by students should be a close match with a task that would typically be undertaken in the relevant professional environment (Oliver 2015).

Methods

Professional Training Year Context

Psychology students at the University of Surrey embark upon their final year of undergraduate study having just completed a placement year where the student works within a chosen, Psychology relevant, field. The placement year is a specific means of providing experiences intended to enhance employability. More commonly known as the Professional Training Year (PTY), the aim of this training year is to ensure transfer of learning back to the final year of study:

> The aims of the Transfer of Professional Training Year Learning are: to enable students to transfer their PTY learning other than placement related situations such as completion of assessment in the final year, communication with peers and tutors and effective, informed and well-targeted search for graduate employment.

Although this is a desirable aim, the true extent to which this is being integrated into Level 6 (final year undergraduate) module learning objectives, and thus facilitated by teaching activities and assessments, is questionable. To what extent do current learning activities and assessments in Level 6 Psychology modules actually require students to verbalise and reflect on their PTY experience in ways that encourage future transfer of that learning?

It is currently argued that in the teaching of Psychology, endeavouring to construct learning, teaching and assessment activities that specifically require students to reflect upon their applied placement experience will encourage future transfer of that learning to the workplace. It is proposed that embedding within curriculum specific Level 6 modules activities which provoke 'practice to theory' and well as a 'theory to practice' thinking will result in beneficial outcomes including preparedness for work and real-world transfer of knowledge. The final year of undergraduate study following a PTY experience is a critical period for the HE educator to foster employability and transfer of learning.

Participants

Approximately 30 students were enrolled on a Level 6 Psychology module entitled 'Psychology and Education', and approximately 30 students were enrolled on a Level 6 Psychology module entitled 'Work and Organisational Psychology'. All students were invited to complete our evaluation measures; a total of 54 students completed the measures at Time 1 (27 students from each module), and a total of 48 students also completed the measures again at Time 2 (21 students from 'Work and Organisational Psychology' and 27 students from 'Psychology and Education'). The mean student age was 23 years and all students had undertaken a PTY experience. Institutional ethical approval for the study was granted, and all students who completed the measures gave informed consent for their participation.

Interventions Embedded Within Modules

'Psychology and Education'

Authentic Activity

A group problem-based learning activity, designed to simulate a real-world decision-making situation, and to enable students to develop and apply their learning from engaging with course content, was developed. Within the module, students learnt about Special Educational Needs (SEN) in several different domains, such as literacy, numeracy, and movement/coordination. Students then learnt about the history of policy regarding the inclusion of children with SEN in mainstream education. When translating policy and theory into practice, many complications and barriers arise and it is difficult to 'teach' students about these complexities. In order for students to experience the decision-making process for themselves, they undertook an activity in groups of four or five. Each group was provided with a dossier of information of the kind that might be presented to a panel when deciding whether a child with SEN should be educated within a mainstream or special setting. Included within the dossier were: (1) a report from an Educational Psychologist; (2) a Paediatrician's report; (3) a report from the child's class teacher and Head Teacher; (4) a statement from the child's parents; (5) a statement from the child; (6) some artefacts from the child's assessment with the Educational Psychologist; and (7) classroom observation notes. In their groups, students were asked to decide what recommendation they would make for the child's placement, and to discuss their justification for the decision, as well as the resources that may be required for the child in that placement. Students were able to make any recommendation on the whole spectrum of inclusion, from full-time residential special setting, through to full-time mainstream placement, with intervening options including settings like full-time special unit within mainstream school, or full-time mainstream with in-class support, for example. Students were then asked to present their decision and justification to the rest of the class. What followed was a class discussion about the difficulties in assimilating evidence to reach a clear decision about a child's placement.

Guided Reflection

Students were supported in their reflection through a reflective learning log, posted on the Virtual Learning Environment, which supported them to surface their perspectives prior to each lecture and revisit them later, and consider how their learning might be transferred to future learning and work. For example, for the topic of 'Learner differences and learning needs', students were given the following reflection questions to consider prior to the lecture, and to revisit following the lecture: 'How might individual learners differ from one another?'; 'what do we mean by 'Special Educational Needs?''. Students were then encouraged to consider their response to the following reflection prompts: 'Do I think differently in any way?' and 'How will what I have learnt be relevant to my future work and study?'. Finally, students were provided with a space to record any other thoughts or reflections.

'Work and Organisational Psychology'

Authentic Activity

A group activity that provided students with a detailed workplace case study example was developed. This example case study is carefully written by the module leader to ensure that it provides enough detail so that students can really contemplate the 'practice to theory' link without having to be concerned about the quality of the contextual issues being discussed. Students were randomly allocated into groups of five and read the example case study in full. This example case-study was relevant to a core area of the module curriculum (e.g., psychology of leadership; case study overview of a leader's behaviour towards employees). The student groups were then asked to prepare answers to a set of questions designed to prompt 'practice to theory' thinking (e.g., 'How would you summarise the respective leader's style, using theories and terminology from the literature?' and 'Would it be worthwhile investment for each party to run a leadership development programme, and if so, how might they go about this?'). The groups then presented their responses to the questions back to the class.

Authentic Assessment

This intervention method required each student to write up (in an 8 page case study report format) an experience that relates to their placement organisation. Experiences included observations of variable performance/motivation at work and poor psychological health. According to the 4 RBL principles (Smith and Van Doren 2004), this assignment required the student to describe the context very clearly in terms of what the exact organisational issue observed was. Then, the student was required to consider which of the psychological theories and/or research covered in the module might explain and enable diagnosis of their observations. The student then had to question what could be done about the issue according to psychological theory, and whether one theory could guide thinking or did they need to draw on different orientations? Finally, they were asked to call upon the literature to indicate how their proposed solution/intervention could be evaluated.

> **Work Psychology—Case Study Assignment**
>
> *The aim of this assignment is to write up an experience that relates to your placement experience.*
>
> For the purposes of this assignment, we would like you to imagine that you are a junior occupational psychologist, whose task is to provide advice on how your placement organisation could benefit from the application of psychological theories and frameworks to the workplace. In order to write up this assignment, you need to consider the following:
>
> Describe the context very clearly in terms of what the organisation is/does, who works within it, what the issue that you observed is?
>
> Once you have described this context, you will then need to diagnose for this what you think the core issues are, but you can also indicate what information you have not got but might need access to, and how you could obtain this.
>
> You will also need to consider:
>
> 1. Which of the areas of work psychology does the issue link to? You can call upon any of the topics covered so far in this module but you can also think outside of the content of the core lectures. Indeed, evidence of independent reading and research will be one of the criteria that your assignment is marked on.
> 2. What could be done, and which psychological theories/arguments might offer a framework? Can any one theory guide your thinking or do you need to draw from different orientations?
>
> Preliminary conclusions: what would you recommend as a solution/intervention to address the diagnosed issue? You could offer some insight about what might be particularly important for a successful solution (e.g. making everyone motivated to do their bit, or offering some ideas for how success could be evaluated in research and/or practice). Strong pieces for work will also indicate how an intervention could be evaluated. What is critical is to say how many suggestions are rooted in evidence.

Measures

Preparedness for Work

The extent to which students felt prepared for the workplace was measured using Borden and Rajecki's (2000) preparedness scale. This scale includes items such as 'How prepared do you currently feel to apply psychological theory to diagnose work issues?'. This consisted of a 12-item scale with all questions being measured on a scale from 1 (very unprepared) to 4 (very prepared). Scores were summed to create a total 'Preparedness for Work' (Time 1 and Time 2) variable (maximum possible score = 48).

Employability Mind-Set

The extent to which students evidenced an employability mind-set was measured using Rothwell et al.'s (2008) Employability Scale.

Six items (e.g., 'People in the career I am aiming for are in high demand in the external work market') were used and all were measured on a scale from 1 (Strongly Disagree) to 5 (Strongly Agree). Scores were summed to create a total 'Employability Mind-Set' variable (maximum possible score = 30).

Intervention Utility

Four direct items were also included (at time 2 only) which asked the students about their reception and perceived utility of the intervention methods specific to each module. For example, students were asked 'The skills I have developed from doing the case study assignment for this module will/have contributed to my employability prospects'. The four items were all measured on a scale from 1 (Strongly Disagree) to 5 (Strongly Agree) and responses to these 4 items were summed to create a total 'Intervention Utility' variable (maximum possible score = 20).

Procedure

The level 6 modules in question were run over the course of 11 weeks. Importantly, the key variables of 'Preparedness for Work' and 'Employability Mind-Set' were measured during the very first session in week 1 (Time 1) and the very last session in week 11 (Time 2). The authentic activity for Work and Organisational Psychology took place during week 5 of the course, a point at which the students were well introduced (in terms of their knowledge base) to the relevant psychological literature/theories (Bloom 1984). The authentic assignment was due in week 8. For Psychology and Education, students participated in the authentic activity in Week 10, in order that they could apply course material from weeks 1 to 9 to the activity. Guided reflection using the learning log spanned weeks 1–10 of the module. Students had time to reflect on the impact of these intervention methods before then completing the 'Preparedness for Work' and 'Employability Mind-Set' measures again in week 11.

Evaluation

Descriptive Statistics

Descriptive statistics and correlation coefficients for all study variables by module are reported in Tables 12.1 and 12.2. Reliability coefficients suggest that all measures used were internally consistent. For both Psychology modules, 'Employability Mind-Set' at time 1 and time 2 is significantly correlated with 'Preparedness for Work' at time 2. This highlights that Psychology students who had heightened awareness of employability were also more likely following the interventions to be ready to join the Psychology job market and act professionally as a psychologist. For 'Work and Organisational Psychology', Intervention Utility significantly correlated with Employability Mind-Set at time 1, suggesting that those who had higher employability awareness at the start of this module were more likely to also report perceiving high utility of the authentic activity and assignment. Descriptive statistics for 'Intervention Utility' (possible

Table 12.1 Descriptive statistics and correlation coefficients for all study variables: 'Work and Organisational Psychology'

	M	SD	α	1	2	3	4
1. Preparedness for Work (Time 1)	29.0	4.4	0.77				
2. Preparedness for Work (Time 2)	35.9	3.5	0.74	0.49*			
3. Employability Mind-set (Time 1)	20.9	2.9	0.62	0.39	0.70**		
4. Employability Mind-set (Time 2)	20.8	3.2	0.83	0.03	0.46*	0.41	
5. Intervention Utility	15.9	2.7	0.78	0.32	0.21	0.54*	0.39

**p < 0.01; *p < 0.05

Table 12.2 Descriptive statistics and correlation coefficients for all study variables: 'Psychology and Education'

	M	SD	α	1	2	3	4
1. Preparedness for Work (Time 1)	29.3	4.6	0.83				
2. Preparedness for Work (Time 2)	34.2	4.9	0.70	0.66**			
3. Employability Mind-set (Time 1)	21.1	2.4	0.88	0.36	0.56*		
4. Employability Mind-set (Time 2)	22.1	3.1	0.77	0.20	0.47*	0.68**	
5. Intervention Utility	16.3	2.4	0.70	0.27	0.25	0.22	0.13

**p < 0.01; *p < 0.05

range from 4 to 20) demonstrate with mean responses of 15.9 (Work and Organisational Psychology) and 16.3 (Psychology and Education) that students perceived the interventions to be very valuable. Interestingly, 76.2% of the student sample reported a response in the range of 15–20, which demonstrates that a strong majority of the students agreed to strongly agree that the intervention methods contributed to their potential employability.

Analyses

In order to assess the effect of the intervention methods on Preparedness for Work and Employability Mind-Set, the questionnaire responses were subject to pretest-posttest analysis; within-subjects t-tests of the pre and post scores on the Preparedness for Work, and the Employability Mind-Set measures were run. This allowed for detection of whether there was any change in these variables as an effect of the intervention methods.

'Psychology and Education'

For Preparedness for Work, it was found that there was a significant difference between students' reported preparedness pre-intervention (M = 29.3, SD = 4.6) and post-intervention (M = 34.2, SD = 4.9) [$t(17)$ = 5.37, p < 0.001, d = 1.25]. Given the items included in this scale, these results illustrate that following the authentic interventions, students felt more prepared, for example, to demonstrate professionalism in the workplace, evaluate whether application of psychology to workplace issues was successful, engage in self-directed learning to increase their employability, and work ethically as a psychologist. For Employability Mind-Set, no significant difference between students' reported employability mind-set pre-intervention (M = 21.1, SD = 2.4) and post-intervention (M = 22.1, SD = 3.1) was found [$t(18)$ = 1.89, p = 0.07, d = 0.45]. This indicates that the experience of the intervention methods had no significant impact on whether students were aware of the employability links/status to engaging with the module in question (e.g., '*I see this module as leading to a specific career that is highly desirable*').

'Work and Organisational Psychology'

Interestingly, consistent patterns of results were evident for this module. There was a significant difference between students' reported 'Preparedness for Work' pre-intervention (M = 29.0, SD = 4.4) and post-intervention (M = 35.9, SD = 3.5) [$t(14)$ = 7.68, p < 0.001, d = 1.73]. This again suggests that the experience of the authentic activity and assignment encouraged a stronger sense of preparedness to communicate effectively with possible colleagues and clients about psychology, and, to apply psychological theory to diagnose real world issues. There was no significant difference between students' 'Employability Mind-Set' pre-intervention (M = 20.9, SD = 2.9) and post-intervention (M = 20.8, SD = 3.2) [$t(14)$ = 0.51, p = 0.61, d = 0.03]. Similar to 'Psychology and Education', the authentic intervention methods here were not observed to bring about change in students' awareness of the demands in achieving, and desirability of, specific Psychology-orientated careers.

Overall, for both modules, students' reported scores for 'Preparedness for Work' at time 2 (post intervention) were significantly higher than scores for 'Preparedness for Work' at time 1 (pre intervention). This outlines that the authentic RBL model-based intervention methods had a positive impact on students' readiness for the workplace.

Implications

The aim of this intervention was to embed within the Level 6 psychology curriculum opportunities for students to apply practice to theory, by using their experiences of PTY/Sandwich placement learning to contribute to their engagement with disciplinary content in Level 6 modules. Whilst opportunities to apply theory to practice abound during periods of work based learning, it is also important to consider how best to capitalise on opportunities to use experience of practice to contextualise and engage with theoretical and conceptual material upon the return to academic study for Level 6 of the degree programme. Our approach to supporting practice to theory learning involved authentic activities, authentic assessment, and structured reflection in two Level 6 Psychology modules.

These elements of instructional design were guided by the reality-based learning model (Smith and Van Doren 2004), in order to align with the principles of co-responsibility through active learning, drawing upon prior experience, developing transferable skills and experiences, and a focus on the skills and attitudes to be developed through learning. Our data demonstrate that application of the RBL model (Smith and Van Doren 2004) and authentic assessment (e.g. Ashford-Rowe et al. 2014) had a positive impact on students' readiness for the workplace. Students in both modules reported significantly higher scores on a 'Preparedness for Work' measure at the end of the modules than they had at the beginning, indicating that the RBL-based intervention methods had a positive impact on students' anticipation for using 'theory to practice' thinking and action. We can speculate that this gain in preparedness was facilitated through reflection, active learning, and opportunities to engage with authentic activities that enabled them to play the role of a professional psychologist. These findings align with other accounts that PTY/Sandwich placements facilitate the development of maturity, work-readiness, and willingness to learn (Morley et al. 2017).

In contrast, we observed no significant increase in students' reported 'Employability Mind-set' over the course of the modules. Closer inspection of the descriptive statistics for both modules indicates that students' scores on this measure were already reasonably high at the beginning of the modules. This may have limited the potential impact of the intervention methods on facilitating further developments in students' employability awareness. Arguably, today's students are keenly aware of factors such as the competitive nature of the psychology job market, and thus the current intervention methods had stronger and more meaningful utility in increasing student confidence that they have skills which could be applied to the workplace (e.g., use psychological theory to diagnose a real-life issue), as measured by the 'Preparedness for Work' measure, than in increasing what is already a strong employability mind-set.

In their ratings of 'Intervention Utility', we can surmise that students believed the intervention methods to serve a useful purpose in terms of advancing their knowledge and skills to give them confidence to transfer their learning to a broader working context. These findings certainly support the propositions of Auburn (2007) that the use of work-reflective activities in the academic year of study following a PTY experience does indeed encourage better anticipated 'induction' and awareness of the transition to a world beyond academic study.

Our work demonstrates that there is potentially much to be gained from directly utilising work based learning experiences to facilitate academic learning; in short, the transfer of learning from 'practice to theory' seems equally important to the transfer from 'theory to practice'. The opportunities afforded by PTY/Sandwich placements for this transfer are important to capitalise upon. It is however imperative to consider that our data are limited to students from two Level 6 psychology modules at a single university, and thus generalisation to the wider final year undergraduate body is limited in scope. Furthermore, all current students received the intervention methods; no comparison/control group was used. We therefore need to be cautious with over interpreting the effect of the intervention methods before effects are replicated, and before we have evidence of the longitudinal impact of RBL-based interventions on graduate employability and the transition to work.

It is also important to note that the two modules in question, 'Work and Organisational Psychology' and 'Psychology and Education' possess particular advantages that support the embedding of reality-based learning. First, regardless of what experiences students gained on their PTY, all students have prior experience of education, and the vast majority of students have experience of the world of work. This may have made it particularly easy for students' learning to draw upon prior experiences (Principle 3 in the RBL model). Second, the applied nature of the subject matter in both modules facilitates the design of active and authentic learning (Principle 2 in the RBL model). Thus, we close this chapter by offering some tentative recommendations as to how the RBL model can inform 'practice to theory' learning in other disciplines.

First, we would argue that any area of the curriculum in any discipline can focus on not only the knowledge, but also the skills and attitudes to be acquired through learning experiences (Principle 1 in the RBL model). For example, the graduate attributes of a discipline (see, for example, Quinlan 2016) specify the characteristics that can be expected of a graduate in a particular discipline, and are becoming more prominent in the minds of educators as they pay greater attention to supporting the employability of their students. Even in an assessment that is not 'authentic' in nature, an assignment can be made relevant to the workplace by showing students which graduate attributes are being developed and assessed through that piece of work. This positions assessment as a driver, not merely a measure, of learning.

Second, learning activities in general, and work-related learning activities in particular, are likely to benefit from being interactive and group-based, thus making the student aware of their co-responsibility for learning (Principle 2 in the RBL model). Framing learning activities involving groups of students in terms of their similarity to work based activities involving teams of co-workers can focus students' minds on how they can use that learning experience to prepare them for employment. When drawing upon students' experiences of PTY/Sandwich placements, group activities are also particularly beneficial, as students are able to apply not only their own practice, but also that of their peers, to the theory they experience in academic learning contexts.

Third, any form of learning, can, we would argue, draw upon students' prior experiences (Principle 3 in the RBL model). When using placement experiences as a basis for learning, students can share problems or assignments they tackled on their placement, and educators can take these real-world, authentic problems and use them as a basis for authentic activities and assignments. This enables students to build upon a broader range of experience than just their own, having the opportunity to work on new problems. Even on programmes where students have not undertaken a PTY, educators can still ensure that learning draws upon prior experience. It might require strategies to surface the wide range of experiences that students bring, but drawing upon their lived realities can be a powerful tool for learning.

Fourth, learning can develop transferable skills and experiences (Principle 4 in the RBL model) through the use of structured reflective activities. Regardless of whether students have strong ideas of where their career will take them upon graduation, the skills they are acquiring through their studies will support their continued learning in the workplace. However, students may find it difficult to recognise the skills being developed, so reflection can be used to bring these skills to the surface, and to encourage students to see, for example, how they can learn from experiencing challenge, disappointment, lack of motivation, or satisfaction, to support their experience of these and similar emotions when they arise in the workplace.

Conclusion

Our data demonstrate much encouragement that (a) the RBL model has potential for the design of work-related activities and assessments, (b) that work-related activities and assessment embedded within Level 6 curricula have potential to contribute to the enhancement of psychology student employability, and (c) that specifically basing these work-related activities and assessments on a PTY experience is a valuable tool in bridging the transition from supervised work experiences, *to* the return to academic work, *to* workplace awareness and induction (Auburn 2007). We cannot expect all students to easily and independently recognise and anticipate the demands of being responsible for their learning and real-world practice. Thus higher education educators really do have much scope to intervene here by keeping teaching activities and assessments relevant and effective, drawing upon students' lived realities to inform instructional design.

References

Ashford-Rowe, K., Herrington, J., & Brown, C. (2014). Establishing the critical elements that determine authentic assessment. *Assessment & Evaluation in Higher Education, 39*(2), 205–222.
Auburn, T. (2007). Identity and placement learning: Student accounts of the transition back to university following a placement year. *Studies in Higher Education, 32*(1), 117–133.
Bloom, B. (1984). *Taxonomy of educational objectives Book 1: Cognitive domain.* New York: Addison Wesley.
Borden, V. M., & Rajecki, D. W. (2000). First-year employment outcomes of psychology baccalaureates: Relatedness, preparedness, and prospects. *Teaching of Psychology, 27*(3), 164–168.
Brooks, R., & Youngson, P. L. (2016). Undergraduate work placements: An analysis of the effects on career progression. *Studies in Higher Education, 41*, 1563–1578.
Burns, C., & Chopra, S. (2017). A meta-analysis of the effect of industry engagement on student learning in undergraduate programs. *Journal of Technology, Management and Applied Engineering, 33*(1), 2–20.
Clark, M., & Zukas, M. (2016). Understanding successful sandwich placements: A Bourdieusian approach. *Studies in Higher Education, 41*(7), 1281–1295.
Crawford, I., & Wang, Z. (2016). The impact of placements on the academic performance of UK and international students in higher education. *Studies in Higher Education, 41*(4), 712–733.
Department for Education. (2016). *Teaching Excellence Framework: Year two specification.* London: DfE.
Drysdale, M. T., McBeath, M. L., Johansson, K., Dressler, S., & Zaitseva, E. (2016). Psychological attributes and work-integrated learning: An international study. *Higher Education, Skills and Work-Based Learning, 6*(1), 20–34.

Elam, E. L., & Spotts, H. E. (2004). Achieving marketing curriculum integration: A live case study approach. *Journal of Marketing Education, 26*(1), 50–65.

Evans, K., Guile, D., Harris, J., & Allan, H. (2010). Putting knowledge to work: A new approach. *Nurse Education Today, 30*(3), 245–251.

Gomez, S., Lush, D., & Clements, M. (2004). Work placements enhance the academic performance of bioscience undergraduates. *Journal of Vocational Education and Training, 56*(3), 373–385.

Gray, B., Stein, S. J., Osborne, P., & Aitken, R. (2013). Collaborative learning in a marketing strategy education context. *Practice and Evidence of Scholarship of Teaching and Learning in Higher Education, 8*(1), 35–55.

Helyer, R. (2015). Learning through reflection: The critical role of reflection in work-based learning (WBL). *Journal of Work-Applied Management, 7*(1), 15–27.

Herrington, J., Parker, J., & Boase-Jelinek, D. (2014). Connected authentic learning: Reflection and intentional learning. *Australian Journal of Education, 58*(1), 23–35.

Hmelo-Silver, C. E. (2004). Problem-based learning: What and how do students learn? *Educational Psychology Review, 16*(3), 235–266.

Hung, W., Jonassen, D. H., & Liu, R. (2008). Problem-based learning. *Handbook of Research on Educational Communications and Technology, 3*, 485–506.

James, L. T., & Casidy, R. (2018). Authentic assessment in business education: Its effects on student satisfaction and promoting behaviour. *Studies in Higher Education, 43*(3), 401–415.

Jones, C. M., Green, J. P., & Higson, H. E. (2017). Do work placements improve final year academic performance or do high-calibre students choose to do work placements? *Studies in Higher Education 42*(6), 976–992.

Lizzio, A., & Wilson, K. (2004). Action learning in higher education: An investigation of its potential to develop professional capability. *Studies in Higher Education, 29*(4), 469–488.

Morley, D. A., Archer, L., Burgess, M., Curran, D., Milligan, V. & Williams, D. (2017). A panel discussion—The impact of students' placements. In *ExcITeS Teaching and Learning Conference*. Guildford, UK: University of Surrey.

Norton, S. (2016). *Embedding employability in higher education for student success*. York, UK: Higher Education Academy.

Oliver, B. (2015). Redefining graduate employability and work-integrated learning: Proposals for effective higher education in disrupted economies. *Teaching and Learning for Graduate Employability, 6*(1), 56–65.

Quinlan, K. M. (2016). Developing student character through disciplinary curricula: An analysis of UK QAA subject benchmark statements. *Studies in Higher Education, 41*(6), 1041–1054.

Rambruth, P., & Daniel, S. (2011). Integrating experiential learning and cases in international business. *Journal of Teaching in International Business, 22*(1), 38–50.

Reddy, P., & Moores, E. (2006). Measuring the benefits of a psychology placement year. *Assessment & Evaluation in Higher Education, 31*(5), 551–567.

Rothwell, A., Herbert, I., & Rothwell, F. (2008). Self-perceived employability: Construction and initial validation of a scale for university students. *Journal of Vocational Behavior, 73*(1), 1–12.

Schambach, T. P., & Dirks, J. (2002). Student perceptions of internship experiences. In *Proceedings of the 17th Annual Conference of the International Academy for Information Management.* Retrieved July 9, 2017, from http://files.eric.ed.gov/fulltext/ED481733.pdf

Smith, L. W., & Van Doren, D. C. (2004). The reality-based learning method: A simple method for keeping teaching activities relevant and effective. *Journal of Marketing Education, 26,* 66–74.

Wilton, N. (2012). The impact of work placements on skills development and career outcomes for business and management graduates. *Studies in Higher Education, 37*(5), 603–620.

Yew, E. H., & Goh, K. (2016). Problem-based learning: An overview of its process and impact on learning. *Health Professions Education, 2*(2), 75–79.

Part VI

Promoting Students' Work Based Learning for International Collaboration and Employment

13

Exploring the Power of High-Level Postgraduate International Partnership Work Based Learning Programmes

P. Weston, D. Perrin, and D. Meakin

Introduction and Context

The academic partnership between the University of Chester and the Mountbatten Institute was the product of two separate developments coming together within UK Higher Education (HE). The first was the expansion of work based learning (WBL). This involved not just the creation of WBL opportunities for full-time undergraduate students on placements but also the development of negotiated WBL frameworks aimed at capturing the learning of adults in the workplace (Talbot 2017). These frameworks were characterised by two key features—the ability to customise learning around workplace opportunities so students could set their curriculum in negotiation with tutors (Perrin et al. 2010). Also, in the prioritisation given to capability and competence alongside more 'traditional' academic preoccupations such as critical engagement with theory (Stephenson and Weil 1992; Stephenson 1998; Lester and Costley 2010).

P. Weston (✉) • D. Perrin • D. Meakin
University of Chester, Chester, UK
e-mail: p.weston@chester.ac.uk

By the turn of the millennium, well over a dozen UK universities had established WBL frameworks with three—Middlesex University, the University of Derby and the University of Chester—developing highly successful programmes attracting large numbers of students (Nixon 2008; Perrin et al. 2010). Furthermore, these universities used their WBL frameworks not only to foster learning of adults in the workplace directly, but also to create partnership arrangements with external parties where high-level vocationally based learning could be assessed and recognised for the purposes of academic credit (see Meakin and Wall 2013; Talbot et al. 2014; Garnett 2016). This usage of WBL frameworks to 'accredit' learning outside of the traditional academy became a significant growth area and market for learning achieved through work.

The second significant development was the internationalisation of HE (Standley 2015) as universities looked beyond their national boundaries not just to attract international students to them but also, through overseas partner organisations, to offer their programmes abroad (Altbach and Knight 2007; Ayoubi and Massoud 2007). The UK has been very much at the forefront of this with 140,000 students in 2002 enrolled on university programmes domiciled outside the UK (Altbach 2002). Since then, students studying UK programmes abroad have grown exponentially with figures for 2015/16 standing at 701,010 (UKCISA 2017). This has resulted in various developments of programme delivery including franchise arrangements with approximately 246,110 students now studying through university-partnership arrangements including collaborative provisions (UKCISA 2017).

The University of Chester's place as a leader in WBL and accreditation for adults in the workplace is well documented (see Nixon 2008; Perrin et al. 2010; Talbot et al. 2014). However, the role of the Mountbatten Institute as a HE level partner and provider of international vocational learning opportunities is less well known.

It was originally created in 1984 at the Anglo American International School in New York as a UK/US GAP year student exchange scheme. In 1986, it was named 'The Mountbatten Internship Programme' in memory of the late Earl Mountbatten of Burma (a noted proponent of international education) and in 1990 it became an all graduate exchange programme organising and administering one-year work experience opportunities in New York for UK graduates. By 1998 a reciprocal programme was developed in London for US students, and in 2000 the Mountbatten Institute was formed in New York to coordinate and direct three regional offices based in London, New York and Bangkok offering international internships with a focus on postgraduate education. Whilst still committed to its US/UK origins the Mountbatten Institute, each year, enrolls students from over 30 nationalities.

Originally, the Mountbatten Institute accredited its programmes through Oxford University Delegacy of Local Examinations and then St Mary's University College, Twickenham. However, the work based nature of their internships led to the Mountbatten Institute incrementally moving its provision from 2014 to the University of Chester's Centre for Work Related Studies (CWRS). Hence a partnership of WBL expertise and high-level international vocational learning provision was formed.

WBL and International Internships

A key strength of WBL is its flexibility to meet the needs of the workplace, evidenced by the many guises in which it appears within HE (Boud and Solomon 2001; Major 2002; Garnett 2007). The necessity that WBL be "grounded in the context, nature and imperatives of work" (Garnett and Workman 2009, p. 3) placing the workplace at the centre of the learning experience (Lester and Costley 2010) emphasises the importance of ensuring this form of experiential learning is both practitioner and academically driven. WBL therefore encourages students to become active learners, drawing on and applying learning gained from both the classroom and workplace in order to adapt and grow (Billett and Choy 2014).

According to Drysdale et al. (2016), this results in WBL students developing greater levels of self-confidence, self-esteem and self-efficacy than if they studied on more conventional HE programmes. In addition, they are likely to be more highly motivated towards their academic studies and show greater concern regarding how they are viewed professionally. WBL can therefore be a key contributory factor in helping an individual consolidate and affirm their professional identify and self-worth (Billett and Choy 2014).

The form of WBL discussed here is a postgraduate international business internship. According to Olsen (2015) an internship is where a student is placed in an organisation for a set time period to gain work experience with no commitment from either party regarding permanent employment once the internship comes to an end. Billett and Choy (2014) assert longer (6–12 month) internships are far more valuable than shorter placements because there is greater opportunity for learning and development.

The Mountbatten Internship programme fits this criteria as it incorporates a 12-month international full-time placement alongside a full-time post-graduate programme of study (Mountbatten Institute 2016). Successful Mountbatten Institute applicants are typically in their mid-twenties who have recently graduated either from an undergraduate or post-graduate degree and who may have some limited work experience. As such, they are at the start of their professional careers.

Internships are a valuable form of experiential learning (Gault et al. 2000; Lang and McNaught 2013; Olsen 2015) as they facilitate the transition from education into the workplace (Mello 2006). In addition, Gault et al. (2000) claim students who take part in internships are more likely to gain job satisfaction and have higher earning potential than those who do not. The value of internships for students is therefore obvious as they provide an opportunity to improve employability prospects in a way that could not be achieved through studying alone (Feldmann 2016). This means internships are a common feature of many business programmes (Moghaddam 2011) with estimates that up to 75% of undergraduate business students take part in some form of work placement as part of their studies (Olsen 2015).

Employers also value internships for similar reasons as they enable students to gain the necessary business knowledge and skills to 'hit the ground running' prior to employment (Mello 2006). The contextualised nature of WBL also means the resultant learning occurs not only at an individual but also at a corporate level (Garnett 2016), therefore organisations also adapt and grow as a result of internships. Finally, they provide a relatively risk free mechanism for employers to observe potential future employees over an extended period of time (Gault et al. 2000).

When internships occur within an international context, they become even more valuable as, in addition to work experience, students develop valuable language, inter-personal and inter-cultural knowledge and skills which are increasingly sought after by global businesses (Dawson 2013). According to Mello (2006), this is further enhanced when students are placed in international operations alongside highly experienced professionals as this exposes them to the intricacies of international business practice which are impossible to replicate either in the class-room or through domestic internships (Mello 2006). In addition, students are more likely to work with senior personnel so raising their profile and strengthening their professional network (Mello 2006). Dawson (2013) asserts this exposure provides a major boost to a student's self-confidence and self-efficacy making them more likely to put themselves forward for challenging roles and projects which place them outside their comfort zone. This makes them highly sought after by global companies (Eaton and Kleshinski 2014).

Offering internships to international students is also highly beneficial for host organisations as it enables them to access a variety of cultural perspectives (ICEF Monitor 2013). They also provide a means of attracting high calibre professionals whilst at the same time reducing the increased risks associated with international recruitment which stem from differences in culture and language (ICEF Monitor 2013).

Regardless of whether or not an internship leads to a job offer, Rigsby et al. (2013) claim the value placed on them by business means internship students are far more likely to gain employment quickly and progress further in their careers. However, when the work placement is international in context, this radically enhances a student's desirability as a potential employee (Dawson 2013) with many global firms paying particular interest to graduate applicants' CVs listing international work experience (Cromm and Kadow 2014).

The value of international work experience for career progression is not lost on students, with increasing numbers targeting programmes with international placements (Dawson 2013). As a result, HE is finding itself under increasing pressure to offer a variety of international work experience opportunities (Lapina et al. 2016) that prepare students for an increasingly competitive and volatile global environment (Shooshtari and Manuel 2014).

Despite clear benefits, Dawson (2013) cautions that international internships present specific challenges. Fox (2017) agrees, claiming they can be very isolating for students who are distanced from people and places they are familiar with. Along with geography, she claims distance is experienced in emotional, cultural, pedagogical and technological forms which intersect in a way that can lead to feelings of loneliness and depression. As such, Dawson (2013) highlights that whilst immersion in a new culture and mixing with new people is important, there needs to be some form of structure and support in place.

The importance of a solid support network means academic providers and host organisations need to work together closely (Billett and Choy 2014) in order to prevent long-term emotional or physical distress to internship students (Richardson and Blakeney 1998). To achieve this, Mello (2006) emphasises that both the academic provider and workplace must oversee the internship and ensure some form of mentoring is provided if students are to take full advantage of their learning experience (Fox 2017).

Alongside this is the need to develop a well-designed academic programme, with highly qualified tutors, to ensure the academic component enhances the experiential learning of the placement (Lapina et al. 2016). To achieve this, care needs to be taken to ensure learning outcomes are specific with deliverables that facilitate and enhance students' knowledge and skills of their workplace context (Fowler and Tietze 1996). Programmes also need to maintain academic integrity and quality standards (Talbot et al. 2014, Olsen 2015) with all associated assessment exhibiting the same degree of academic rigour as conventional HE programmes (Billett and Choy 2014).

A common tool for assessing the more personal and subjective aspects of WBL, including personal growth and development, is the use of reflective essays and reports which are difficult to quantify through other mechanisms (Fowler and Tietze 1996). The use of reified reflection in the assessment process is particularly important when the learning is situated within an international context, as this is a major contributory factor to the enhancement of learning (Webber 2005).

In summary, while international internship programmes can be extremely valuable for both students and employers they also present challenges which need addressing if the full benefits are to be realised. Key to this is the importance of academic providers and host organisations working closely together in order to create internships that are fit for purpose, are academically rigorous and have the necessary support networks in place (Webber 2005; Meakin and Wall 2013; Billett and Choy 2014). Only then will the full benefits of this form of experiential learning be realised.

The Mountbatten Institute Internship Programmes

The University of Chester and the Mountbatten Institute have jointly developed three postgraduate level programmes using the University of Chester's Work Based and Integrative Studies (WBIS) framework from WBL. Currently, two programmes are running; the Postgraduate Certificate in International Business (WBIS), and the MA Entrepreneurial Leadership in Global Business (WBIS); the MBA is in the final stages of academic approval. The partnership agreement means all programmes are managed and delivered by the Mountbatten Institute including student recruitment, module design, delivery and assessment. The University of Chester acts as an advisor and, in addition, co-assesses and quality assures all assessment (Meakin and Wall 2013).

The original and longest-running of the programmes, the MA Entrepreneurial Leadership in Global Business (WBIS), comprises seven modules. Three of these are compulsory for all WBIS masters programmes and consist of an introductory module in the concepts and tools of experiential and reflective learning; a practitioner researcher methods module and a final triple (60 credit) negotiated experiential learning module (Triple NELM). The other four taught modules cover topics including leadership, global business and entrepreneurship.

The 'Triple NELM' is a negotiated work based research project with an output consisting of a report designed to have significant business impact(s), plus a critical reflective learning log where students evaluate and reflect on their internship experience. The Triple NELM is a crucial element of the MA, as the concept of working on a project exploring a real-life workplace issue with outcomes of potential benefit to both the student and their host company is a central feature of WBL (Garnett 2016).

All module assessments include some critical reflection of students' workplace learning in light of theoretical concepts and modules they have been introduced to. The academic component and the work placement are therefore fully integrated with one another (Billett and Choy 2014).

The Mountbatten Institute has agreements with a number of leading international and global companies to offer 12-month full-time work placements in London and New York. Most, although not all, operate within banking and finance with students from Europe and India typically going to New York and students from the US coming to London. Unlike many other internships, applicants must secure their work placement prior to being offered a place. Acceptance of a place also requires students to agree to enroll onto one of the Mountbatten Institute academic programmes which run concurrently with the placement. Module workshops take place in the evenings and/or weekends, and attendance is mandatory. As part of the internship, the Mountbatten Institute provides students with accommodation and a small stipend.

The recruitment process and the inter-connectedness between the work placement and the academic programme create a rare form of WBL that uniquely prepares students for employability (Feldmann 2016).

Because it is the longest running example of the University of Chester-Mountbatten Institute partnership in operation, we have chosen to use the MA as the basis for the evaluation of workplace impacts and graduate employability.

Findings and Analysis

The findings below are taken from data obtained from module evaluation forms and critical reflective learning logs from the final Triple NELM assessment. Unfortunately, due to confidentiality reasons, it was not possible to obtain data direct from companies offering internships through the Mountbatten Institute.

Statistics from the module evaluations give an aggregated overview of student responses to questions focusing mainly on the academic component of the internship. These provide the basis for an analysis of students' critical reflective learning logs. Together they help us develop a unique insight into students' perceptions of what they have learnt from their internship experience.

All data used is either anonymous in origin or has since been anonymised to protect the identity of students and their host organisations.

Module Evaluation Forms

The module evaluations were completed between January 2015 and January 2017. Among a broader set of questions, the following five statements (presented on a Likert scale) measured the impact of students' study on their workplace practice:

1. I feel more confident in managing my own learning
2. I found a balance between my work and my study
3. I felt feedback was helpful to my learning and development
4. I learnt new skills as a result of the module
5. I gained new knowledge as a result of the module

A total of 134 respondents returned an approval rating (satisfactory or better) of 86%. Of 1608 statement responses, only 65 (4%) expressed strong disagreement with any of the statements, whereas over 66% gave a positive evaluation ('Strongly agree'/'Agree').

Over 80% of students reported they gained *"new knowledge as a result of the module"*, with additional free-text comments added of which these were typical:

I gained a much better understanding of how global markets fit together and interact.

Learning (how to) apply new frameworks (such as the Belbin team roles) offered a fresh perspective on workplace dynamics and an idea of how improvements to efficiency can be facilitated.

I have gained a better understanding of management behaviour.

As well as knowledge, 65% of respondents reported acquisition of new skills and acknowledged the positive impact of tutor feedback upon learning and development. In addition, several students commented favourably on the enthusiasm and energy of certain tutors, and a wish for more opportunity to work together within the classroom setting: *"More class time", "More time for simulation", "More time for discussion"*.

These responses indicate students' view the MA as an important mechanism for gaining academic underpinning to underpin their experiential learning within their work placement. It also shows the value students place on social and professional support from their tutors and peers. This concurs with Webber (2005) and Lapina et al. (2016) regarding the importance of designing academic programmes that are relevant to the workplace context, and Fox (2017) who emphasises the need for support networks.

It was pleasing to see 64% of students reported a noticeable gain in confidence to manage their own learning, typically:

I have gained confidence in (my) capabilities to study alone outside of class, judge the right supporting reading materials, etc.

with several making reference to the realisation of the power of reflective practice:

I am more conscious of my reflective practice and I have started using self-assessment tools and journals to enhance my practice at work.

This aligns with the general ethos of WBL to develop students as active learners (Billett and Choy 2014), as well as highlighting the importance of critical reflection to facilitate experiential learning (Fowler and Tietze 1996).

The findings from the module evaluations show students are generally positive about the academic component of the internship programme. The evaluations also highlight some important themes which can be explored in greater depth within the critical reflective learning logs. These include the relationship between active learning and self-confidence (Billett and Choy 2014), the interrelatedness of the academic programme and the workplace (Richardson and Blakeney 1998; Fox 2017), the role of support networks (Wall et al. 2016; Fox 2017) and finally the role of critical reflection to support experiential learning (Fowler and Tietze 1996).

Critical Reflective Learning Logs

Building on these themes (Silverman 2006) nine students' critical reflective learning logs were analysed to draw out their perceptions of their internship experience.

All students stated they found their internship challenging and often, at least initially, highly stressful: *"when my line manager dropped this task … my immediate instinct was to feel overwhelmed"* (student 1); *"when I first [started] my placement, the behaviours I demonstrated were inconsistent and fell into two extremes such as being self-assured and apprehensive or being relaxed and tensed"* (student 2); *"since joining Mountbatten, I stepped out of my comfort zone"* (student 4). Part of this can be attributed to being placed in a new and unfamiliar working context, however it is also clear students struggled with balancing work commitments alongside studying full-time: *"the Mountbatten year was a stressful one and having to combine academic studies with a full time employment could be very demanding"* (student 2); *"I was mentally exhausted from the stress of working full time in addition to being a full time student"* (student 9).

It is also clear the international context presented students with specific challenges including: *"language barriers and varying time zones"* (student 1); *"I began to miss home, the food I loved, people I enjoyed and culture I was used to"* (student 2). Whilst these mirror concerns raised by Fox (2017) regarding the potentially isolating nature of international placements, it was also apparent many students thrived on meeting new people and submerging themselves in new cultures: *"I moved across an ocean and started a new job in an unfamiliar professional industry, pursued higher education … and travelled to a dozen cities in half a dozen countries"* (student 7); *"living with people from various cultures, working with brilliant professionals has been eye-opening"* (student 9).

Almost without exception, students described how many of their initial feelings of stress and discomfort were replaced with more positive emotions which resulted in them having a more open, 'can do' attitude to their work and academic studies: *"The more I got involved … the more energised I felt and the more my capacity grew"* (student 1); *"The initial culture shock I experienced preceded my adaptation to a new environment"* (student 2). As a result, students have developed more confidence and also more curiosity to step outside their comfort zone and embrace new challenges (Dawson 2013).

Whilst the workplace may provide the context, students clearly view their learning in a holistic way with emphasis on both the workplace and the academic programme: *"the work exposure, academic courses and programme as a whole has provided me with the tools needed to solve real life problems"* (student 2); *"a key learning brought about through the combination of my Mountbatten traineeship and the deep learning facilitated through the MA coursework has been harnessing a much stronger sense of my own strengths and weaknesses"* (student 5); *"I have been exposed to new concepts, new information and new ways of conducting business … Not only has this come from the workplace, but also in the classroom"* (student 9). The importance students place on the classroom as well as the workplace to support their experiential learning highlights why care is required when designing internship programmes (Fowler and Tietze 1996; Meakin and Wall 2013).

Students' proactivity and their openness to new challenges appears to have been recognised by their host companies as several describe how and why they were given increased responsibility during their placement: *"My managers always delegate that task to me as they know I am good at approaching and solving problems"* (student 4); *"I am now the one having to schedule, plan for and lead"* (student 5). These comments indicate both students and host companies can benefit immensely from international internships (ICEF Monitor 2013) and there is real potential that they can lead to permanent employment (Eaton and Kleshinski 2014): *"I was approached by the MD … and offered a new role with larger responsibilities and management opportunities. If done well, the job would be mine on a full-time basis"* (student 9).

Students' self-confidence and their willingness to take on new responsibilities and challenges appear to be highly influenced by how they are viewed by their managers and work colleagues (Drysdale et al. 2016): *"I began to see value in the fact that my manager left the autonomy of the task to me"* (student 1). *"Achievements … [were] brought to my attention at my end of year review by my manager"* (student 3). *"I even received an e-mail from my department head and the chief [professional] appreciating my work. It was the most fulfilling feeling!"* (student 8). This creates a virtuous circle where both the student and their host company benefits (Dawson 2013): *"my managers were very pleased … my innovation was adopted"* (student 7). As such, international internships as a means for developing an individual's self-efficacy and self-worth comes through as an extraordinarily powerful theme (Drysdale et al. 2016).

Another crucial theme is the importance students place on having a strong professional and social support network around them: *"My interactions with [individuals] infused me with the energy I needed to perform my other roles"* (student 1); *"friendship and connections made … is valuable for my personal development"* (student 4), *"it was not just about the job it was also about the people I have met"* (student 9). For many, their interactions with others, and the support they gained from this, has been a key factor in helping them develop their resilience in order to thrive in a challenging and potentially stressful environment (Richardson and Blakeney 1998): *"The effectiveness and support of the team at work is largely what made this year so rewarding for me"* (student 6); *"embracing new tasks, building dynamic relationships and being open to new cultural experiences are some of the vital learning curves I have encountered"* (student 1). The emphasis students place on their support network in enabling them to take full advantage of their internship highlights why academic providers and placement providers need to collaborate with one another to ensure this is in place (Mello 2006; Fox 2017).

Finally, all the critical reflective learning logs emphasised the role and importance of reflection in helping students assess and evaluate their learning experience whilst on the internship, and in developing them as active learners (Billett and Choy 2014): *"[the] more I critically reflect on these skills/attributes, the more they become embedded in me, helping me thrive"* (student 1); *"My reflections and application of theory … have helped me better understand my values and motivations"* (student 7). Whilst the emphasis on the value of critical reflection of the internship experience is not surprising given the focus of the assessment, what is interesting is students' assertions they intend to use critical reflection as part of their ongoing self-development: *"The ability to reflect my feelings and experience … [has] contributed to the move to another stage of my career change journey"* (student 4). This perhaps more than anything else highlights the true power of WBL as part of lifelong learning, particularly when undertaken as part of an international internship.

Conclusion

The findings from this limited study support the contention that international internships can be a very powerful mechanism for experiential learning, personal growth and of enabling WBL for the purposes of HE credit.

Overall, the Mountbatten Institute internship experience—whilst clearly challenging—appears to be extremely rewarding, helping students develop their self-worth and self-esteem both professionally and personally. Whilst some of this comes from within, much of it is derived from external loci with several references to the impact of positive feedback from managers, achievements gained from the academic programme and good interactions with tutors and peers.

Although no data could be obtained directly, it is clear from students' learning logs that their host companies also benefited from the internship programme; with several accounts of students taking on increased responsibility such as running projects and introducing new processes and procedures. This illustrates how potentially valuable international internship programmes are for both students and host companies, not just in terms of future recruitment but also in terms of adapting and growing. Further study on the destination of graduates would highlight the longitudinal impact of this experience on future employability in the international context.

The importance of emotional, social support networks is crucial with many students focusing on friendships with fellow internees and work colleagues, the need for support and approval from their line managers and tutors as well as the general thrill of meeting and making new friends. Through taught workshops and shared accommodation, in addition to the work placement, the Mountbatten Institute facilitates students in developing these vital support networks. As such it is extremely effective in enabling students to develop resilience strategies to not only cope, but excel, with respect to challenges they face working whilst studying full time.

The value students attribute to the process of critical reflection to support their learning throughout their internship appears to be immense. This is fundamental as it underpins the ethos of all forms of WBL and is an integral part of almost all WBL assessments. The process of reflection enables students to recognise not only how to apply and embed academic learning to inform working practice and vice versa, but also to develop a greater self-awareness of their strengths and self-worth. This in turn helps embolden their relationships with others, particularly those which occur in a professional context. As such, the process of reflection is pivotal in helping students develop their self-confidence, team-working abilities and social networks which are so crucial to a positive learning experience. The effect of students' cultural differences on this type of learning would be worthy of further investigation.

Finally, and perhaps most interestingly, students perceive the value of critical reflection not only in terms of the internship experience itself, but also in the way it will influence their future career strategies and longer-term professional development. As such, developing the ability to critically reflect appears, for these internship students at least, to be a capability that has the potential to be genuinely life changing.

References

Altbach, P. G. (2002). Perspectives on internationalizing higher education. *International Higher Education, 27*(Spring), 6–8.

Altbach, P. G., & Knight, J. (2007). The internationalization of higher education: Motivations and realities. *Journal of Studies in International Education, 11*(3–4), 290–305.

Ayoubi, R. M., & Massoud, H. K. (2007). The strategy of internationalization in universities: A quantitative evaluation of the intent and implementation in UK universities. *International Journal of Educational Management, 21*(4), 329–349.

Billett, S., & Choy, S. (2014). Integrating professional learning experiences across university and practice settings. In S. Billett, C. Harteis, & H. Gruber (Eds.), *International handbook of research in professional and practice-based learning* (1st ed., Vol. 18, pp. 485–512). Dordrecht: Springer.

Boud, D., & Solomon, N. (Eds.). (2001). *Work-based learning: A new higher education?* Open University Press.

Cromm, P., & Kadow, K. (2014). Internships abroad: A career booster for German students. *A I B Insights, 14*(4), 10.

Dawson, J. (2013). International exposure'. *CMA Magazine, 87*(5), 33–36.

Drysdale, M. T. B., McBeath, M. L., Johansson, K., Dressler, S., & Zaitseva, E. (2016). Psychological attributes and work-integrated learning: An international study. *Higher Education, Skills and Work-Based Learning, 6*(1), 20–34.

Eaton, T. V., & Kleshinski, A. S. (2014). Improving undergraduate learning for employability through international exposure. *American Journal of Business Education, 7*(1), 49.

Feldmann, L. (2016). Considerations in the design of WBL settings to enhance students' employability. *Higher Education, Skills and Work-Based Learning, 6*(2), 131–145.

Fowler, G., & Tietze, S. (1996). A competence approach to the assessment of student placements. *Education + Training, 38*(1), 30–36.

Fox, M. (2017). Student isolation: The experience of distance on an international field placement. *Social Work Education, 36*(5), 508–513.

Garnett, J. (2007). Challenging the structural capital of the university to support work-based learning. In *Work-based learning futures* (pp. 21–27). Bolton: University Vocational Awards Council.

Garnett, J. (2016). Work-based learning: A critical challenge to the subject discipline structures and practices of higher education. *Higher Education, Skills and Work-Based Learning, 6*(3), 305–314.

Garnett, J., & Workman, B. (2009). The development and implementation of work based learning at Middlesex University. In J. Garnett, C. Costley, & B. Workman (Eds.), *Work based learning: Journeys to the core of higher education* (Vol. 1, pp. 2–14). Middlesex: Middlesex University Press.

Gault, J., Redington, J., & Schlager, T. (2000). Undergraduate business internships and career success: Are they related? *Journal of Marketing Education, 22*(1), 45–53.

ICEF Monitor. (2013). *International internships are increasingly valued by employers*. Retrieved August 3, 2018, from http://monitor.icef.com/2013/04/international-internships-are-increasingly-valued-by-employers/

Lang, R., & McNaught, K. (2013). Reflective practice in a capstone business internship subject. *Journal of International Education in Business, 6*(1), 7.

Lapina, I., Roga, R., & Müürsepp, P. (2016). Quality of higher education: International students' satisfaction and learning experience. *International Journal of Quality and Service Sciences, 8*(3), 263.

Lester, S., & Costley, C. (2010). Work-based learning at higher education level: Value, practice and critique. *Studies in Higher Education, 35*(5), 561–575.

Major, D. (2002). A more holistic form of higher education: The real potential of work based learning. *The Journal of Widening Participation and Lifelong Learning, 4*(3), 12.

Meakin, D., & Wall, T. (2013). Co-delivered work based learning: Contested ownership and responsibility. *Higher Education, Skills and Work-Based Learning, 3*(1), 73–81.

Mello, J. A. (2006). Enhancing the international business curriculum through Partnership with the United States Department of Commerce: The "E" award internship program'. *Journal of Management Education, 30*(5), 690–699.

Moghaddam, J. M. (2011). Perceived effectiveness of business internships: Student expectations, experiences, and personality traits. *International Journal of Management, 28*(4), 287.

Mountbatten Institute. (2016). Information about Mountbatten Institute. *Mountbatten Institute—Our Organisation* [web page]. Retrieved April 10, 2016, from http://www.mountbatten.org/about-us

Nixon, I. (2008). *Work-based learning: Impact study*. York: Academy, H. E.

Olsen, P. E. (2015). Use of positive psychology to enhance the undergraduate business internship experience. *Journal of the Academy of Business Education, 16*, 156.

Perrin, D., Weston, P., Thompson, P. A., & Brodie, P. (2010). *Facilitating employer engagement through negotiated work based learning: A case study from the University of Chester*. University of Chester.

Richardson, S., & Blakeney, C. (1998). The undergraduate placement system: An empirical study. *Accounting Education, 7*(2), 101–121.

Rigsby, J. T., Addy, N., Herring, C., & Polledo, D. (2013). An examination of internships and job opportunities. *Journal of Applied Business Research, 29*(4), 1131–1143.

Shooshtari, N. H., & Manuel, T. A. (2014). Curriculum internationalization at AACSB schools: Immersive experiences, student placement, and assessment. *Journal of Teaching in International Business, 25*(2), 134–156.

Silverman, D. (2006). *Interpreting qualitative data* (3rd ed.). London: Sage Publications Ltd.

Standley, H. J. (2015). International mobility placements enable students and staff in higher education to enhance transversal and employability-related skills. *FEMS Microbiology Letters, 362*(19), 1–5.

Stephenson, J. (1998). The concept of capability and its importance in Higher Education. In J. Stephenson & M. Yorke (Eds.), *Capability and quality in higher education*. London: Stylus Publishing, Inc.

Stephenson, J., & Weil, S. W. (Eds.). (1992). *Quality in learning: A capability approach in higher education*. London: Kogan Page.

Talbot, J. (2017). Curriculum design for the post-industrial society: The facilitation of individually negotiated higher education in work based learning shell frameworks in the United Kingdom. In R. V. Nata (Ed.), *Progress in education* (Vol. 5, pp. 127–160). New York: Nova Science Publishers.

Talbot, J., Perrin, D., & Meakin, D. (2014). Risk management and cultural virtue in HE co-delivery arrangements. *Quality Assurance in Education, 22*(2), 109–124.

UKCISA. (2017). *International student statistics: UK higher education*. Retrieved August 8, 2017, from https://institutions.ukcisa.org.uk/Info-for-universities-colleges--schools/Policy-research--statistics/Research--statistics/International-students-in-UK-HE/#Students-studying-wholly-overseas-for-a-UK-qualification

Wall, T., Tran, L. T., & Soejatminah, S. (2016). Inequalities and agencies in workplace learning experiences: International student perspectives. *Vocations and Learning, 10*(2), 141–156.

Webber, R. (2005). Integrating work-based and academic learning in international and cross-cultural settings. *Journal of Education and Work, 18*(4), 473–487.

14

Developing Global Citizenship: Co-creating Employability Attributes in an International Community of Practice

N. Radclyffe-Thomas, A. Peirson-Smith, A. Roncha, A. Lacouture, and A. Huang

Introduction

According to the UK's Higher Education Academy (HEA) increasing pressure to meet multiple stakeholder expectations is driving the employability agenda and has prioritised the integration of employability skills and attributes for all higher education providers (HEA 2016). The notion of enhancing graduates' employability is of course not a new one, but in the

---

N. Radclyffe-Thomas (✉) • A. Roncha
University of the Arts, London, UK
e-mail: n.radclyffethomas@fashion.arts.ac.uk

A. Peirson-Smith
City University, Kowloon Tong, Hong Kong

A. Lacouture
RMIT, Ho Chi Minh, Vietnam

A. Huang
LASALLE College of the Arts, Singapore, Singapore

'Embedding Employability Framework' the HEA recognise the significance of graduate employability extends beyond prospective students and employers to include the 'supportive others': families, communities and industries. Furthermore, national and international institutional employability rankings impact both reputation and recruitment. Stakeholders have become more vocal in their calls that universities evidence how their curricula, pedagogies and additional activities enable graduates to showcase specific 'knowledge, skills, experiences, behaviours, attributes, achievements and attitudes' to 'make successful transitions and contributions benefitting them, the economy and their communities' (HEA 2016, p. 2).

Equally, talent is identified as the driver of the Cultural and Creative Industries (CCIs) and the university sector has been recognised as a seedbed of creative talent. In his book, 'The Rise of the Creative Class' Florida (2002) suggested that three 'Ts' (technology, talent and tolerance) would attract and develop creative talent thus driving local and regional economic development in creative hubs. Universities have been cited as the stimulus for the 'spillover' of the three 'Ts' given that the new urban-based, creative class, tend to be young, productive, entrepreneurial and highly educated (Florida et al. 2006). One critique of contemporary higher education is that a 'vocationalist' agenda focuses on workforce needs rather than education for global citizenship (Arambewela 2010), yet regardless of career path, the authors believe graduates need to be well-connected, culturally intelligent, strong communicators, and capable of working effectively both autonomously and as part of a team.

This chapter discusses an example of a global classroom project that provides tangible learning gain through simulating some of the complexities of working in the modern creative industries. It demonstrates a commitment to creating authentic experiential learning activities engendering both professional and intercultural communication competences. By designing a Collaborative Online International Learning project, with multiple touchpoints between remotely situated students, tutors aimed to create 'Personalised Learning Environments' for students reflecting lived experiences and creating multiple online learner communities (McLoughlin and Lee 2010, p. 29). Students from University of the Arts London (UAL) work collaboratively with peers studying in Asia at three partner institutions: City University Hong Kong, LASALLE College of the Arts Singapore and RMIT Vietnam. Students support each other's development through a private Facebook group adopting multiple roles as researcher, advisor and expert reviewer and co-create learning outcomes which facilitates the development of attributes and capabilities required by the future creative industries.

A detailed case describes and evaluates this flexible informal collaboration which adopts a blended learning approach (delivery combining classroom and online learning) and has established a 'community of practice', (an informal learning group organised around a common interest) (Wenger 1998), with over 450 students internationally. The role of higher education as a boundary spanner between cultures is critical (Byram and Fleming 1998) and the impact of this project on teaching and learning was monitored and analysed using evaluative individual and team-based student feedback and interviews with individual students. To further support the discussion, the UAL employability initiative the Creative Attributes Framework will be introduced.

Background: International Industry Context and the Complexities of Working in the Modern Creative Industries

The World Economic Forum reports that although the employment and environmental implications of the Fourth Industrial Revolution are unpredictable, cross-sector partnerships are likely to be necessary to meet the challenges of "global instability and economic transformation"; these partnerships will require "new ways of working together" (Albrectsen 2017, p. 31). The twenty-first century business environment is in flux creating 'new market ecosystems' (Denning 2014); established divisions between businesses and their competitors are being replaced by non-traditional, collaborative working practices (OECD 2013). Companies have become increasingly lean due to rapid technological advancements and globalisation, and the established working practices of creative industries have been adopted more widely as innovative businesses move towards open forms of innovation (Chesbrough 2003; Mathe 2015).

CCIs represent not only 'soft' cultural power but also a substantial contribution to national economies (DCMS 2016). Creative industry jobs entail economic and cultural creativity and innovation concerning "forms of cultural production and consumption that have at their core a symbolic or expressive element" (UNESCO 2013, p. 20). Assuring the future of the creative sector in any geographic or cultural context is predicated on an ability to provide the future workforce with the relevant knowledge and skill-set and in the post-industrial knowledge economy universities are reframing what a career in the creative industries is or could be. Concurrently, globalisation and digital technologies have transformed business practices and require graduates to have the resources and resilience to manage extended supply chains and successfully work remotely with colleagues who could be situated almost anywhere in the world. Collaboration has become key to foster innovation facilitating richness of perspectives, better approaches to problem solving, knowledge and ideas exchange, and creativity is increasingly integrated into the curriculum at all levels and across geographic regions (Radclyffe-Thomas 2015).

The World Economic Forum (2015) identified 16 skills for school students; skills that should be further enhanced in higher education. Creative industries undergraduates require foundational literacies and core domain skills and additionally need to develop competencies and character qualities to thrive in increasingly connected work environments and tackle complex problems that require multi-disciplinary solutions. Competencies include: critical thinking and problem-solving, creativity, communication and collaboration; and character qualities include: curiosity, initiative, persistence/grit, adaptability, leadership and social and cultural awareness. Creative Industries graduates should adopt a 'glocal' mindset adopting global best practices meaningful to their own region to address localised issues, values, and preferences as well as being confident in creating innovative local work for regional and global markets.

Developing Collaborative Skills for Future Employability and Sustainable Development

Understanding how CCIs use collaboration to stimulate innovation has prompted a whole new employability skillset. Equipping students with capabilities to develop their personal and professional networks and establish open forms of communication is a key learning gain. Students' prior experiences of networking and online communities mean they are often accustomed to building knowledge collaboratively (Ulbrich et al. 2011). Hence teachers can design curricula which demonstrate and enhance digital literacies; furthermore, social media networking is an ideal way to foster communities of practice which are shown to improve student self-efficacy (Junco 2012; Morley 2014; Radclyffe-Thomas 2012). Some of the benefits of building collaborative networks and enhancing these skills amongst students include: knowledge and experience acquisition, competitiveness, possibility to differentiate themselves from other peers and the ability to build long-term relationships that provide an added value regarding employability. Several features of modern CCI working practices are also evident in students' habitus; social media can empower students to be active co-producers of knowledge and for learning to become a "participatory and social" process "supportive of personal life goals and needs" (McLoughlin and Lee 2010, p. 31).

Case Study: The International Fashion Panel Global Classroom

In this connected and mobile society both learners and teachers are increasingly involved in complex relationships and networks, through information exchange and knowledge sharing (Rheingold 2002). The global classroom project, (the 'International Fashion Panel'), was initiated between partner colleges to mirror collaborative knowledge building and exchange evident in the CCIs. Staff in Higher Education institutions based in the UK and Asia created a community of practice hosted in a private Facebook group that supports learning and builds community (Morley 2014) in a blended model. To simulate the culture of work based learning tutors set separate but aligned assignment briefs which required students to co-create learning with peers across the globe.

The initiative aimed to create an effective learning environment and tested out a range of assumptions about the use of virtual platforms and blended learning in attaining learning and employability outcomes.

Following previous work on the educational affordances provided by the application of this type of technology in educational settings, Dickey (2003) suggests that educational affordances of virtual worlds enhance collective team based communication skills. Others have suggested that individual learning is also a key by-product of this process (Scardamalia 2002).

Internationalising the curriculum through collaborative international learning can expose students to alternative learning and cultural environments and enhance their intercultural empathy but only if students commit to this outcome (Arambewela 2010; Caruana 2010). Initially run between London and Hong Kong, and subsequently expanding to include Singapore and Vietnam, the global classroom grows students' professional networks and allows personalisation of the learning experience as students act as experts in their own domain.

The International Fashion Panel Partners

The International Fashion Panel was initially conceived as a partnership between students at UAL's London College of Fashion (LCF) and City University Hong Kong. Meeting at an international popular culture conference the course tutors discovered a shared interest in pedagogic uses of social media and cross-cultural education (Radclyffe-Thomas et al. 2016). Working in discipline areas that include international marketing we wanted a way to bring our students in London and Hong Kong together to share their experiences of international fashion brand marketing communications, conceiving of a global classroom that could provide a shared space to analyse, research and co-create knowledge. The students participating in the global classroom are connected by a shared interest in communications but are not necessarily from the same discipline or year groups; for example, the first iteration of the global classroom connected first year LCF BA (Hons) Fashion Design and Marketing students with higher year-groups at City University Hong Kong taking either a Popular Culture or Advertising course. The partnership has extended to include students in Singapore and Vietnam with each iteration of the collaboration adding to the pool of expertise and industry network so now 450 students currently comprising the Panel. The authors were intrigued to discover how cultural factors might affect the collaboration, and saw such interdisciplinarity as adding further value in simulating industry work experiences where creative professionals are required to collaborate both internationally and across job roles. The local industry context and brief institutional profile of each partner is introduced below.

London College of Fashion, University of the Arts London, United Kingdom

The UK's CCIs have become an integral marker of differentiation for 'Brand Britain' competing in the global economy (CIF 2014) estimated to contribute £10m per hour to the Economy (UK.gov 2016). London is the UK's creative hub providing 40% of all creative industry jobs, supplemented by nearly 50 'creative clusters' across the UK (Winston 2016a). Education is key to the UK's creative economy, with its distinctive art and design pedagogies fostering creativity, problem-based learning and innovation (Radclyffe-Thomas 2015) and the significance of the CCIs has been further highlighted in post-EU-referendum lobbying of the government to support creative education including exchange programmes (Winston 2016b).

UAL is the largest art and design institution in Europe and its alumni practice their diverse crafts internationally and across disciplines ranging from fine arts to management. UAL's 2015–2022 Strategic Plan entitled 'Transformative Education for a Creative World' specifically highlights its aspiration to be a global university through communication and collaboration. In 2016 UAL launched its Creative Attributes Framework (UAL n.d.) to articulate the centrality of employability and enterprise to a creative education. Graduates of UAL's Fashion Business School join an industry that requires facility with working locally and internationally and across disciplines with colleagues in design, operations, finance and promotions. The International Fashion Panel has become an integral part of the year one experience for the BA (Hons) Fashion Marketing with an intake of approximately 100 students.

City University Hong Kong, Hong Kong

Hong Kong's recent secondary school curriculum liberalisation introduced more creative subjects to foster more fully-rounded citizens (Peirson-Smith et al. 2014). In line with global trends the CCIs in Hong Kong are seen by policymakers, opinion formers and educators (Lau 2015) as an engine of economic growth and future prosperity. Asia Pacific is the fastest growing CCI market generating US$743bn of revenues (33% of global CCI sales) and 12.7m jobs (43% of CCI jobs worldwide) (Santiago 2015). Hong Kong has over 39,200 CCI-related establishments, representing around 5% of Hong Kongs GDP (HKSAR 2016a) and employing around 200,000 practitioners. Hong Kong has actively branded itself as a creative city and creative hub in the Asian region in recognition of the increasing relevance of the 'knowledge economy' as a driver of employment and prosperity (HKSAR 2016b).

City University Hong Kong's guiding principles and goals highlight personal career development, innovation, creativity and global outreach. Its Strategic Plan 2015–2020 includes aspirations for internationalisation and global partnerships. City University's Discovery Enriched Curriculum (DEC) aims to prepare globally aware, self-driven, technically competent and creative young professionals and enhance global and flexible learning through digital pedagogies. The International Fashion Panel students come from a range of disciplines taking optional Media Communication or Advertising courses in the School of English, class sizes are approximately 40 students and in different years either one or two classes have joined the International Fashion Panel.

LASALLE College of the Arts, Singapore

Singapore's Creative Industries Development Strategy (CIDS) was launched in 2003 to develop a 'vibrant and sustainable creative cluster to propel the growth of Singapore's Creative Economy' (WCI 2002, p. v). The strategy saw significant infrastructure investments and efforts to embed arts, design and media into mainstream education. Singapore's small domestic market requires creative enterprises to "adopt a global mindset" (p. 7) and "an export-driven approach" (p. iv) to drive sustainable growth. A challenge for Singapore's creative industries, particularly in fashion, is to move beyond its shopping destination image and increase international recognition for its domestic fashion industry.

LASALLE College of the Arts Singapore is a practice-led industry focused art school. LASALLE's alumni are employed throughout Singapore's creative industries and LASALLE's mission statement, 'To nurture enterprising and employable graduates who will become cultural influencers and leaders' places employability as a key focus but also alludes to the hope for graduates to be more than just workers. The BA (Hons) Fashion Media & Industries programme at LASALLE is a three-year programme focusing on the business side of the fashion industry and fashion business environment that is increasingly global and digital. Approximately 50 students joined the International Fashion Panel in 2015–16.

RMIT Vietnam, Ho Chi Minh City, Vietnam

Since adopting '*doi moi*' (economic renovation) in the late 1980s Vietnam's economic and political reforms have raised income levels and developed its position as an international trade partner (World Bank n.d.). Vietnam's 2011–2020 Socio-Economic Development Strategy (SEDS) drives investment in innovative business and start-ups e.g. a $45m start-up fund in the southern economic hub of Ho Chi Minh City (Heles 2016). Growing consumer spending is 'spurring the demand for greater choice in products, brands, and product categories' (Deloitte 2014); the fashion industry is a significant contributor to the economy likely to extend from a manufacturing base into retail. CCI employment has typically been perceived as riskier due to lower wages and job instability, however, Vietnamese students and their parents are increasingly seeing the CCIs as a viable career.

RMIT is one of the world's most globalised institutions; its Ho Chi Minh City campus is the world's largest off-shore campus with goals to promote innovation and nurture creativity locally and internationally. The ability to work globally is a key attribute required of Vietnamese fashion business graduates who aspire to work in leadership roles in global fashion retail as well as promoting the burgeoning local fashion industry. RMIT Vietnam Fashion Business students are competitive graduates with high rates of employment in the local fashion industry, notably because students are bilingual with English being the language of instruction. A class of 11 students from the BA Fashion (Merchandise Management) joined the International Fashion Panel in 2016–17.

Learning Activities

This collaborative project was designed to internationalise the curriculum, to increase students' agency undertaking research, and to showcase their individual cultural capital. For this type of collaboration to have authentic value it was aligned to assessment tasks within specific units, and an integral part of planning was to map curriculum across partner institutions and find commonality. Having identified marketing communications as a common subject area, tutors deliberately designed assessments that required students to analyse both their local and international creative industry context. Students in each location worked on their own assignments relating to international fashion business practices e.g. the London-based students were tasked with analysing a UK fashion brand and proposing a brand extension to be launched in one of the partner institution's locations: Hong Kong, Singapore or Vietnam requiring research into retail practices, consumer behaviour and the marketing landscape in the UK and in Asia.

The global classroom forms part of a blended learning approach and is supplementary to regular lectures, seminars and tutorials of each partner. It was decided to host the global classroom in a private Facebook group due to the facility of the platform to share text and visual data, to curate online communications and to avoid institutional firewalls. In planning the interactions tutors identify touchpoints across the project that take place during formal teaching time and include:

- *Discussion*: e.g. tutors posted questions such as 'what is global fashion?' for students to respond to
- *Market analysis*: commenting on fashion branding examples posted into the group by staff

- *Information sharing*: photos of local retail design concepts posted by students
- *Peer review*: critiquing students' formative presentations posted by students following a real-time formative presentation in their home institution

Additional planned activities take place outside formal class sessions and include:

- *Introductions*: students introduce themselves, their career aspirations via a Facebook post
- *Market research*: students post surveys to collect data on the target market and consumer behaviour

Initially tutors limited online activity to a few seminar activities that could be shared via the Facebook group and delivered asynchronously. Subsequently we have seen the value of delivering more content through the group as students' familiarity with the Facebook platform as an ad hoc communication platform (Selwyn 2007) enables cross-group interaction to develop even within one institution. One activity uses a series of brand-based visual resources with prompts for students to discuss in groups and post a summary of their discussion; the nature of Facebook means that comments are collated and visible to all. Additional activities contribute to each other's knowledge base by sharing local knowledge on retail, customer and marketing activities and this was an area which increased students' self-efficacy as they identified themselves as subject-knowledge experts. In addition, this type of boundary-spanning activity (Tsui and Law 2007) closely aligns with professional practice e.g. global client-based consultancy in the creative industries where local knowledge is increasingly valuable and sourced from cultural informants on the ground. The value inherent in sharing knowledge and co-creating creative outputs was clearly demonstrated through students posting questionnaires into the group space to inform their own projects. Additionally, students in each location critiqued the other's formative projects offering local expertise and in turn experienced diverse approaches to similar creative industry projects.

Although for the majority of students' participation was not mandatory, participation rates were very high with almost all students joining the group and only minor differential engagement from the partners. Class-based activities were mostly facilitated in small groups with one student acting as scribe and posting their group-generated responses or resources. Students in Hong Kong are obliged to comment on their participation as part of their assignment which undoubtedly encourages visible participation. Students in Singapore have been the most reluctant to engage; nearly half the LASALLE group did not have Facebook accounts at the outset and this may have been a factor, although our review showed that students were happy to contribute to tasks that were directly assessed but less so otherwise. Students in London have generally shown a high level of participation although feedback shows that they have not always connected the activities directly to their assessment tasks; this is most evident with more general sector discussions rather that the targeted activities. The group from RMIT Vietnam was small but showed a high level of engagement with peer review tasks and expressed great interest in the London students' proposals for bringing UK brands to Ho Chi Minh City.

Project Evaluation

In terms of the benefits of the course experience, the private Facebook group was a useful communication platform for all students. While the use of Facebook as a pedagogic third space (Bhabha 1994) could be regarded as the misappropriation of social media for formal purposes, student responses suggested that this was a positive and purposeful experience for them.

> … Interactive and interesting … perfect for meeting students from London, Singapore and Vietnam. … we were allowed to share and see a lot of information about the fashion industry… this Facebook platform and the international interaction… allowed such a fruitful engagement with fascinating insights to the fashion industry. (Hong Kong student)

As an emerging player in the international fashion industry RMIT Vietnam students were proud to 'represent' their country and were glad to be able to exchange knowledge about their local fashion environment in an international professional environment. Through the process of peer exchange they were able to easily assimilate knowledge, took the peer review very seriously and exercised international academic standards, whilst becoming more aware of the challenges of working across time zones, and cultural differences in terms of communication and exposure. Amongst all the students the common consensus appears to suggest that this application of digital literacy was a useful way of sharing ideas and knowledge multi-modally and encouraged active, transactional communication and useful feedback on work projects such as the moodboard representing their chosen fashion brand for analysis:

> *I was delighted to have an exchange of thoughts… we were really surprised to have received so many feedback and comments, either telling us how to work better for the mood board or complimenting on it. It was really encouraging.* (Hong Kong student)

> *I learned a lot about communicating with other people, it's great that I can just open my Facebook page and find someone from the group with the same interest from a different country. I also learned about Hong Kong in general and I got to know many new brands. It is nice to see so many different moodboards and visuals, it is easy to get tips from the group….* (London student)

Many students observed that they acquired new, marketable skills based on the interaction between the students from different geographic locations and studying different majors. Students recognised that communicating online in the context of a borderless classroom was very useful in preparing them for their future workplace, especially in the East-West context of Hong Kong where many creative industry workplaces comprise international teams who need to communicate using English as the lingua franca:

I enjoyed working as a team in this Facebook group as I could understand more about people's views towards certain topics of fashion from their own cultural perspectives and this certainly broadened my horizons and has equipped me with a flexible mindset and the confidence to use technology to communicate with people in a common language from other parts of the world… which is really helpful for my future creative career. (Hong Kong student)

Participants noted the value to their own lives and future careers—both within the fashion industry or the wider CCI sectors:

Participating in this very resourceful fashion panel has allowed me to dig deep into the professional and sophisticated sides of the fashion world-marketing, brand extension, advertising and promotions, etc. (Hong Kong student)

I think that it is really interesting and different to be able to interact with students from other universities with similar interest… I am able to see different perspective and their view of fashion as well as how they approach their work. … students also get the opportunity to network… which could be of help… in the future. (London student)

It was evident that students were acquiring an awareness of cultural differences that heightened their understanding of how fashion brands adapt when positioning themselves in global markets. They recognized that cultural knowledge is specific to its place of origin, but general industry knowledge can also be usefully applied to assist and inform when managing brands in other markets:

It's like being a part of this creative learning community and people from different cultural backgrounds coming together to talk about the same topic. … it helped understand the perspective of people from the countries we based our project on. I also learnt so much about what people from other countries thought about my own culture. It was a very helpful learning experience. (London student)

Some students noted cultural challenges of working internationally, however they also showed self-reflexivity aligned with industry experiences:

…The students in London were not always very familiar with the fashion brands in Asia, making it harder for them to give us the critical responses that

we wanted sometimes. However, they were still very passionate to use what they had learnt to answer our questions… And this is how we can test out and modify our promotional ideas in other marketplaces when we are launching a new brand or going onto a new market. (Hong Kong student)

Cultural and linguistic challenges were largely overcome as students could spend time preparing responses which were typed into posts. Additionally, when linguistic and semantic meanings failed then the ubiquitous visual language could be used to convey shared meaning:

… Since we mainly communicated with students on Facebook the distance between us was rather wide. But thanks to the universally understood emoticons we could break the ice and understand them better and get to know them using these useful non-verbal cues to analyse the brands and our respective takes on these brands that were foreign and new to each side as it would be in the business world. (Hong Kong student)

Faced with the need to problem solve by creating a brand for a global launch, the students had to knowledge-build through community-knowledge creation to fulfil the project and core assignment brief. On one level, individual team members questioned, researched, and worked with their team members and their overseas student partners. This knowledge was subsequently shared in the Facebook group and coalesced to build community-knowledge in the form of their brand project and the brand artefact itself as created in the multi-user virtual environment platform. Here, student as 'knower' (Maton 2007) experiences a discursive shift from traditional approaches to one where their subjective view and agency becomes a legitimate part of knowledge enquiry through critical engagement in an interpretative community (Miller and Peirson-Smith 2014).

Conclusion and Recommendations for Future Practice

Working in emerging and global markets will require new levels of cultural awareness, empathy and agency (Routledge 1996) that can be engendered through more internationalised in-class and online cross-cultural exchanges such as the International Fashion Panel experience. The International Fashion Panel can be judged as a successful community of practice allowing its members to meet and participate according to their shared interests (Wenger et al. 2002). The affordances of Facebook technology for global pedagogical purposes, as tested out in this longitudinal study, included enhanced communication competencies, greater intercultural awareness, a sense of immersive reality, increased student engagement and the professional benefits of being actively engaged in a collaborative effort. The online interaction enabled generic information to be shared and local knowledge to be imparted simulating creative work in the increasing borderless real and virtual world.

Our review has resulted in several recommendations such as allowing planning time to share curriculum, to identify an overall project lead and key moderators/facilitators in each institution. Although one should avoid being overly concerned where course disciplines and year-groups or class-sizes are not identical it is important to establish shared teaching philosophies, to identify common subjects, activities and key deliverables and it is likely to increase engagement when student and staff participants are briefed on the benefits and challenges of such a project. It is efficacious to and build in both formal and informal activities and find ways to surface students' skills and self-development e.g. through reflective writing and to debrief staff and students to inform plans.

Employability can be significantly enhanced through curriculum alignment that develops relevant graduate knowledge, skills and attributes (HEA 2016). Providing 'real-life' work practices in collaborating with fashion business and international peers is offering learners a way to be initiated into the competitive employment market environment, to demonstrate their personal skills and attributes building on their self-confidence regarding individual creativity and cross-cultural communication. Studies of international educational collaborations have shown success can be designed-in with a focus on shared understandings between partners and about partnerships (Ayoubi and Massoud 2012). Yet, it is important to recognise that inter-cultural empathy amongst students is not engendered by merely 'connecting up' with culturally different others. Rather, the inter-cultural interaction should be based on active engagement—necessitating reflection, analysis whereby action and extended and 'deep' encounters should be facilitated by educators (Byram 2008). Although the challenges of integrating professional competencies into formal educational processes should not be underestimated (García-Peñalvo et al. 2013) the consequence of successful collaboration is the ability to implement ideas and push boundaries in a way that would not be possible for a single party.

Tribute for Anais Lacouture (1987–2017)

We are sad to inform readers that our friend and colleague Anais Lacouture passed away in August 2017. Anais was a passionate educator and inspiring teacher who relished the opportunity to showcase her students through our international collaborative project. Although she was at the early stages of her teaching career she had already gained a strong reputation as a dedicated, energetic and creative educator who practiced her belief that education should be informed by life experience and self-development. Anais was a young, enthusiastic and fabulous woman and an inspirational teacher and she will be much missed by all who knew her.

References

Albrectsen, A. (2017). Why collaboration will be key to achieving the sustainable development goals. *World Economic Forum*. Retrieved June 10, 2017, from https://www.weforum.org/agenda/2017/01/realising-the-potential-of-cross-sector-partnerships/

Arambewela, R. (2010). Student experience in the globalized higher education market: Challenges and research imperatives. In F. Maringe & N. Foskett (Eds.), *Globalisation and internationalisation in higher education* (pp. 155–173). London: Continuum International Publishing Group.

Ayoubi, R. M., & Massoud, H. (2012). Is it because of partners or partnerships? An investigation into the main obstacles of developing international partnerships in four UK universities. *Educational Management, 26*(4), 338–353.

Bhabha, H. K. (1994). *The location of culture*. New York: Routledge.

Byram, M. (2008). *From foreign language education to education for intercultural citizenship: Essays and reflections* (Vol. 17). Languages for Intercultural Communication and Education. Clevendon: Multilingual Matters.

Byram, M., & Fleming, M. (Eds.). (1998). *Language learning in intercultural perspective*. Cambridge: Cambridge University Press.

Caruana, V. (2010). Global citizenship for all: putting the 'higher' back into UK higher education? In F. Maringe & N. Foskett (Eds.), *Globalisation and internationalisation in higher education* (pp. 51–64). London: Continuum International Publishing Group.

Chesbrough, H. W. (2003). *Open innovation: The new imperative for creating and profiting from technology*. Boston, MA: Harvard Business School Press.

Creative Industries Federation. (2014). *Creative industries federation*. Retrieved March 1, 2015, from http://www.creativeindustriesfederation.com/about/

Deloitte. (2014). *Retail in Vietnam: Emerging market emerging growth*. Retrieved June 1, 2017, from https://www2.deloitte.com/content/dam/Deloitte/ie/Documents/ConsumerBusiness/2014-deloitte-ireland-retail-vietnam.pdf

Denning, S. (2014). Navigating the phase change to the creative economy. *Strategy & Leadership, 42*(2), 3–11.

Department for Culture, Media and Sport. (2016). *Creative industries economic estimates*. Retrieved April 5, 2017, from https://www.gov.uk/government/uploads/system/uploads/attachment_data/file/523024/Creative_Industries_Economic_Estimates_January_2016_Updated_201605.pdf

Dickey, M. D. (2003). Teaching in 3D: Pedagogical affordances and constraints of 3D virtual worlds for synchronous distance learning. *Distance Education, 24*(1), 105–122.

Florida, R. (2002). *The rise of the creative class: And how it's transforming work, leisure, community and everyday life*. New York: Perseus Book Group.

Florida, R., Gates, G., Knudsen, B., & Stolarick, K. (2006). *The university and the creative economy*. Fairfax, VA; Pittsburgh, PA; and Los Angeles, CA: George Mason University, Carnegie Mellon, UCLA. Retrieved June 10, 2016, from http://creativeclass.com/rfcgdb/articles/University_andthe_Creative_Economy.pdf

García-Peñalvo, F. J., Conde, M. Á., Johnson, M., & Alier, M. (2013). Knowledge co-creation process based on informal learning competences tagging and recognition. *International Journal of Human Capital and Information Technology Professionals, 4*(4), 18–30.

HEA. (2016). *'Embedding employability in higher education'* frameWORKS 02. Higher Education Academy. Retrieved May 10, 2017, from https://www.heacademy.ac.uk/individuals/strategic-priorities/employability

Heles, T. (2016). *Ho Chi Minh City to establish $45m vehicle*. Retrieved June 1, 2017, from http://globalgovernmentventuring.com/news/ho-chi-minh-city-to-establish-45m-vehicle

Hong Kong Special Administrative Region. (2016a). *The culture and creative industries in Hong Kong*. Retrieved June 10, 2016, from https://www.censtatd.gov.hk/hkstat/sub/sp80.jsp?productCode=FA100120

Hong Kong Special Administrative Region. (2016b). *Creative industries*. Retrieved June 12, 2016, from https://www.gov.hk/en/about/abouthk/factsheets/docs/creative_industries.pdf

Junco, R. (2012). Too much face and not enough books: The relationship between multiple indices of Facebook use and academic performance. *Computers in Human Behavior, 28*, 187–198.

Lau, S. (2015, August 17). Push creative industries in Hong Kong to stay a 'world city'. *SCMP.com*, Monday. Retrieved June 12, 2016, from http://www.scmp.com/news/hong-kong/economy/article/1850072/push-creative-industries-hong-kong-stay-world-city-says

Mathe, H. (2015). *Living innovation: Competing in the 21st century access economy*. Singapore: World Scientific.

Maton, K. (2007). Knowledge-knower structures in intellectual and educational fields. In F. Christie & J. Martin (Eds.), *Language, knowledge and pedagogy: Functional linguistic and sociological perspectives* (pp. 87–108). London: Continuum.

McLoughlin, C., & Lee, M. (2010). Personalised and self regulated learning in the Web 2.0 era: International exemplars of innovative pedagogy using social software. *Australasian Journal of Educational Technology, 26*(1), 28–43.

Miller, L., & Peirson-Smith, A. (2014). Football for all, organic living, and MK culture: Teaching popular culture by turning theory into practice. In P. Benson & A. Chik (Eds.), *Popular culture, pedagogy and teacher education: International perspectives* (pp. 97–109). London: Routledge.

Morley, D. A. (2014). Supporting student nurses in practice with additional online communication tools. *Nurse Education in Practice, 14*(1), 1–7.

Organisation for Economic Co-operation and Development. (2013). *Interconnected economies: Benefiting from global value chains*. Retrieved June 1, 2017, from https://www.oecd.org/sti/ind/interconnected-economies-GVCs-synthesis.pdf

Peirson-Smith, A., Chik, A., & Miller, L. (2014). Teaching popular culture in a second language university context. *Pedagogies: An International Journal, 9*, 250–267.

Radclyffe-Thomas, N. (2012). Blogging is addictive! A qualitative case study on the integration of blogs across a range of college courses. In C. Wankel & P. Blessinger (Eds.), *Increasing students engagement and retention using online learning activities: Wikis, Blogs and Webquests, cutting-edge technologies in higher education* (pp. 75–107). Emerald.

Radclyffe-Thomas, N. (2015). Fashioning cross-cultural creativity: Investigating the situated pedagogy of creativity. *Psychology of Aesthetics, Creativity and the Arts, 9*(2), 152–160.

Radclyffe-Thomas, N., Peirson-Smith, A., Roncha, A., & Huang, A. (2016). Creative cross-cultural connections: Facebook as a third space for international collaborations. In P. Blessinger & B. Cozza (Eds.), *University partnerships for academic programs and professional development* (pp. 243–266). Emerald.

Rheingold, H. (2002). Rethinking virtual communities. Developing a sense of place. In *Proceeding of the Richard A. Harvill Conference on Higher Education*.

Routledge, P. (1996). The third space as critical engagement. *Antipode, 8*(4), 399–419.

Santiago, J. (2015). What is creativity worth to the world economy? *World Economic Forum*. Retrieved May 10, 2016, from https://www.weforum.org/agenda/2015/12/creative-industries-worth-world-economy/

Scardamalia, M. (2002). Collective cognitive responsibility for the advancement of knowledge. In B. Smith (Ed.), *Liberal education in a knowledge society* (pp. 67–98). Chicago: Open Court.

Selwyn, N. (2007). "Screw blackboard… do it on Facebook!": An investigation of students' educational use of Facebook. Paper presented to the Poke 1.0 Facebook social research symposium, University of London, 15 November 2007.

Tsui, A. B. M., & Law, D. Y. K. (2007). Learning as boundary crossing in school-university partnership. *Teaching and Teacher Education, 23*, 1289–1301.

Uk.gov. (2016, January 26). Creative industries worth almost £10 million an hour to economy. *Press Release*. Retrieved March 1, 2016, from https://www.gov.uk/government/news/creative-industries-worth-almost-10-million-an-hour-to-economy

Ulbrich, F., Jahnke, I., & Mårtensson, P. (2011). Special issue on knowledge development and the net generation. *International Journal of Sociotechnology and Knowledge Development, 2*(4), i–ii.

United Nations Educational, Scientific and Cultural Organisation. (2013). *Creative economy report*. Paris: UNESCO. Retrieved May 10, 2015, from http://www.unesco.org/culture/pdf/creative-economy-report-2013.pdf

University of the Arts, London. (n.d.). *Creative Attributes Framework*. Retrieved February 10, 2017, from http://www.arts.ac.uk/about-ual/teaching-and-learning/careers-and-employability/creative-attributes-framework/

Wenger, E. (1998). *Communities of practice: Learning meaning and identity*. New York, NY: Cambridge University Press.

Wenger, E., McDermott, R., & Snyder, W. M. (2002). *Cultivating communities of practice*. Boston: Harvard Business Press.

Winston, A. (2016a, July 26). Creative industries booming across the UK, according to new report. *Dezeen*. Retrieved June 1, 2017, from https://www.dezeen.com/2016/07/28/creative-industries-booming-across-uk-creative-clusters-outside-london-nesta-geography-of-creativity-report/

Winston, A. (2016b, August 16). Creative industries must present a united front to make best of Brexit says John Sorrell. *Dezeen*. Retrieved June 1, 2017, from https://www.dezeen.com/2016/08/16/creative-industries-must-present-united-front-post-brexit-john-sorrell/

Workgroup on Creative Industries. (2002). *Creative industries development strategy: Propelling Singapore's creative economy*. Workgroup on Creative Industries.

World Bank. (n.d.). *Vietnam overview*. Retrieved June 1, 2017, from http://www.worldbank.org/en/country/vietnam/overview

World Economic Forum. (2015). The skills needed in the 21st century. *New vision for education—Unlocking the potential of technology*. Retrieved June 14, 2017, from https://widgets.weforum.org/nve-2015/chapter1.html

Index

A

Argyris, C., 3, 76, 176

B

Belbin, R.M., 96, 102, 103
Benner, P., 97, 105, 106, 183–187

C

Communities of practice, 43, 47, 134–138, 257, 259, 270

D

Degree apprenticeship, 2, 5, 51–53, 57, 59–61, 63, 65, 173
Dreyfus, S.E., 185

E

Ellstrom, P.-E., 3, 155, 176

K

Kolb, D.A., 19, 40, 55, 76, 81, 117–119, 122, 126, 131

L

Lave, J., 136, 147, 174, 185
Learning gain, 1, 2, 134, 153

S

Schön, D., 3, 7, 19, 20, 39, 40, 55, 76, 95, 176

T

Teaching Excellence Framework, 2, 34, 64, 114, 169, 214
Theory practice gap, 3, 184

V

Vygotsky, L.S., 41, 136, 174

W

Wenger, E., 43, 134–137, 146–148, 174, 184, 185, 257, 270

CPSIA information can be obtained
at www.ICGtesting.com
Printed in the USA
LVHW04*1241280518
578670LV00011B/746/P